Be a part of the Dalmatian Press Puppy Pack™!
Your pictures and ideas could be *spotted* on our new books!

"I like all the different things you can do in this book. We love this book."
— Katie T., age 4 ½
Orlando, FL

"I love your books, especially the <u>God Loves Me</u> book... Well, I have to go."
— Kayla E., age 8 ½
Bentonville, AR

"It is fun, and it helps you understand God...I like the puzzles and games."
— Casandra M., age 8
Tioga, WV

"I like your pictures. I love your books and would never change them! I have a lot of your books."
— Tiffany O., age 5
Glenn Allen, AL

Noah's Ark

"I would like coloring books like this about Bible people."
— Timothy G., age 9
Westville, OK

"I like this book because I love God, and I like Dalmatians. I really like them."
— Amanda S., age 8
Mooresville, NC

"Thank you for your coloring books. I like them. So, thank you Dalmatian Press. I love your books."
— Allyson T., age 8
Florence, AL

"They're fun. I want a coloring book about Jesus. I don't know anything to change about your books."
— Kadie K., age 6
Salina, KS

Be a part of the Dalmatian Press Puppy Pack!

We want you and your ideas to be spotted in our new books!

✂ cut along dotted lines

Dear Dalmatian Press,

_____

_____

_____

_____

_____

_____

_____

Your Friend,

_____

10013ULTHOLI   (write your name here)   (write your age)

Here is how to join the Puppy Pack:

1. **Ask your mom or dad for help to cut out the letter.**

2. **Tell us what you like about Dalmatian Press Coloring Books. What do you want Dalmatian Press to make a coloring book about? What would you change about our books? Your mom or dad can help.**

3. **Ask your mom or dad for an envelope and stamp. Fill out the envelope like this.**

Your name
and address

STAMP

Dalmatian Press
P.O. Box 1823
Brentwood, TN 37024

4. **Now, put your letter and a picture you have colored in a mailbox.**

5. **Who knows, maybe your drawings and ideas will be spotted in the next Dalmatian Press Book!**

All rights in and to the works submitted to Dalmatian Press, become the sole and exclusive property of Dalmatian Press. Each person submitting works to Dalmatian Press gives it his or her permission to use his or her name and likeness for any purpose.

✂ cut along dotted lines and *keep for yourself*

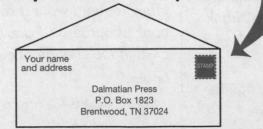

Dalmatian Press

Dalmatian Press Puppy Pack™

YOUR NAME

I am a member of the DPPP because I wrote Dalmatian Press on _____.

DATE

Old Testament

New Testament

Editorial and Layout by Yellowhouse, Inc.

First printed in the U.S. in 1997 by Dalmatian Press, U.S.A.

™

Dalmatian
🐾 **Press**

Genesis 1•1

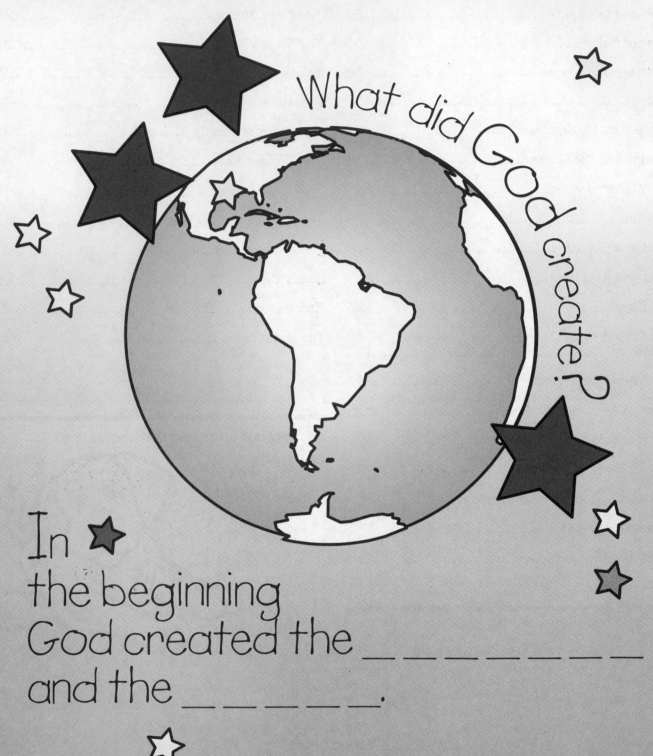

What did God create?

In ⭐
the beginning
God created the _____
and the _____.

ANSWERS IN BACK

Can you get through the Heavenly Maze & the Earthly Maze?

START

END

God is so A-mazing!

5

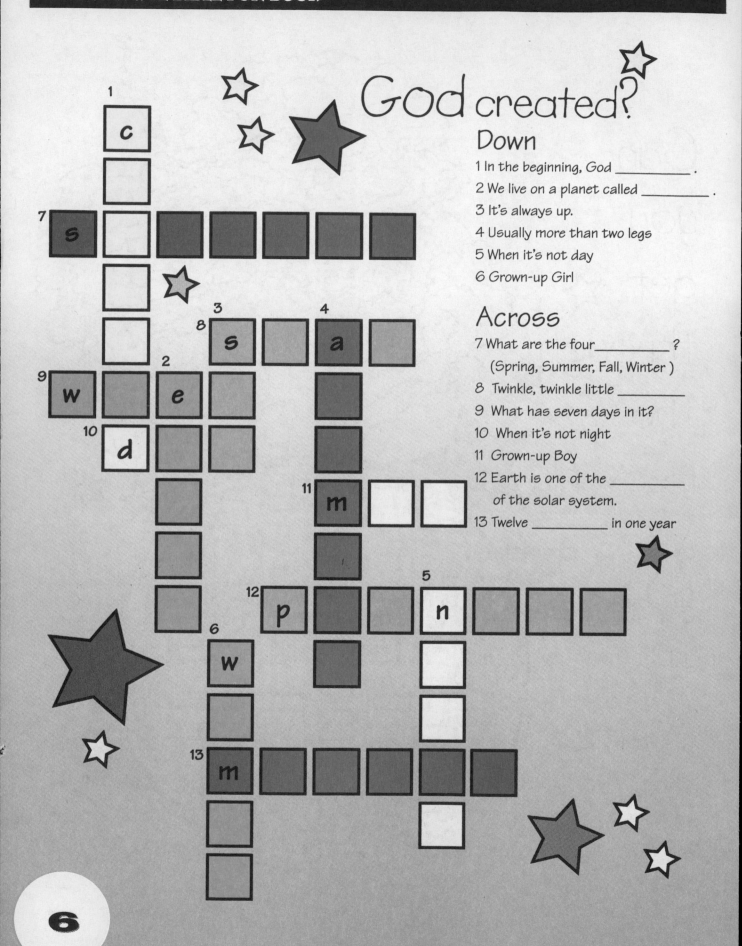

God created?

Down

1 In the beginning, God _____ .

2 We live on a planet called _____ .

3 It's always up.

4 Usually more than two legs

5 When it's not day

6 Grown-up Girl

Across

7 What are the four _____ ?
   (Spring, Summer, Fall, Winter)

8 Twinkle, twinkle little _____

9 What has seven days in it?

10 When it's not night

11 Grown-up Boy

12 Earth is one of the _____
   of the solar system.

13 Twelve _____ in one year

ANSWERS IN BACK

All the words below have to do with creation.

Can you find and circle them?

A	B	I	R	D	S	B	C	S	T	A	R	S
N	Y	D	F	E	F	O	U	R	T	H	I	G
I	R	L	H	I	M	L	P	M	S	X	M	R
G	X	J	F	V	W	O	Z	N	T	H	Q	P
H	K	T	M	A	N	Y	O	H	C	E	L	U
T	H	S	D	G	A	S	U	N	I	A	T	C
W	U	Y	T	R	A	T	E	W	N	V	Q	R
H	T	R	A	E	X	I	S	T	O	E	P	E
A	G	H	S	R	J	K	S	R	L	N	T	A
L	F	D	E	S	L	A	N	D	I	X	S	T
E	N	T	C	B	V	C	X	A	Z	F	E	U
S	A	M	O	U	T	Q	O	Y	E	A	R	R
W	S	L	N	S	E	A	D	R	I	H	T	E
X	G	O	D	V	E	W	O	M	A	N	F	S
T	H	G	I	L	X	S	E	V	E	N	T	H

birds	creatures	day	earth	fifth	first
fly	fourth	God	heaven	land	light
man	moon	night	plants	rest	sea
seasons	second	seventh	sixth	stars	sun
third	water	whales	woman	year	air

7

ANSWERS IN BACK

Genesis 1•3
Day (1)

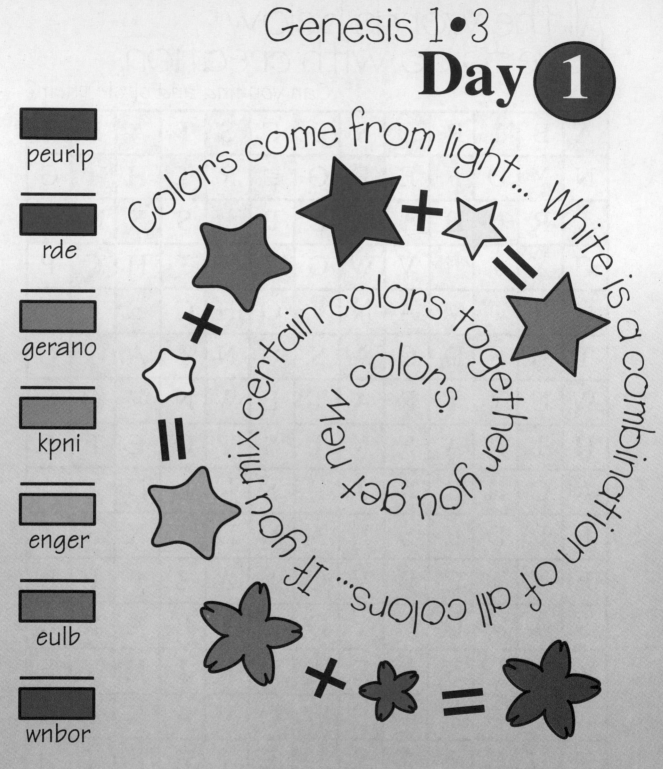

peurlp

rde

gerano

kpni

enger

eulb

wnbor

Colors come from light... White is a combination of all colors... If you mix certain colors together you get new colors.

Can you unscramble the color names?

God created Light!

ANSWERS IN BACK

Cool•Things to Know

Did you know,

on the first day, when God created light,

it was the first time earth had a day

and then a night?

We wake up at Day•Time
and go to bed at Night•Time.
When do you do the things listed below?

Day•Time

Night•Time

snore	bath	dinner	lunch
breakfast	pj's	dream	nap
bicycle	sleep	play	chores
school	dress	homework	snack

9

Genesis 1•8
Day 2

God called the sky heaven...

odlscu _____

idnw _____

dbisr _____

nsu _____

omon _____

astrs _____

oerwrksfi _____

nlpea _____

olnalob _____

itgnhilgn _____

biwanor _____

wosn _____

veaenh _____

You can find many of these things in the sky!
Can you unscramble these words?

ANSWERS IN BACK

Sometimes clouds can look like funny things!

What do you think these clouds look like?

Next time you're outside,
look at the clouds and see if you can see some funny things!

Genesis 1•9-13

Day 3

God created the seas, land, and vegetation...

At this time God created fruit trees. Can you put the fruit in its proper place?

apple • lemon • plum • papaya • cherry
avocado • fig • kumquat • peach • banana
orange • mango • apricot • grapefruit

12

Genesis 1•11-13

God said they would grow
after their kind because of the seed
He put in the fruit...

Each tree was created to grow one kind of fruit. In this orchard some of the trees are growing the wrong kind of fruit. Can you find and circle them?

God made sure that
an apple tree
would only grow apples
and a plum tree
would only grow plums.

13

Genesis 1•14

"Let there be stars in heaven to separate day from night, and to make known the seasons, days and years."

START

In 1 year we have 4 seasons: Winter, Spring, Summer, and Fall.

Skate into Winter, Jump into Spring, Swim into Summer, and blow into Fall where you will be the winner of all!

YOU WIN

14

The earth is where we live. Can you build off the word blocks starting here?

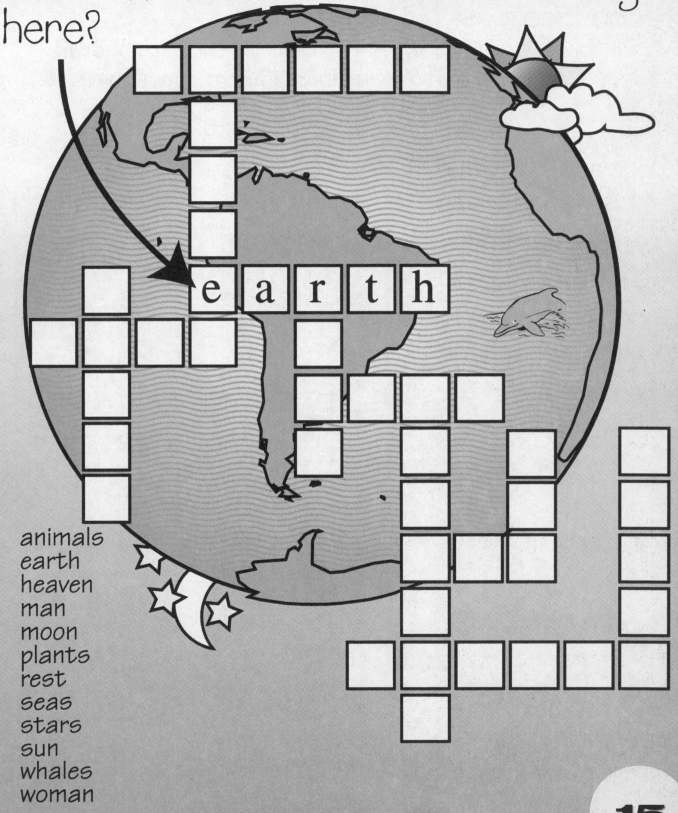

e a r t h

animals
earth
heaven
man
moon
plants
rest
seas
stars
sun
whales
woman

15

Genesis 1•16
God placed stars in the sky for signs and seasons!

Connect the sets of stars
to reveal four different constellations.

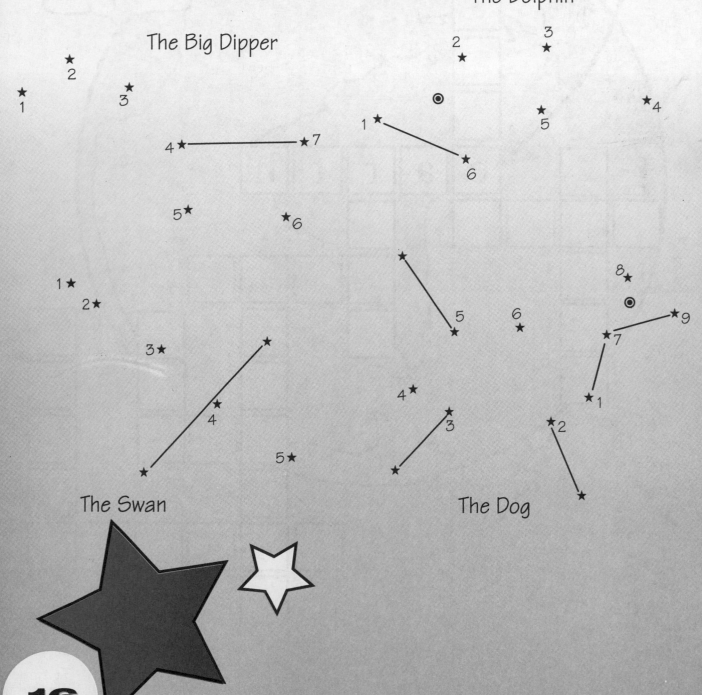

The Dolphin

The Big Dipper

The Swan

The Dog

ANSWERS IN BACK

Genesis 1•15-18
Day ④

Let's create a MOBILE
for you to hang up in your bedroom!

You will need: scissors, string, something to punch holes, and sticks.

1. Cut out shapes along dotted lines
2. Punch a small hole where you see the "X"

On the 4th day God created the Sun, Moon, & Stars!

3. Tie one end of a string to each shape and the other end to the sticks.
4. Balance the mobile pieces by moving them on the sticks from the outside toward the center.

Origami Stars
"He made the stars also."

You can make stars out of paper.
Just follow these simple steps.

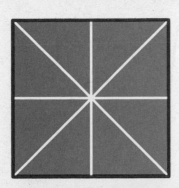

1. Fold a square of paper four times along the white lines, making sharp creases. Open it out.

2. Fold it over diagonally. If one side is colored, fold it outside.

3. Fold the right hand side up toward you.

4. Open the right hand side out and press it down into itself.

5. Make a sharp crease.

6. Fold the new wing back to the right. Repeat steps 3, 4, and 5 for the left side.

Continue to next page

7. Flatten your shape out.

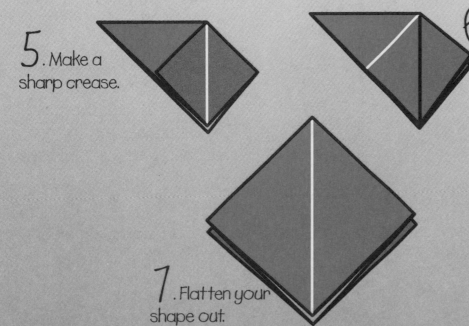

19

Origami Stars
Continued

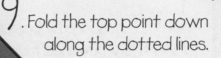

8. Fold the left and right flaps into the center along the dotted lines.

9. Fold the top point down along the dotted lines.

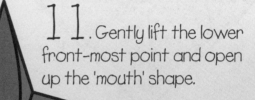

11. Gently lift the lower front-most point and open up the 'mouth' shape.

10. Unfold the last three folds.

12. Flatten it down so that the sides meet in the middle. Sharpen all of your creases. Turn the shape over and repeat steps 8 - 11 on the other side.

13. This is the basic shape that will be used to make the star on page 21.

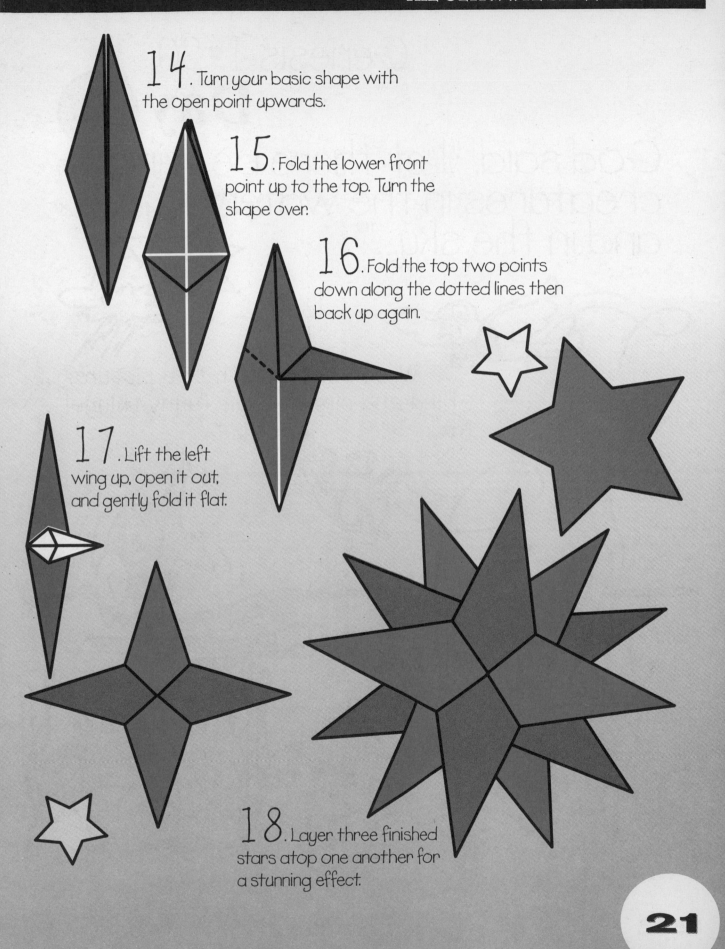

14. Turn your basic shape with the open point upwards.

15. Fold the lower front point up to the top. Turn the shape over.

16. Fold the top two points down along the dotted lines then back up again.

17. Lift the left wing up, open it out, and gently fold it flat.

18. Layer three finished stars atop one another for a stunning effect.

Genesis 1•20
Day 5

God said, "Let there be living creatures in the water and in the sky..."

What's wrong with this picture?
Find and circle all the funny things!

22

There are many kinds of creatures in the ocean...

...can you match these creatures with their names?

Whale
Sea Horse
Starfish
Dolphin
Shark
Sea Turtle
Octopus
Sea Snail
Clam
Swordfish
Sea Lion
Sea Otter
Eel
Crab
Squid
Jellyfish
Lobster
Seal

ANSWERS IN BACK

Genesis 1•24

God created cattle and living creatures to fill the earth.

Day 6

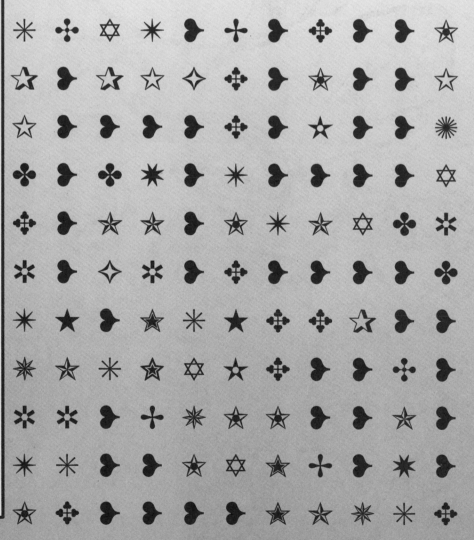

Can you circle the creatures after decoding the symbols

A
B
C
D
E
F
G
H
I
J
K
L
M
N
O
P
Q
R
S
T
U
V
W
X
Y
Z
•

Ant
Beetle
Bull
Cat
Cow
Deer
Dog
Elk
Goat
Horse
Lamb
Lizard
Mouse
Pig
Sheep
Snake
Spider
Toad
Turtle
Worm

24

God gave
man dominion...

... over all the animals.
Help the man by finding as
many animals and creatures
as you can!

25

Genesis 1•3-27

Day 7 God
created the heavens & the earth
in 7 DAYS!

In the first six days of creation God made certain things each day.
Can you match the correct item with the day God made it?
Don't forget that God rested on the Seventh day.

SUNDAY	MONDAY	TUESDAY	WEDNESDAY	THURSDAY	FRIDAY	SATURDAY
	1	2	3	4	5	6
7	8	9	10	11	12	13
14	15	16	17	18	19	20
21	22	23	24	25	26	27
28	29	30	31			

ANSWERS IN BACK

You can create a small portion of the universe ...

Take:

 1 cup of Flour

 Mix with 2/3 cup of water

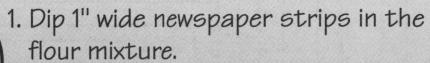

1. Dip 1" wide newspaper strips in the flour mixture.
2. Wrap around blown-up balloon, covering fully.
3. Let dry completely. Then when the paper maché is dry, pop balloon with a pin.
4. Paint with bright color tempera paints.

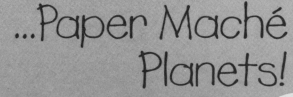

...Paper Maché Planets!

God created Eve as a friend and helper for Adam...

... Can you tell Adam which path he should take to find Eve?

28

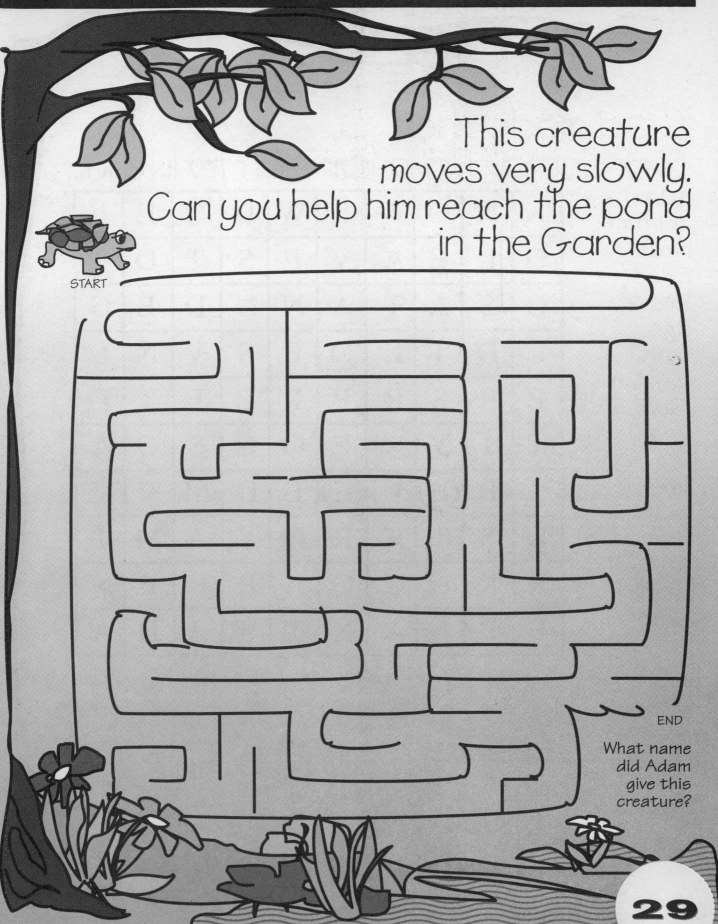

This creature moves very slowly. Can you help him reach the pond in the Garden?

START

END

What name did Adam give this creature?

29

ANSWERS IN BACK

God made the Garden of Eden for man to live in...

Adam
animals
birds
Eden
Eve ✔
figs
fruit
garden
God
knowledge
leaves
life
plants
rivers
Satan
serpent
tree
water

K	N	O	W	L	W	D	G	E	F
G	L	E	A	V	E	S	T	D	I
O	S	A	T	A	N	N	D	E	G
L	D	T	E	O	E	S	V	N	S
E	R	S	R	P	R	E	F	I	L
T	I	Y	R	E	O	U	S	O	A
I	B	Ⓔ	Ⓥ	Ⓔ	E	D	M	V	M
U	S	I	E	R	O	Y	A	M	I
R	R	U	C	G	A	R	D	E	N
F	P	L	A	N	T	S	A	H	A

...Find all the words about the Garden of Eden in this puzzle.
Then fill in the secret phrase below with the uncircled letters!

_ _ _ _ _ _ _ • _ _ _ _ _ • _ _ _ _ • _ _ _ _ _ • _ _ _ _ _ !

30

ANSWERS IN BACK

Adam lived to be a very old age!

Do the math and get the answer.

Can you guess Adam's age?

Add 657 and 242 then subtract 503

$$657$$
$$+242$$
$$-\!-\!-$$
$$-503$$
$$-\!-\!-$$

Take that number and divide it by 3

$$3\overline{)}$$

Take your number and add 846

$$+846$$
$$-\!-\!-$$

Now subtract 132

$$-132$$
$$-\!-\!-$$

Take this number and divide it by 2

$$2\overline{)}$$

Take your number and add 452

$$+452$$
$$-\!-\!-$$

Now subtract 410 and add 465

$$-410$$
$$-\!-\!-$$

How old was Adam?

$$+465$$
$$-\!-\!-$$

31

Genesis 2•15

Watch me grow!

You will need:

1. a clear plastic jar or cup
2. a natural sponge or paper towel
3. six dried lima beans

What to do...

Take your clear plastic jar or cup and fill it snugly with your sponge or paper towel.

Then put the lima beans about half way down, between the sponge and the sides of the jar.

Now add water to the jar, allowing the sponge or paper towel to soak it up, not leaving standing water. Place in a bright window. Then check it each morning to make sure it is moist.

Soon you will see your beans begin to grow!

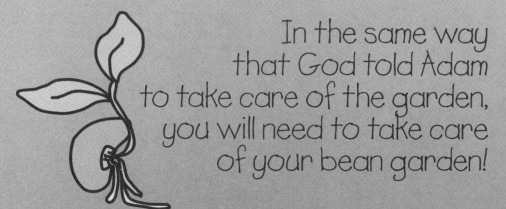

In the same way that God told Adam to take care of the garden, you will need to take care of your bean garden!

Genesis 2•8

God planted the Garden of "Eden" and put Adam there.

One of the first things God asked Adam to do was to name all the animals!

Can you help give names to these animals?

2•8

On the following pages...

...you will be asked to guess what type of animals you see.

A	B	C	D	E	F	G	H	I	J	K	L	M	N	O	P	Q	R	S	T	U	V	W	X	Y	Z

If you don't know...

...just use 1 of the 3 codes on this page.

try out this phrase for practice

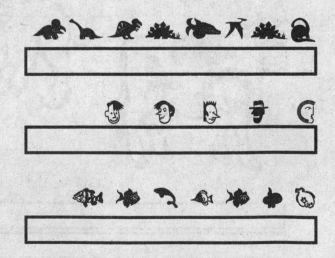

ANSWERS IN BACK

beginning in
Genesis 2•8

God created the animals!

God brought the animals to the man one by one and asked what he would name them.

Do you know what name Adam gave to this animal?
Use the code!

Genesis 1•21
God brought forth...
...every winged fowl after its kind.
Unscramble the names of these winged fowl.

ARPORT

LCRIAADN

LEJY BUA

ODEKRWOPCE

ODUNRRARNE

How are bird babies born?

OINBR

36

ANSWERS IN BACK

Genesis 2•19
God created the animals...
...and brought them to Adam
to see what he would name them.

Looking at the picture above,
can you draw this bird?

Did you know that this
is the only bird that
can fly backward!?

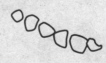

ANSWERS IN BACK

God created the animals!

What is this
animal called?

What type of sound
does it make?

38

ANSWERS IN BACK

Never forget that this animal loves peanuts!

Make your own edible peanut butter play dough.
You won't forget how much fun you had doing it!

Edible Peanut Butter Play Dough!

You will need

- 1 cup powdered milk
- 1 cup peanut butter
- 1/2 cup honey
- bowl

Combine dry powered milk, peanut butter, and honey in bowl.
Mix* with hands until smooth.

This makes modeling and sculpting a SUPER TREAT.
Make animals, people, and funny shapes. When you're done,
eat the results.

*Be sure to wash hands before playing with play dough,
and, if you plan to eat this, play on a clean surface!

End

Genesis 2•19-20

What would Adam...

...call this little creature when God brought it to him?

Can you help point the way to the acorn?

Start

ANSWERS IN BACK

Genesis 2•19-20

Adam called these?

Cool•Things to Know

Did you know that this animal is in a group called "amphibians?" This means they live both in water and on land.

What sound do they make?

41

God created the animals!

God brought the animals to the man one by one and asked what he would name them.

Genesis 2•19-20

ANSWERS IN BACK

How many Horses do you see on this page?

Cool·Things to Know

Did you know that except for the ostrich, the horse has the largest eyes of any other land animal? These eyes can move separately from each other so a horse can look forward and backward at the same time.

43

God is so creative!

God created the creeping
things that crawl
on the earth.

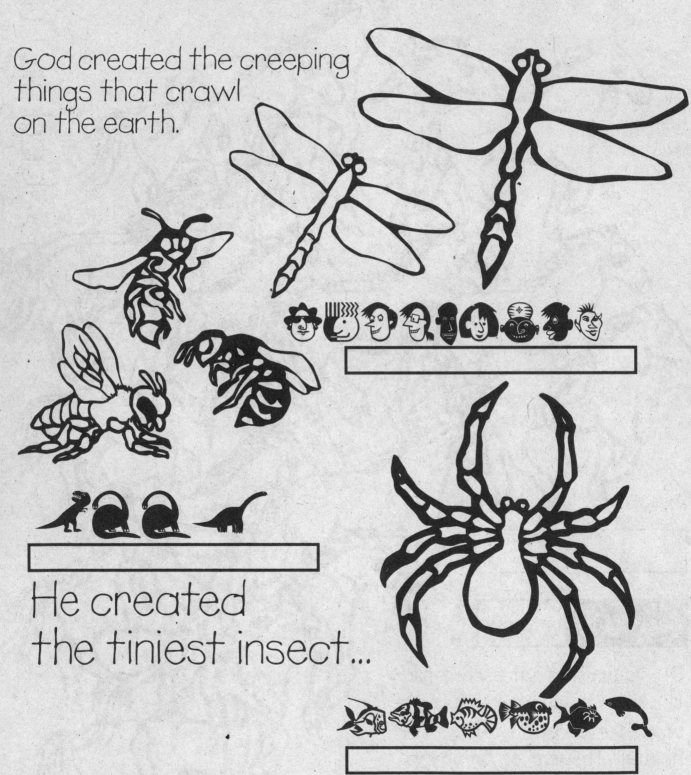

He created
the tiniest insect...

ANSWERS IN BACK

Adam named the animals!

How long do you think it took for Adam to name all the living creatures?

...to the largest animals.

45

God created unique and individual animals!
Some animals seem fun and friendly.

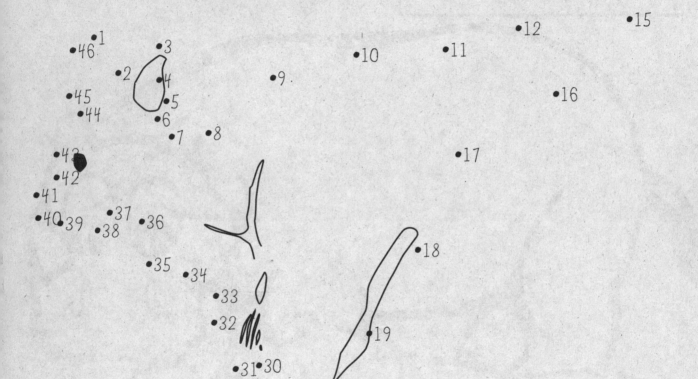

Just connect the dots to see
what comes from down under.

Cool•Things to Know

Did you know that a nickname
given to the kangaroo is "Joey?"

46

Cool·Things to Know

Did you know that this animal
is mentioned in the Bible 9 times?

ANSWERS IN BACK

God created Camels...

...perhaps to become transportation in the desert.

Cool·Things to Know

Did you know that when a Camel gets thirsty it can drink up to 40 gallons at a time?

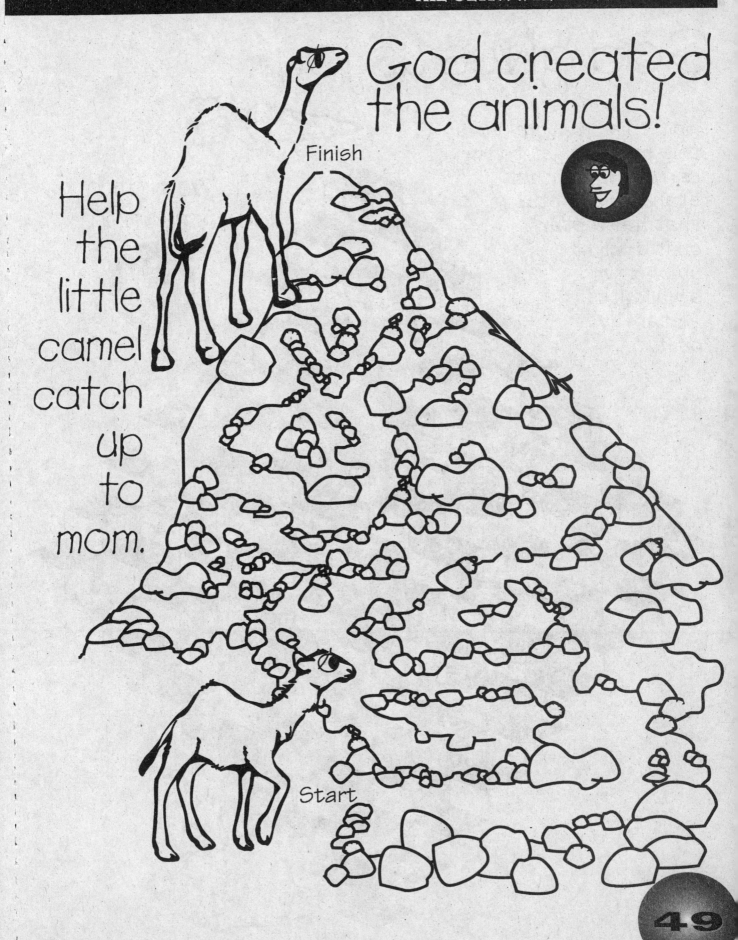

God created the animals!

Help the little camel catch up to mom.

Finish

Start

49

God gives us joy...

Help this creature hop up this maze to get to the carrot. He may not stand on any step that has a star on it or climb up or down a wall with a star on it.

End

...as we watch his creation.

Start

ANSWERS IN BACK

Adam took care...

...of the garden for God, and you can take care of the garden here.

Decode the name of this little creature that likes to eat in your garden for a clue.

1.
2.
3.
4.
5.
6.

1. When the leaves fall you use this to put the leaves in a pile.
2. These grow from seed, flower and die in one year.
3. Within each one is a flower and all its leaves just waiting for spring.
4. This vegetable sometimes has the word "string" in front of it.
5. This is another word for "trimming the trees."
6. This is what you're doing when you put a seed or plant in the ground.

ANSWERS IN BACK

"Word Games"
Combine these pictures to find the animal name!
You may want to draw and color it in.

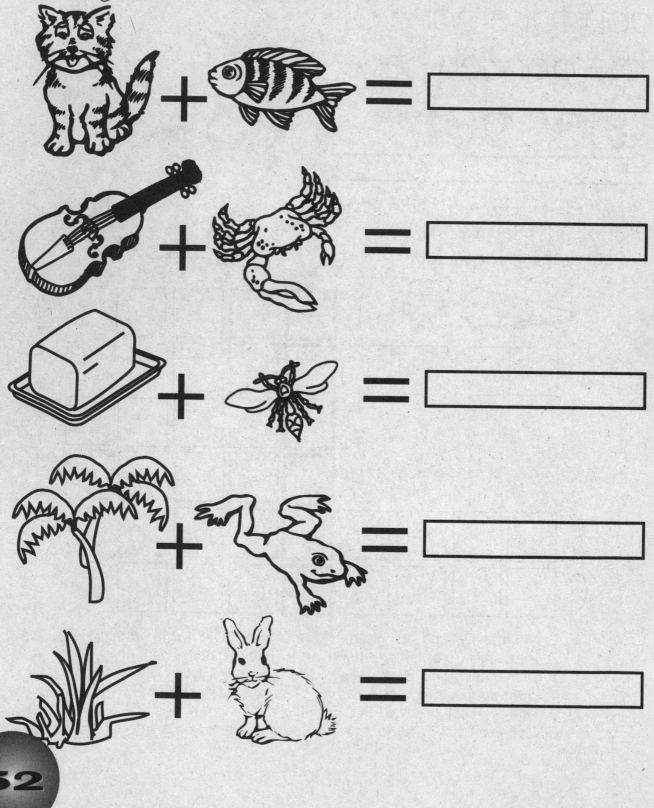

ANSWERS IN BACK

The Lion is known as the King of the Jungle.

Connect the dots and color him COOL!

Start

End

What sounds do Lions make?

53

God created the animals!

Can you draw the other half of this Butterfly? Color it with bright colors!

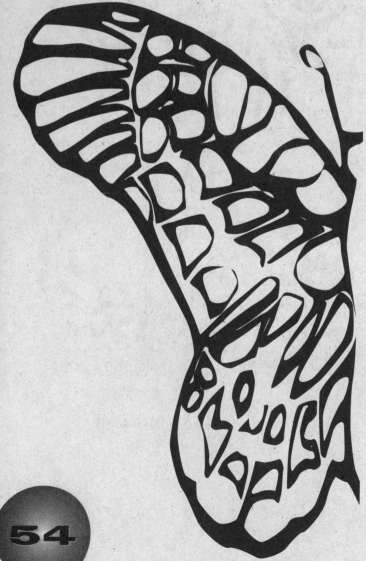

Genesis 2•10-14

- A river ran through Eden to water the garden and then split off into four separate rivers.

- The first was Pison, which means to surround the land of Havilah. This land was rich in gold.

- The second river was called Gihon and it surrounded Ethiopia.

- The third river was called Hiddekel as it went towards the east of Assyria.

- And the fourth river was called Euphrates.

Garden of Eden

NSPOI

UHRESTRPE

_____

_____ 1

Havilah

IDKLEEDH _____ 4

INGHO

_____

Ethiopia

2

Cool•Things to Know

Did you know that the Euphrates river can still be found on a map of the middle east?

3

55

Genesis 2•17

God's one rule was that Adam and Eve could not eat of the tree of

_____

_____ .

God said "For on that day you shall surely ____!"

God kept them from eating from the tree of

_____ .

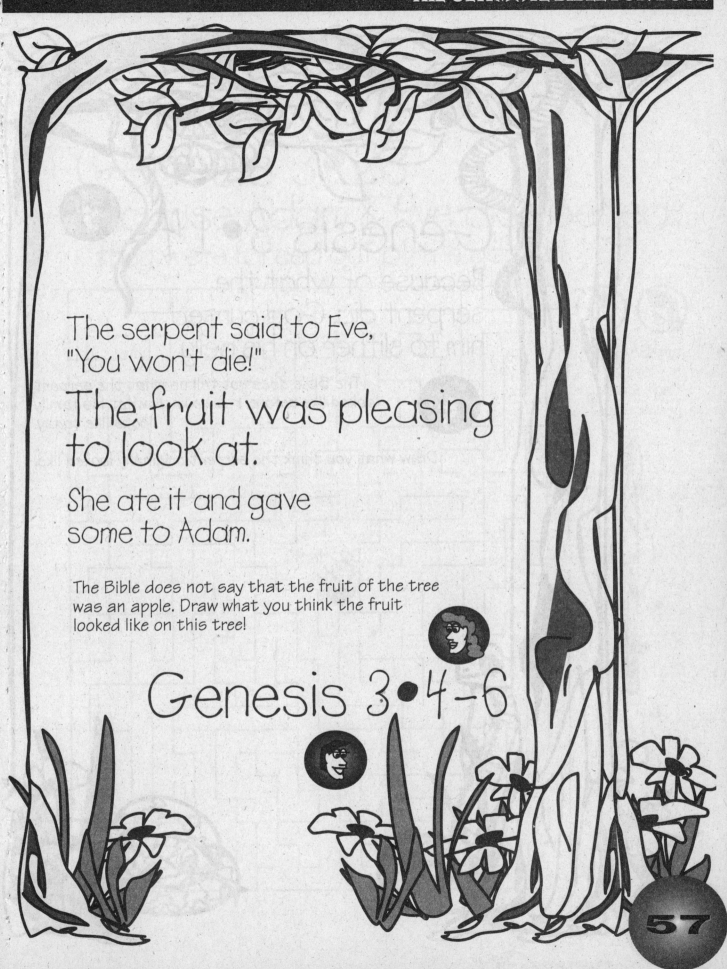

The serpent said to Eve, "You won't die!"

The fruit was pleasing to look at.

She ate it and gave some to Adam.

The Bible does not say that the fruit of the tree was an apple. Draw what you think the fruit looked like on this tree!

Genesis 3•4-6

Genesis 4•1-2

Adam and Eve
had two sons...

Adam

Eve

Cain

Able

More to Come

...Cain, which means "brought forth",
& Able, which means "breath".
Cain would become a tiller
of the ground and Able
would be a keeper
of the sheep.

Genesis 4•3-5

God was very pleased with Abel's offering and accepted it.
But Cain's offering did not please God because it was not his best.

How can we always give God our best?

LIE•   •I will always try to put others _ _ _ _ _.

LOVE•   •I will not be _ _ _ _ _ _ _.

COMPASSION•   •I will _ _ _ _ my Mom and Dad.

SELFISH•   •I will have _ _ _ _ _ _ _ _ _ _ towards others.

TRUTH•   •I will _ _ _ _ to God.

FAITH•   •I will _ _ _ _ God.

PRAY•   •I will have _ _ _ _ _ in God.

OBEY•   •I will not _ _ _.

FIRST•   •I will always tell the _ _ _ _ _.

61

"Cain & Able," being brothers,...

...had a rivalry and would compete with each other. Have fun competing with a friend. See who can get through the maze first.

Able

Cain

START

START

END

END

One of you take the gray trails, the other the black. If you're gray you can cross black lines; if you're black you can cross gray lines!

62

Cain & Able Genesis 4

Can you find all of the words listed below in this puzzle?
Color in the letters

O	A	T	L	P	O	R	T	I	O	N	D
T	F	A	V	O	R	O	R	D	S	E	I
I	R	F	L	O	C	K	E	E	H	R	S
U	P	K	E	X	A	J	M	A	B	E	L
R	P	R	B	R	O	T	H	E	R	S	I
F	D	E	L	L	I	K	P	I	T	H	K
C	P	R	I	E	L	N	S	C	E	V	E
U	A	L	C	A	I	N	G	L	O	R	D
R	M	O	N	S	O	N	S	M	A	R	R
S	A	E	T	R	S	M	A	N	G	R	Y
E	D	O	N	R	O	B	T	S	R	I	F
W	A	N	D	E	R	E	R	N	G	E	Y

ADAM • EVE • SONS • CAIN • ABEL • FLOCK • SOIL • FRUIT
OFFERING • FAT • FIRSTBORN • PORTION • FAVOR • LORD
DISLIKED • ANGRY • SIN • KILLED • BROTHERS • CURSE
WANDERER

Cain   Able

63

Genesis 5
The generations of Adam to Noah.

Figure out the centuries, decades, and years each person lived.

Cool·Things to Know

Did you know that a DECADE = 10 years and a CENTURY = 100 years?

Adam Lived to be 930 years					
9 Centuries	**3** Decades	**0** Years

Adam had a son named Seth. He lived 912 years.

☐ Centuries ☐ Decades ☐ Years

Seth had a son named Enosh. He lived 905 years

☐ Centuries ☐ Decades ☐ Years

Enosh had a son named Kenan. He lived 910 years

☐ Centuries ☐ Decades ☐ Years

Kenan had a son named Mahalalel. He lived 895 years.

☐ Centuries ☐ Decades ☐ Years

Mahalalel had a son named Jared. He lived 962 years.

☐ Centuries ☐ Decades ☐ Years

Jared had a son named Enoch. He lived 365 years.

☐ Centuries ☐ Decades ☐ Years

Why is Enoch so young compared to the others? Genesis 5:24 says that Enoch walked with God; then he was no more, because God took him away!

Enoch had a son named Methuselah. He lived 969 years.

☐ Centuries ☐ Decades ☐ Years

Methuselah had a son named Lamech. He lived to be 777 years.

☐ Centuries ☐ Decades ☐ Years

Lamech had a son named Noah...

64

ANSWERS IN BACK

Beginning
Genesis 6•8

The Story of Noah and the Ark

BibleTells

After God created Adam and Eve,
people began to multiply on
the earth.

As their numbers increased they
began to forget God
and they

became very evil and wicked.
God became very sad and was sorry he created them.

But there was one man who found favor with God and
that was Noah.

Because Noah loved God and was obedient to God, God wanted
to save him, his wife, their three sons, Shem, Ham, and Japheth,
and their families. God decided to destroy the wickedness
by covering the whole earth with water.

To protect Noah and his family from the flood, God told Noah
to build a very large boat called an ark.

God gave Noah all the measurements he wanted
Noah to construct the boat by.

Noah and the Ark

The reason God wanted Noah to build such a large structure was so Noah could save not only his family but also two of every living creature so they could multiply after the flood.

Once the boat was built and everyone was on board, God closed the door and allowed the heavens to pour out rain upon the earth for forty days and forty nights.

BIBLE TELLS

Noah and the Ark

After the earth was filled with water, Noah had to wait a long time for all the water to dry up before he and his family and all the animals could leave the Ark.

To find out if he could leave, he sent a raven out. The raven flew and flew around the earth but never came back. After more time had passed, Noah sent out a dove. The dove flew out into the earth and then returned with an olive branch. This told Noah that the land was now ready to welcome Noah and his family and all the animals.

They were very happy that God had saved them and God was happy that they were obedient. God told Noah to "be fruitful and multiply and fill the earth."

God also promised Noah that He would never flood the earth again, and as a sign of His promise He sent a beautiful rainbow in the sky. So every time you see a rainbow, remember that God loves you and that He always keeps His promises.

BIBLE TELLS

Noah and the Ark

Put on your thinking Cap

Can you list 7 ways to keep busy if you were on an Ark for over a year?

Cool•Things to Know

Although the rain lasted 40 days and 40 nights, Noah and his family, along with all the animals, actually lived on the Ark for over 1 year!

ANSWERS IN BACK

Noah and the Ark

"Brain Power"

Test your memory.
Study these pictures, then answer the questions on the next page!

Can you be like the elephants and never forget?

"Brain Power"
Question & Answers

1. Why did God send the flood?

2. Why did God save Noah?

3. What did God tell Noah to build to be ready for the flood?

4. Who helped Noah in his building?

5. How many animals did God tell Noah to gather?

6. What sign did God create as a promise between Him and Noah that He would not flood the whole earth again?

ANSWERS IN BACK

Noah and the Ark

Noah's son Shem is using the hammer at the far end of the Ark. Can you help Shem get the hammer back to Noah quickly?

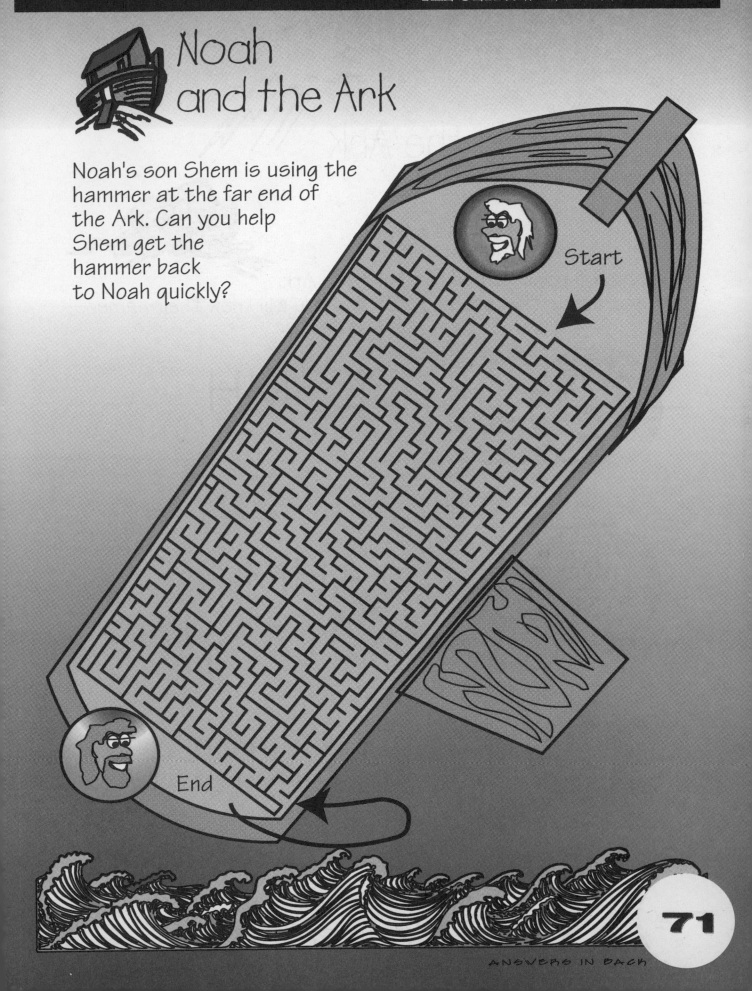

Start

End

ANSWERS IN BACK

Noah and the Ark

Noah's 3 sons helped him build the Ark.
Unscramble the letters below and you will know their names.

ESMH

AHM

PEJTAHH

ANSWERS IN BACK

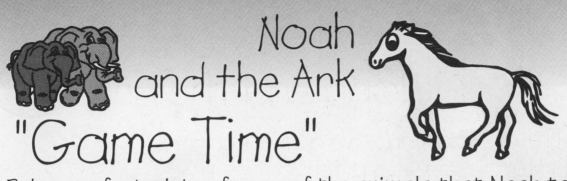

Noah and the Ark "Game Time"

Below are footprints of some of the animals that Noah took on the Ark. Cut on the dotted lines and tape to your "walking" fingers.

Have a guessing game with your friends and see if they can identify the footprints of the animals.

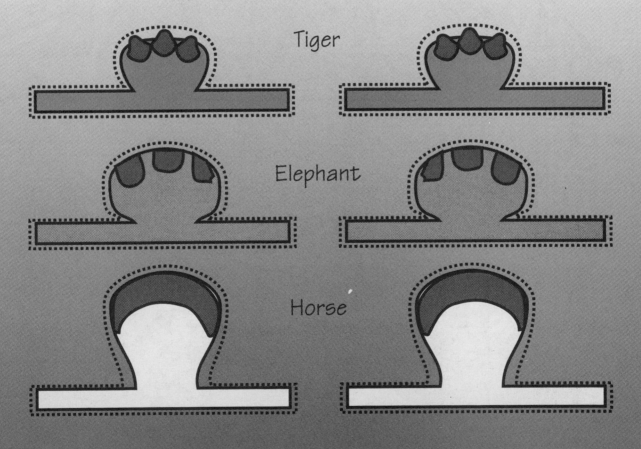

Tiger

Elephant

Horse

The Story of Noah and the Ark

The animals may have gotten a little topsy-turvy after the storm!

Circle the animals that look mixed-up.

ANSWERS IN BACK

Noah and the Ark

GOD   NOAH   ANIMALS   EARTH
EVIL   LOVE   ARK   DOVE
DESTROY   HONEST   RAIN   OLIVE BRANCH
SAVE   FAMILY   FLOOD   RAINBOW

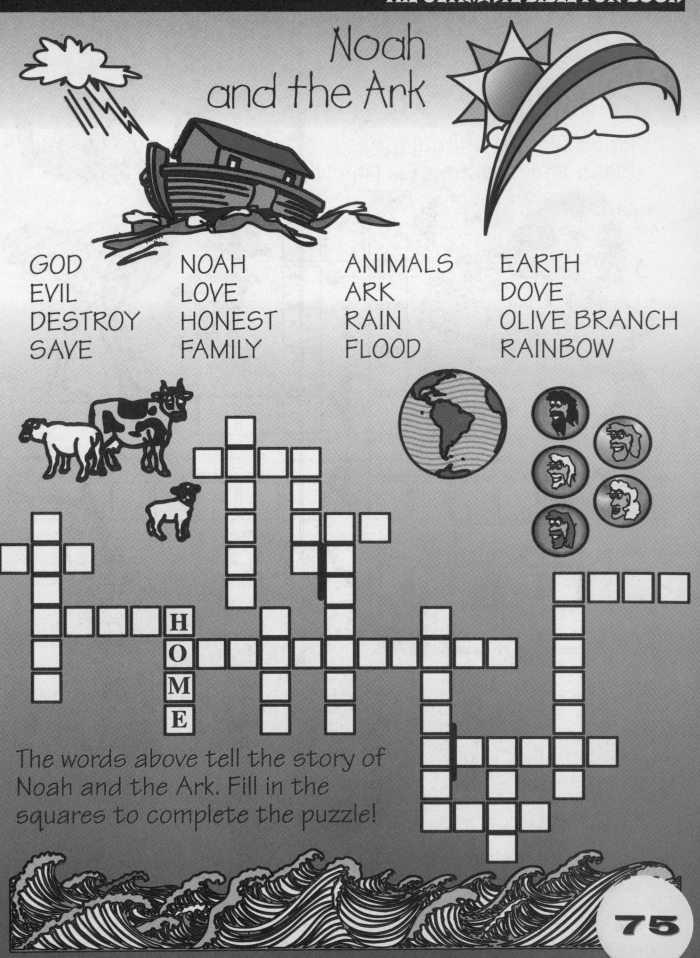

H
O
M
E

The words above tell the story of Noah and the Ark. Fill in the squares to complete the puzzle!

75

Noah and the Ark

Have a little animal fun!
Fill in the spaces starting with clue 1.

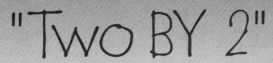

"TWO BY 2"

"They went in two by two unto Noah into the ark."

Genesis 7:9

Find the animal names hidden in Noah's Ark!

```
B S Z E K S A J C M N N R R G O A S T E X L J H N K
I K R L M O N K E Y K O H O Q D Z N P R T R V U A N
L N B P G P S M O O E R P O G J A F O E S L J N H T
Y E A E R D T N A H P E L E O D W T P O I B G A C L
G A Z H A I A W W R Y M O F T G B Y I R N A O R T Y
O Q W T R E O R H I R E J F M I D L P H R K V J L H
T R O N O H B O E O E A S A R L L E N O B E J F S N
A E E A O R I R N D I G N R O M T A O L V U R T Q V
T E A L H G H N C E I T R I E D V T R T B B C L A J
U D G Y D A F M O D N P F G O A T G E S O P P I H Z
R N L G O N R F W T D E S K F R W N I V J I N R V T
T I E R I G L F L A R N Q A L T Z S N M R O W A T N
P E C N P L T A R B E Z Z N H V N L D U S P I D R E
N R O H O E B E E H D S H E L T R U T W G T O A L Z
```

cow	turtle	worm	eagle	monkey
zebra	elephant	fly	spider	reindeer
giraffe	rhino	kangaroo	hippo	goat

ANSWERS IN BACK

"Match Mate"
Noah and the Ark

Help each animal find its mate. Don't get confused and take the wrong path.

ANSWERS IN BACK

Noah and the Ark

•43
42•
•46
•41 •44
•60
•61
•64
•58
•62
•66
•67 •65•63 •57
•47
•68
•37 •69 •59
•36 •40•45
•48 •56
•39
•70
•35 •38
•49
•55

Noah knew

that the water

level had lowered

enough to reveal

dry land when a

dove that he sent

returned with an

olive branch.

•34
•32 •33 •50
•31 •54
•30
•29 •53
•51
•28
•27
•52
•21 •26 •1
•18 •20 •22 •25
•17 •24 •2
•16 •19 •23
•15 •5 •4 •3
•10
•14 9••6
13• •12 •11
8•
•7

Noah and the Ark

"Science Fun"

You can easily create your own rainbow at home! All you need is:

1. a flashlight
2. a clear glass of water

Turn your flashlight on; point it toward the glass of water. When the light hits the water it will break into several colors.

What colors do you see?

Congratulations! You've made a rainbow!

Noah and the Ark

"Shadow Fun"

One thing Noah, Shem, Ham, Japheth, and their families might have done to pass time on the Ark was to create shadow puppets by candle light!

Position your hands and fingers between a light source and the wall. Put your hands together in different configurations, watching what types of shadows appear.
You never know what you might discover!

What do you think this is?

81

Noah and the Ark

"Shadow Puppets"

On the following pages are some examples of shadow puppets!

Can you do this?

Cool·Things to Know

Not only can you make cool pictures on the wall, but you can spell words with hand gestures! This is called sign language.

Noah
and the Ark

Sign language is a way of talking to a person who can't hear.

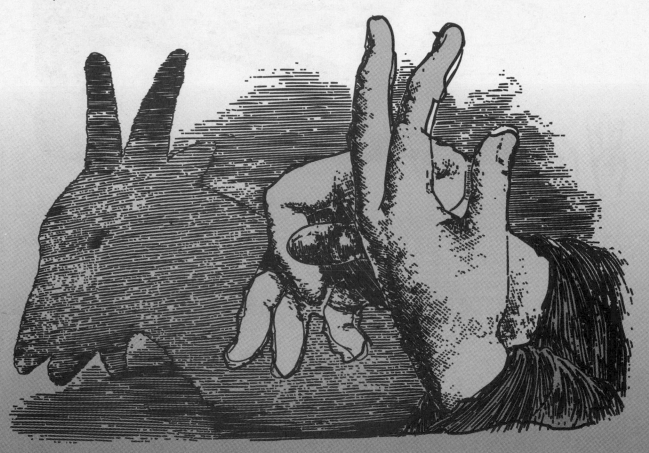

What is this animal?

"Shadow Puppets"

"Shadow Puppets"

Guess what these animals are!

If you need help, look on the next page for the sign language alphabet.

ANSWERS IN BACK

Here is the alphabet in sign language.
Can you spell your name?

Can you figure out
what these signs mean?

Noah
and the Ark

85

"Shadow Puppets"

ANSWERS IN BACK

Can you make this dog Bark?

Just have a friend hold up a flashlight
and imitate the hands below.

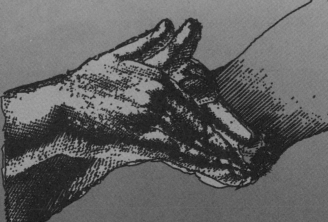

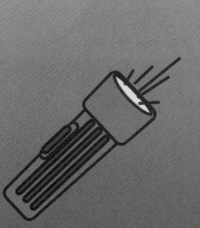

Noah
and the Ark

Flashlight Fun

Take turns holding the flashlight and trying to guess what the shadow is.

Noah
and the Ark

ANSWERS IN BACK

These dogs want to be
your friends.

"Shadow People"

Now that you are an expert...

...try to do these shapes!

Noah
and the Ark

Who built the Ark?

_ _ _ _ Look at the puzzle below. How many times can you find his name?

Hint: Look in all directions!

N	O	A	H	O	A	O	H	N	H
A	N	O	A	H	A	O	N	O	A
O	H	A	O	H	N	O	O	H	O
H	A	H	N	O	A	H	A	A	N
N	O	A	A	H	O	N	A	O	O
O	N	O	N	O	A	H	A	N	H
O	H	N	O	A	O	H	A	O	N
A	A	H	O	A	H	O	H	N	A
N	O	N	N	O	A	H	O	A	H
O	N	O	A	H	O	N	A	O	A
A	A	H	H	A	O	N	H	O	O
H	O	H	A	O	N	H	A	A	N

ANSWERS IN BACK

Color the Rainbow 1-2-3.

How many colors do you see?

God promised Noah that He "would never destroy the earth with a flood again." As a sign God created a rainbow and placed it in the sky!

2
5
3
7
1
6
4

Noah
and the Ark

1. Blue   2. Red
3. Yellow   4. Violet
5. Orange   6. Indigo
7. Green

Help Noah navigate...
...these rough ocean waves!

Start

Noah and the Ark

End

95

Search & Read

If you would like to read the story of Noah and the Ark in the Bible, search for the scripture below in the red squares.

N	O	A	H	T	A	O	H	N	H
G	N	O	A	H	H	O	N	O	A
O	E	A	O	H	N	G	O	H	O
H	A	N	N	O	A	H	I	A	N
N	O	A	E	H	O	N	A	E	O
O	N	O	N	S	A	H	H	N	H
O	H	N	O	A	I	G	A	O	N
A	A	H	O	A	U	S	H	N	A
N	O	N	N	O	A	H	S	I	X
O	N	O	R	H	O	N	A	O	A
A	A	H	H	A	O	N	H	O	O
H	T	H	A	O	N	H	A	A	N

ANSWERS IN BACK

"Rainstick"

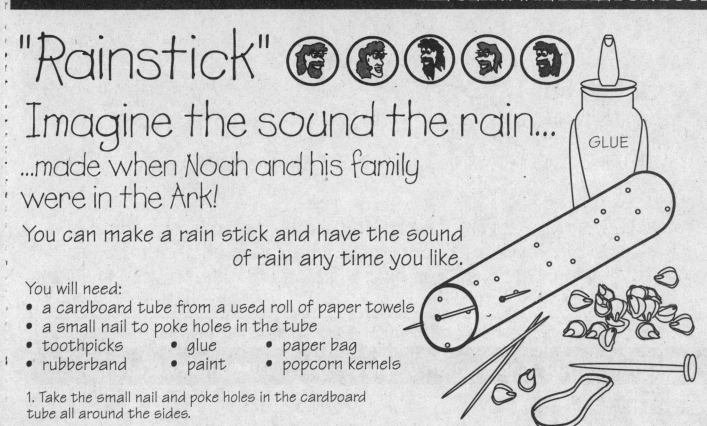

Imagine the sound the rain...

...made when Noah and his family were in the Ark!

You can make a rain stick and have the sound of rain any time you like.

You will need:
- a cardboard tube from a used roll of paper towels
- a small nail to poke holes in the tube
- toothpicks
- glue
- paper bag
- rubberband
- paint
- popcorn kernels

1. Take the small nail and poke holes in the cardboard tube all around the sides.

2. Poke the toothpicks through the holes to holes on the other side. Do this with several toothpicks until the toothpicks are crossing over each other inside the tube. Use another toothpick to dot a little glue at each hole. Them let them dry!

3. While holding the tube over a wastebasket cut off the ends of the toothpicks so they are smooth with the tube. Nail clippers will work well for this.

4. Now is a good time to paint the rainstick. Make it as colorful as you like.

5. Take your paper bag and cut two large circles. Glue one of these circles to the end of your rainstick. Put a rubberband around it until it dries.

6. Take as many popcorn kernels as your hand can hold and put them into the stick. Then take the other paper circle and glue it to the end to close the rain stick. Again, put a rubberband around it to hold until it dries.

As you gently turn the rain stick from side to side you can hear the soothing sound of rain!

Noah and the Ark

97

Genesis 7•1-3

Noah and the Ark

The Lord told Noah, "Go into the Ark, you and your family. I have found you to be good people in this generation.

Take with you seven of every kind of clean animal, male and female, and two of every kind of unclean animal, male and female. Also take seven of every kind of bird, male and female, to keep them alive throughout the earth."

Clean = God approved for food or sacrifice • Unclean = Not to be eaten or sacrificed

Unscramble the names of these clean and unclean animals

Clean:	Unclean:
UATN	AELMC
RUTOT	ABTIBR
OUTSCL	IGP
ETEBLE	OPINHLD
RSHPERPOSAG	OSERTBL
XO	ALEGE
HEEPS	UTREULV
OTGA	AENVR
ERED	WLO
ABLM	AKWH
HCENKIC	WNAS
	EIANCLP
	OSEUM
	OTIESORT
	IADRZL

98

Genesis 7•1-3

From the previous page, can you circle which animals and birds were clean? Noah would have seven of these on the Ark.

Noah
and the Ark

99

Help Noah feed the animals!
Draw a line and match the food with the animal.

Cool·Things to Know

One of the largest animals living on land is the elephant.
They also have the largest nose (called a "trunk"), the
largest ears, and the largest teeth (called "tusks").
They are very strong and very very smart!

Noah
and the Ark

ANSWERS IN BACK

"Cow"

Can you find the matching cows
that went on Noah's Ark?

Two are the
same.

Can you
spot them?

Noah
and the Ark

101

What kind of animal games might

Draw a line from the letter of the alphabet

A
B
C
D
E
F
G
H
I
J
K
L
M

ANSWERS IN BACK

Noah and his family play on the Ark?

Draw a line to the animal that begins with that letter!

N O P Q R S T U V W X Y Z

Noah
and the Ark

103

The Ark was so big that these ants got separated!

Help them find each other.

Start

End

Noah
and the Ark

ANSWERS IN BACK

"Play Dough Animals"

Make a batch of play dough...

...then roll in different size balls to create animals for the Ark!

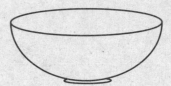

You will need:

- 1 cup flour
- 1/2 cup salt
- 2 tsp. cream of tartar
- pan
- 1 cup water
- 1 Tbl. cooking oil
- 1 tsp. food coloring
- small bowl

1. Mix flour, salt, and cream of tartar in pan.

2. Combine water, oil, and food coloring in small bowl; mix until smooth. Add to dry ingredients; mix well.

3. Cook over medium heat, stirring constantly, until mixture forms ball.

4. Knead ball until mixture is cool and smooth before using.

Use for modeling and sculpting as desired. Store in airtight container.

Noah and the Ark

"Bears"

Can you find the matching pair of bears?

Noah and the Ark

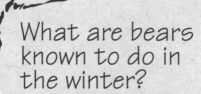

Cool·Things to Know

Did you know that Genesis 7:15-16 tells us that pairs of all the creatures came to Noah? When they were all there and in the Ark God shut the door to the Ark!

What are bears known to do in the winter?

ANSWERS IN BACK

Noah and the Ark

"Zebra"

How many Zebras
can you find?

107

ANSWERS IN BACK

"Animal Guess"
Do you know your animals?

A _____ is good for wool.

A _____ has nine lives.

I never forget: I'm an _____.

I jump high; I jump low; I'm a _____.
I store my baby in a pouch.

The _____ is known for desert travel.

I swing from tree to tree. You're right—
I'm a _____.

Is a _____ white with black stripes
or black with white stripes?

I love to eat hay, and I love to nay.
I'm a _____ of course!

Noah
and the Ark

108

"Fun with Fishing"

Turn the page to see how you can
play this great game!

"Fun with Fishing"

All you need is:

- ✦ A long stick or wire coat hanger that has been untwisted
- ✦ A long piece of string
- ✦ A magnet
- ✦ Paper clips

Assemble "Fishing Pole"

Tie string to one end of stick or coat hanger. Attach magnet to the other end of the string.

"Fish"

Cut out Fish below and slide paper clip on each fish. Place "Fish" number side down and see how many points you can catch. First Fisherman to 100 points wins the "Catch of the day!"

Noah and the Ark

Noah and the Ark

"Mind Recall"

Test your memory. Turn the page to see how!

Noah
and the Ark

Noah
and the Ark

Noah
and the Ark

Noah
and the Ark

Noah
and the Ark

Noah
and the Ark

"Mind Recall"

Cut out individual playing cards

Object of game: Get as many pairs of animals as you can. When all cards are gone the player with the most pairs wins!

Noah and the Ark

Rules:
- Place all the cards animal side down.
- First player picks two cards and turns them over.

(Rules continue on next page)

115

Rules: (Cont.)

- If player gets a matching pair, he/she keeps the matching cards and takes another turn.
- If no match, turn both cards over and the next player takes his/her turn.

Noah and the Ark 	Noah and the Ark 	Noah and the Ark 
Noah and the Ark 	Noah and the Ark 	Noah and the Ark 

"Mind Recall"
Match the pairs of animals!

"Mind Recall"

Animal match game! See previous pages for rules.

Noah
and the Ark

Noah
and the Ark

Noah
and the Ark

Noah
and the Ark

Noah
and the Ark

Noah
and the Ark

"Spot Blots"

Noah and the Ark

You can create art by blotting paint on paper and folding it together. Here's how!

Materials needed:
• thick tempera paint
• spoon or brush
• paper that has been folded in half and then opened flat again.

How to do it:
• drop or brush the thick tempera paint down the fold mark (or only down one side of the fold mark)
• fold the paper over and press gently
• unfold and allow to dry

You should have a mirror image on both sides of the fold mark

"Color me two by two"

Color the pairs of animals
as they are allowed
to go free from the Ark!

Noah
and the Ark

120

Noah
and the Ark

Noah
and the Ark

"Color me two by two"

Noah and the Ark

Noah
and the Ark

"Color me
two by two"

Noah
and the Ark

Genesis 9•9-11

God's Covenant with Noah

Using the code, read what God's covenant was.

A = ❄
B = ⚲
C = 🏭
D = ▲
E = ☆
F = 👫
G = ⚑
H = 〰
I = ⬠
J = ✝
K = ⟩
L = ▢
M = ⛏
N = ☢
O = ⬭
P = ▽
Q = 🏛
R = ✪
S = 🕊
T = ◎
U = 〰
V = ⚑
W = 🍁
X = ♿
Y = 🛡
Z = ⟨

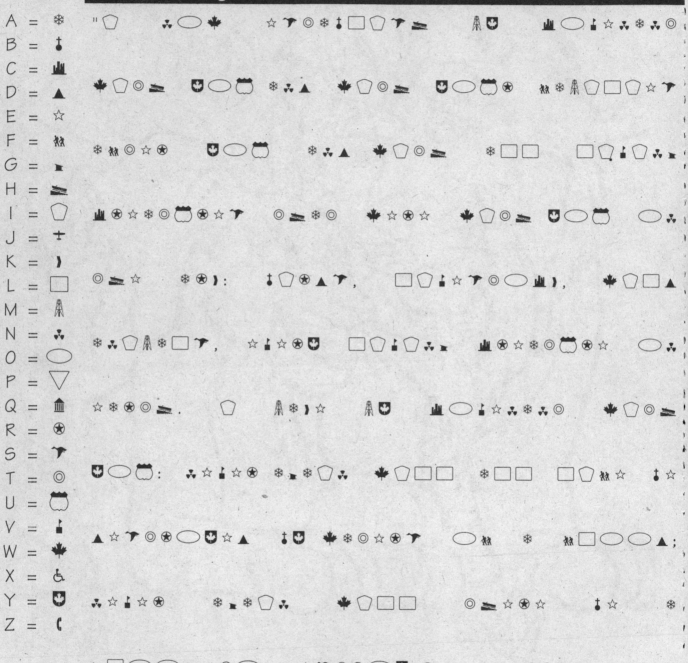

ANSWERS IN BACK

Genesis 9•20

Noah and the Ark

Cool•Things to Know

Noah was also a tiller of the ground.
After the flood he planted a vineyard.

Grapes are grown in a vineyard. After coloring
these grapes, can you list several things that grapes
are used for?

Noah lived
to be a very old age!

Do the math
and get the answer.

Can you guess Noah's age?

400
x2

Multiply 400
by 2 then
subtract 375
$- - -$

-375

Take that
number and
add 95
$- - -$

+95

Take this
number and
divide it by 5
$- - -$

$5\overline{)}$
$- - -$

Take your
number and
multiply by 10
$- - -$

x10

Now
subtract 205
$- - -$

-205

$- - -$

Take this
number and
add 175
$- - -$

+175

Take this
number and
divide it by 5
$- - -$

$5\overline{)}$
$- - -$

$- - -$

Now
multiply your
number by 3
then
add 344
x3

$- - -$

+344

How old was Noah?

$- - -$

ANSWERS IN BACK

Genesis 8•11

...and the dove came back to Noah with a newly sprouted _____; Noah knew that the waters had dried from the land.

ANSWERS IN BACK

Genesis 11•9
The Lord God confounded all the languages of the earth.

End

Follow the arrows
to reveal why God caused
speech to be confused!

Start

Use the code from page 24
to figure out what this says!

130

ANSWERS IN BACK

Cool•Things to Know

There are over 5 billion people in the world and they speak over 9,000 languages.

New languages are still being discovered in remote places.

African
Aramaic
British
Celtic
Chinese
Dutch
English
French
German
Greek
Hebrew
Hindi
Irish
Italian
Japanese
Latin
Mandarin
Norwegian
Polish
Portuguese
Russian
Spanish
Swedish

```
A Z W N I R A D N A M E X J
U F R E N C H W E R B E H A
A Z R W A B R I T I S H A P
Y N W I K A C H I N E S E A
N A J E C V A I S Z C H R N
A M E A E A Q N W E A A L E
I R B Z L A N D E A M C A S
G E A C T R A I D A Z A P E
E G J A I W A H I K A A A X
W D U T C H A C S A N H W N
R R U S S I A N H I A W B I
O A K I A Z Q C S A L A P T
N Q L I R I S H A C A G A A
A O B N A I L A T I A V N L
P O R T U G U E S E W Y T E
```

Look at the list of languages and find them in the puzzle - Look backwards and forwards, up then down. Color them in with green or brown!

131

This **MAN** is lost in the Tower of Babel. He can't find anyone who speaks his language. Can you help him get out?

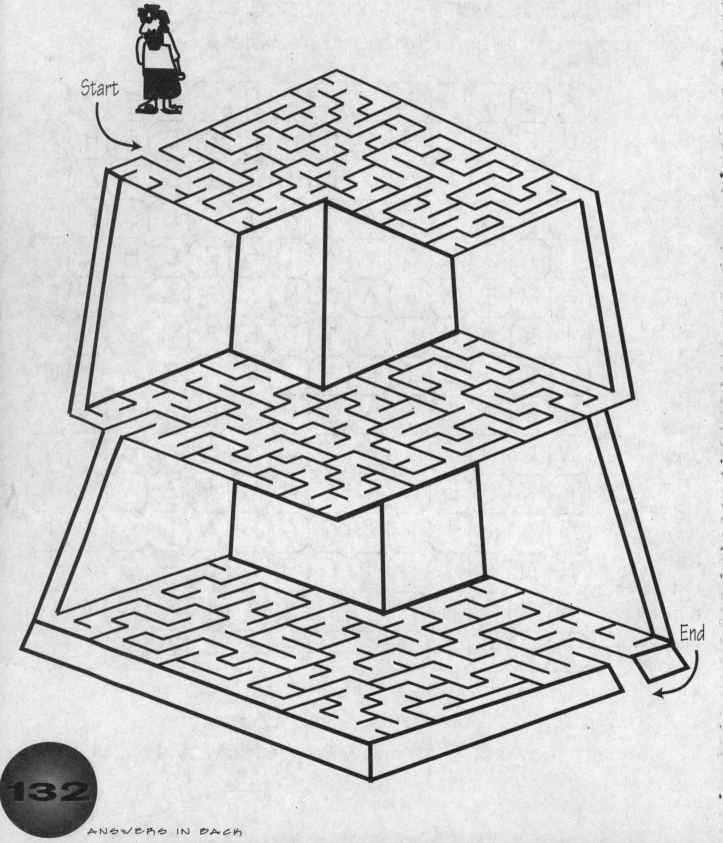

Start

End

132

Start with Tower of Babel.

See how many words you can make that have to do with TYPES OF communication. Use the tiles below!

A word does not have to be created in all directions but you must use all tiles.

133

Learn to Measure

Measuring Abbreviations

tsp. = teaspoon
Tbl. = tablespoon
c. = cup
qt. = quart

fl. oz. = fluid ounce
pt. = pint
gal. = gallon
lb. = pound

How to Measure

Use clear glass or plastic liquid measuring cups for all liquids.

Measure liquids by reading the lines on the cup at eye level.

Use dry or stacking measuring cups for dry ingredients.

Measure by spooning into the cup until it's completely full, then levelling off with the straight edge of a knife or rubber spatula.

For spoons, first check the measurement on the spoon to select the correct one.

Fill measuring spoon as closely to the top as possible with liquids. With dry ingredients, level off with the straight edge of a knife or rubber spatula.

Kitchen Math

3 tsp. = 1 Tbl.
4 Tbl. = 1/4 c.
8 Tbl = 1/2 c.
16 Tbl = 1 c.
2 c. = 1 pt.
4 c. = 1 qt.
4 qt. = 1 gal.
1 fl. oz. = 2 Tbl.
1/2 stick butter = 1/4 c.
1 stick butter = 1/2 c.

Make An Easy Apron

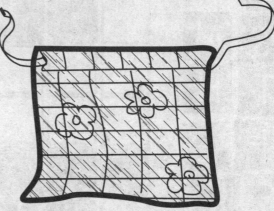

You Will Need:
- 2 yards cotton cording
- 1 kitchen towel
- needle and thread.

1. Fold one long side of the towel down 1/2"
2. Sew 1/4" in from the edge.
3. Thread cording through opening.
4. Knot both ends.

Fun Cookies to make from other countries

Italian Cookies

1. These are all the ingredients you will need to make the cookies. With help from Mom and/or Dad turn the oven on to 300° to preheat. Next get all your ingredients and place them on the kitchen table.
   - 1 cube room temperature Butter
   - Sugar
   - 1 egg
   - Vanilla extract
   - All-Purpose Flour
   - Salt
   - Bag of Shredded Coconut

2. Now you will need to get the correct amounts of each of these ingredients. Use the chart on the previous page to help you if you're not sure what the abbreviations mean. You can also learn how to measure from the previous page so you know you are getting the right amounts of each item.

3. Let's start by measuring all the dry ingredients:
   - 1/3 c. sugar
   - 1 c. + 2 Tbl. all purpose flour
   - 1/2 tsp. salt
   - 1 c. shredded coconut

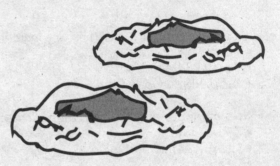

4. Now let's measure all the liquid ingredients:
   - 1/2 c. butter
   - 1/4 tsp. vanilla extract

5. With help, separate the egg white and yolk into two separate bowls.
   - 1 egg yolk (that's the yellow part of the egg)
   - 1 egg white

6. Now you are ready to mix everything together in its proper order:

In a large mixing bowl mix together butter and sugar. Mix until light and fluffy.
Now add the egg yolk (yellow part) and vanilla. Once again mix really well.
Mix the flour and salt into your bowl a little at a time. Make sure all the ingredients are mixed together really well.

Now you will need to put the dough in the refrigerator until it is easy to handle (about 30 minutes).

Roll spoonfuls of dough into balls; dip ball into egg white and then roll in coconut. Place on lightly greased cookie sheet about 2 inches apart. You can put your thumb print in the middle of each cookie to leave a dip.

Bake at 300° for 20 to 25 minutes. Cool on wire racks and fill dip with preserve of your choice.
Makes 3 1/2 dozen cookies

Fun Cookies to make...

Norwegian Almond Cookies

1. These are all the ingredients you will need to make the cookies. With help from Mom and/or Dad preheat the oven to 375°. Next get all your ingredients and place them on the kitchen table.

- 1 cube room temperature Butter
- Powdered Sugar
- All-Purpose Flour
- Flaked almonds
- 1 Lemon
- 1 egg

2. Now you will need to get the correct amounts of each of these ingredients. Use the chart on page 134 to help you if you're not sure what the abbreviations mean. You can also learn how to measure from the previous page so you know you are getting the right amounts of each item.

3. Let's start by measuring all the dry ingredients:
- 1/2 c. powdered sugar
- 1 c. flaked almonds
- 1/2 c. all-purpose flour

4. Now let's measure all the liquid ingredients:
- 3/4 c. butter
- 1 tsp. fresh lemon juice
- 1 egg

5. Now you are ready to mix everything together in its proper order:

In a large mixing bowl mix together butter and sugar. Mix until light and fluffy.
Now add the flaked almonds to the mixture. Once again mix really well.
Now add the lemon juice and the egg. Once this is mixed really well add the flour a little at a time.
Make sure all these ingredients are mixed together really well.

Roll teaspoonfuls of dough into balls (or use a cookie press). Place 2 inches apart onto an ungreased cookie sheet. Bake at 375° for 10 to 15 minutes. Cool on wire racks.
Makes 5 1/2 dozen cookies

Fun pudding to make...

English Flummery - a type of rice pudding

1. These are all the ingredients you will need to make the flummery. With help from Mom and/or Dad, get all your ingredients and place them on the kitchen table.

- 1 bag of round-grain rice, soaked in cold water for 30 minutes
- Milk
- Heavy cream
- Sugar
- 1 Lemon
- Ground Cinnamon

2. Now you will need to get the correct amounts of each of these ingredients. Use the chart on the page 134 to help you if you're not sure what the abbreviations mean. You can also learn how to measure from the page 134 so you know you are getting the right amounts of each item.

3. Let's start by measuring all the dry ingredients:
- 2/3 c. round-grain rice
- 1/4 c. sugar
- 1 Tbl. finely grated lemon rind
- 1 tsp. ground cinnamon

4. Now let's measure all the liquid ingredients:
- 1 1/4 c. milk
- 1 1/4 c. heavy cream

5. Now you are ready to mix everything together in its proper order, Make sure Mom and/or Dad are there to help you since this is made on the stove!:

In a double saucepan combine all the ingredients in the top part of the pan. Fill half the bottom part with boiling water.
Place the double saucepan over low heat. Cover the double saucepan and let cook, stirring the mixture every few minutes.
Once the rice has absorbed all the liquids (about 1 hour) remove the pan from the heat.
Pour the mixture into pudding cups and allow to cool to room temperature.
Refrigerate for 3 hours or until the flummery is set and firm.
Enjoy eating it cold with whipped cream on top!!

Cool·Things to Know

What's a "Double Saucepan" or
    "Double Boiler"?
Two pans fitting into each other
    so that the contents of the upper pan can be cooked
    by boiling water in the lower pan.

Genesis 12•1

In the old times of the Bible God wanted people to understand Him better...

BIBLE TELLS

...He would test their faith by asking them to do certain things. Abram was one of those people. God asked him lo leave his homeland and go to a new place. Because Abram loved God, he wanted to obey. So he left his city called Ur, in a country called Mesopotamia, and began to venture out into the wilderness. He took with him all his possessions: his sheep, goats, cattle, donkeys, his servants, his wife Sarai, and his nephew Lot. Together they traveled across the countryside to reach the land of Canaan, which God designated for them.

Sometimes it would be very difficult for Lot and Abram to feed all their flocks in the same place because there were so many animals. So Abram and Lot decided to go to different places to feed their animals because there was so much land that they could share. Abram settled in Canaan and Lot settled in a city called Sodom which was by another city called Gomorrah. This way everybody could be happy. When Abram arrived in Canaan, God told him to look north, south, east, and west, and all the land he could see would be the land of Abram's descendants, which means his children's children's children, and so on and so on.

Abram's wife Sarai had grown very old and still had no children. She decided Abram should have a child with her maid-servant Hagar, and so they had a son and called him Ishmael. God told Abram that he would be the father of many nations. As a sign of this promise, God told Abram his name would be changed to 'Abraham' and that all male children would be required to be circumcised as a sign of this covenant. God also told Abraham that He would change Sarai's name to 'Sarah" as a sign of Abraham's promise to God.

Abraham's Family History

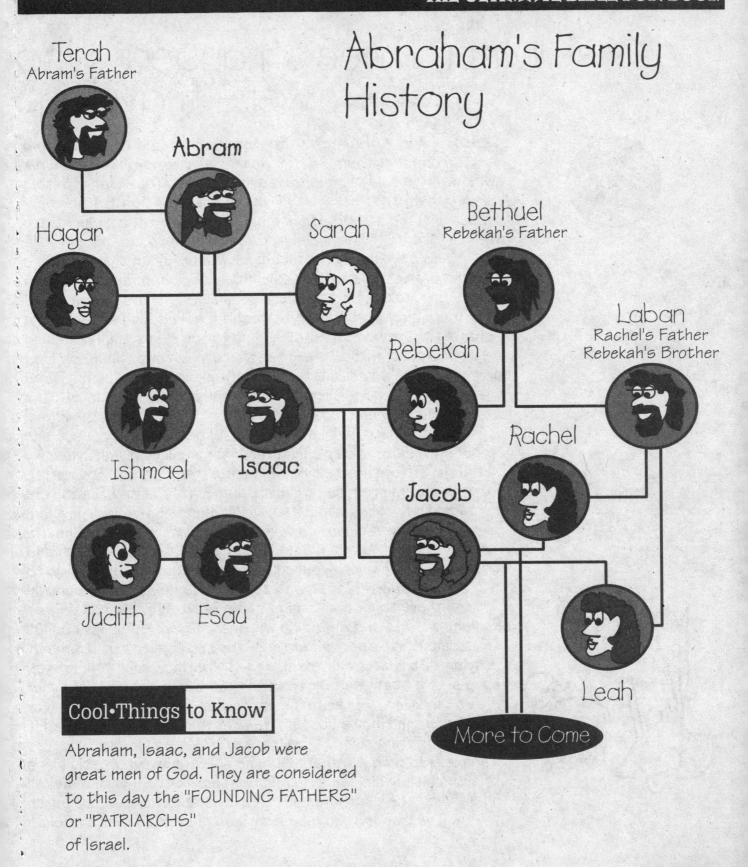

Terah
Abram's Father

Abram

Hagar

Sarah

Bethuel
Rebekah's Father

Laban
Rachel's Father
Rebekah's Brother

Rebekah

Ishmael

Isaac

Rachel

Jacob

Judith

Esau

Leah

Cool•Things to Know

Abraham, Isaac, and Jacob were great men of God. They are considered to this day the "FOUNDING FATHERS" or "PATRIARCHS" of Israel.

More to Come

Later, three strangers who were traveling...

...stopped by Abraham's tent. Abraham offered them food and drink, to comfort them. The strangers asked Abraham where his wife was. He told them she was in the tent. The strangers told Abraham that his wife Sarah would bear a son. Sarah, over-hearing the conversation, laughed, because she thought she was way too old to have children. God spoke to her and said, "Is there anything too difficult for the Lord?" In the meantime Abraham and Lot saw that the cities of Sodom and Gomorrah were very wicked, and that the people living there were very evil and had no respect for God. Abraham asked God to spare the cities if there were at least 10 good people, but the Lord could not find 10 that had their hearts turned toward him. So God sent two angels to tell Lot and his family to leave because God was going to destroy these cities because they were so evil. The angels also instructed them to not look back at the cities' destruction, but Lot's wife could not resist. Because she disobeyed God's order she turned into a pillar of salt. The only things left of these cities were smoke and ashes. Soon after, God fulfilled his promise to Sarah, and Abraham and Sarah bore a son. They called him Isaac, which means laughter. Abraham and Sarah loved their son very much and were proud to have a child of their own. But God still wanted to test their faith and trust in Him. The Lord spoke to Abraham and told him to go to a place called Moriah and to sacrifice Isaac on a mountain there to God as a sign of his faith. Abraham again was obedient to God and did as he was instructed. As he was about to sacrifice Isaac, an angel of the Lord called out his name, saying "Abraham, Abraham, do not sacrifice your son, for you have shown that you fear God and you would not withhold your only son for Him." Abraham then heard a noise close by and saw a ram caught in the bushes. He went and got it and offered it up as an offering to the Lord instead of his son Isaac. God was so pleased with Abraham that he said He would greatly bless him and multiply his seed, as all the stars in the heavens and all the sand on the seashore, and that all the nations of the earth will be blessed because Abraham obeyed the voice of God.

Abraham, God's friend

My Family History

Make your own family tree in the space below. You can draw pictures or ask your mother or father to help you cut out photographs and glue them down with a glue stick.

Connect with lines and label with name and relationship.

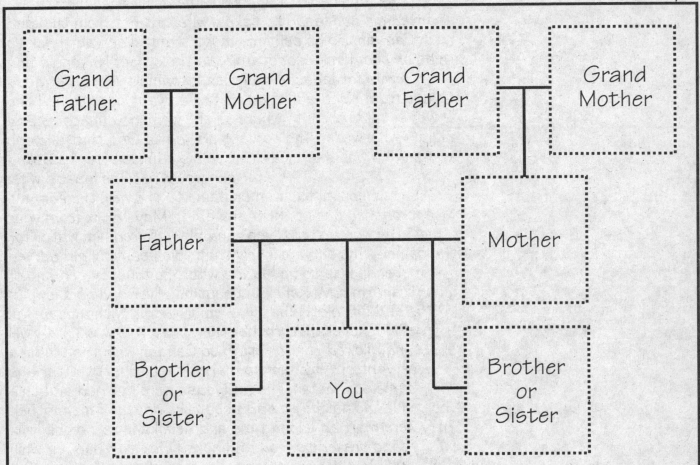

This is a fun project to do with your friends. Everyone's family tree looks different: Step Moms and Dads, Half Brothers and Sisters, Aunts and Uncles. Families are made up of all kinds of people and they are all very important!

Abraham returned home a very happy man.

But a very sad thing happened soon after. His wife Sarah died at the age of one hundred twenty seven. Abraham was very sad and grieved over her death; he knew he was getting very old and would be dying soon himself. He wanted his son Isaac to take a wife, but not from the land of Canaan. So he sent his most trusted servant back to his homeland in Mesopotamia, to the city of Nahor, to find a wife for Isaac. Along with 10 camels and other good things from Abraham, the trusted servant approached the well outside the city where all the women would come and fill jars with water. The servant prayed to God that the one woman who would offer a drink to his camels after he asked for one would become Isaac's wife.

When all the women came to the well, the servant approached one of them and said, "May I drink from your jar?" The woman said "yes" and also offered him water for the camels. The servant knew that this beautiful girl named Rebekah was to be Isaac's wife. The trusted servant of Abraharm gave Rebekah beautiful silver and gold jewelry and fine cloth that was embroidered with a beautiful design. Rebekah's brother knew that this was God's will and allowed her to return to Canaan with the trusted servant of Abraham to marry Isaac. Shortly after she came to Canaan, she and Isaac were married and this helped Isaac not be so sad about the death of his mother. They were married a long time and Rebekah had no children. Isaac prayed to God and asked God to bless her with children. She soon conceived and bore twin sons. The firstborn son was covered in red hair and they named him 'Esau'. The second was holding onto the first one's heel and they called him 'Jacob'.

Genesis 12•1

God tells Abram to move...

...from the land where he and his family lived and to go to the land that God would show him.

Haran

Start here

Abram was a very obedient man of God. Can you help him and his family get from Haran to Canaan? Along the way they stopped at Sichem.

Go from Haran to Sichem and then to Canaan.

End here

Canaan

143

The story of these two brothers is quite interesting...

...because they were so different from each other. Esau loved to hunt and Jacob was very peaceful and liked to stay in the tent. One day Esau came in from hunting and was very hungry. Jacob had a big pot of lentil stew cooking and it smelled so good to Esau that he wanted to eat right away. Jacob said, "you can have some stew if you will give up your birthright as firstborn to me." Esau thought it was so funny and said to Jacob, "What good is my birthright when I'm going to die of hunger?" So Jacob made Esau give him his word that indeed he had given away his birthright for a bowl of lentil stew. As time passed their father began to get very old. He could not see very well anymore and was near death. He wanted Esau, his favorite son to prepare a special dish of venison which he could taste for one last time. Rebekah, the boy's mother, overheard the conversation and told Jacob, her favorite son, to disguise himself as Esau so he could receive his father's final blessing. Rebekah told Jacob that she would cook the meal that Isaac requested, and she wanted Jacob to go and cover himself with the hair of an animal so when Isaac touched him he would think it was Esau. After the meal was prepared, Jacob covered himself with fur and went to see his father. Isaac knew that the voice he was hearing was Jacob's but when he touched him he felt hairy like Esau. Isaac asked his son to come close and kiss him, but because Jacob was covered in animal skin he smelled like Esau. Isaac believed it was his firstborn and began to bless him. When Esau returned from hunting it was too late. Isaac had already given everything to Jacob. Esau was very upset that Jacob had taken away his birthright and his blessing from his father. He was so angry with Jacob that he planned to kill him after his father died. His mother heard this and told Jacob to go back to Mesopotamia to her brother's house where he would be safe until his brother calmed down. Rebekah assured Jacob she would let him know when it would be safe to return.

BibleTells

What's in a name?
Fill in the puzzle below

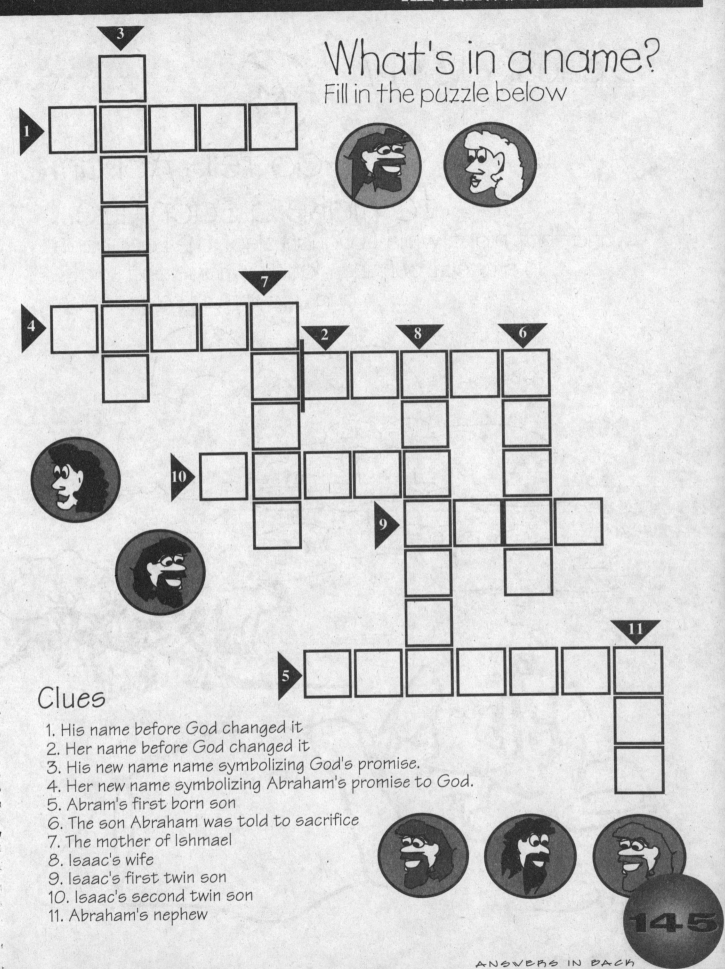

Clues

1. His name before God changed it
2. Her name before God changed it
3. His new name name symbolizing God's promise.
4. Her new name symbolizing Abraham's promise to God.
5. Abram's first born son
6. The son Abraham was told to sacrifice
7. The mother of Ishmael
8. Isaac's wife
9. Isaac's first twin son
10. Isaac's second twin son
11. Abraham's nephew

145

Genesis 15•17

God tells Abram to make a sacrifice...

...and that night while Abraham slept the Lord came in a great burning cloud of flame and smoke and accepted the sacrifice.

Cool·Things to Know

A camel with one hump is called a dromedary.

A camel with two humps is called a camel!

Genesis 22•13

Abraham

Abraham and Isaac go to give a sacrifice...

...unto God as God has required. God provides a ram caught in a thicket.

Isaac

God changed Abram's name...

...to Abraham. There is a lot to a persons name. Abram means "high" and Abraham means "father of multitudes."

S	P	A	T	R	I	A	R	C	H	S	S
S	A	B	R	A	H	A	M	O	A	H
I	I	S	A	A	C	E	N	C	S	O
C	S	W	O	R	O	A	R	D	A	B
H	A	R	A	D	N	I	H	W	R	E
E	R	M	R	N	F	S	H	D	O	D
M	A	D	A	I	D	W	O	E	R	I
O	H	C	C	I	S	R	A	E	L	E
E	A	E	O	S	H	A	R	A	N	N
A	B	R	A	M	H	W	H	R	O	T

Look at the list of words. Find and color them in..

Abram   Israel
Obedient   Abraham
Haran   Sacrifice
Canaan   Ram
Sichem   Sarah
Patriarch   Isaac

149

Cool·Things to Know

Camels can carry up to 400 lbs and can travel swiftly through the desert at about 8 to 10 miles an hour.

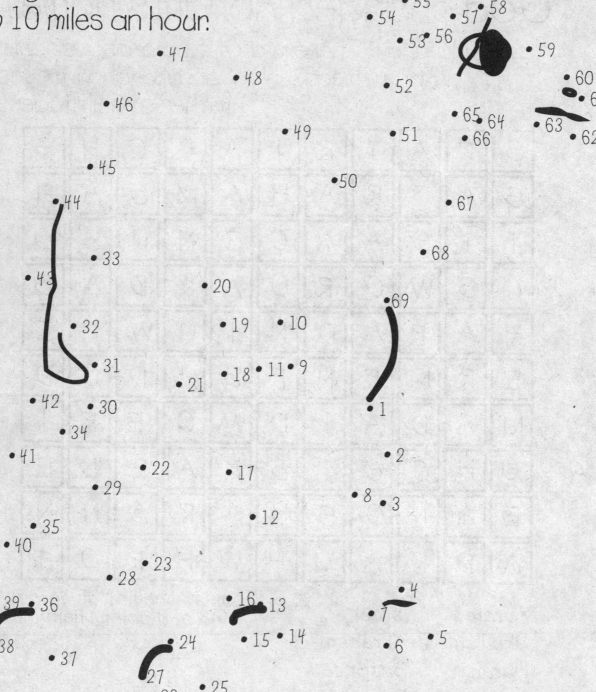

I love to drink a lot of water—especially when the weather's hotter!

ANSWERS IN BACK

God often used Angels as messengers...

...In fact, angel means 'messenger.'

ANSWERS IN BACK

Abram has lost something very important.

Can you help him find it?

1. Start at the palm tree that has 7 fronds.
2. Go north until you reach a tent.
3. Count the number of people by the tent. Go that many inches due west until you come to another palm tree.
4. Turn south until you run into something.
5. If it is a tent, go north.
6. If it is a burning fire, jump to the man selling camels.
7. Follow the path until you come to a lizard.
8. Go southeast to the nearest rock.
9. Walk south until you run into the answer.

North
West ✚ East
South

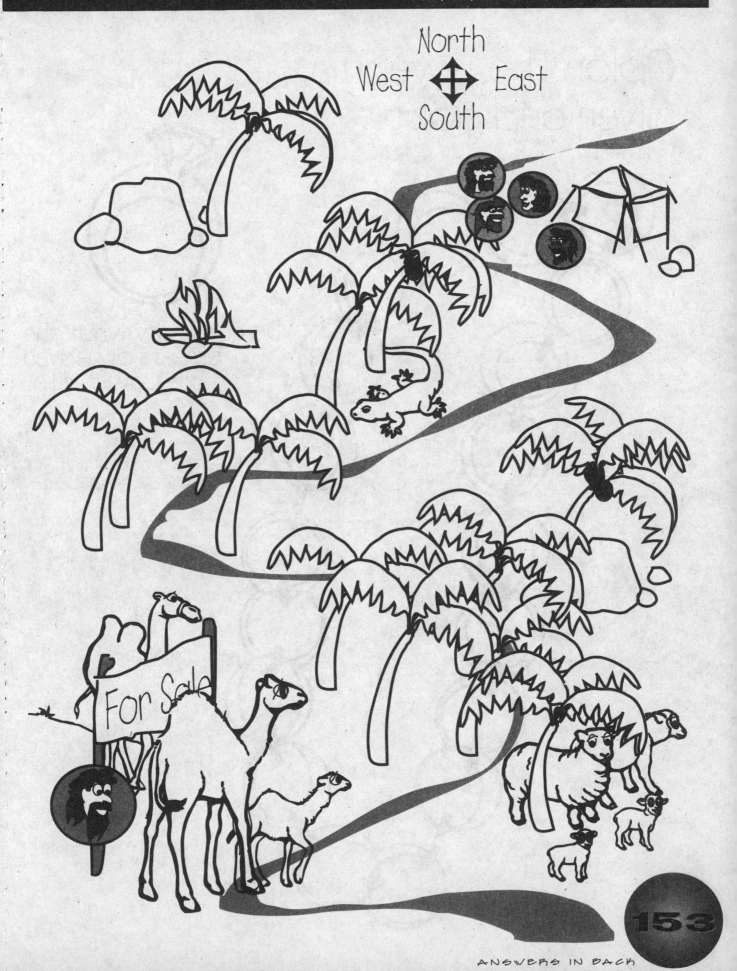

153

Color the jewelry silver and gold.

Do you know what the streets of heaven are paved with?

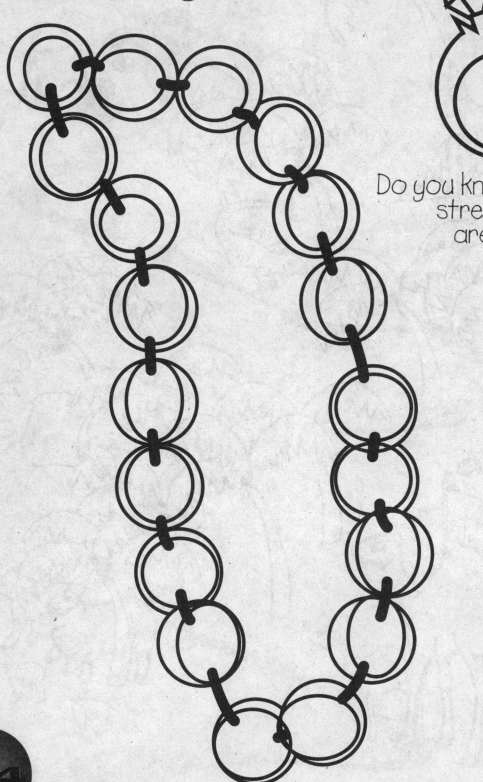

154

Cool·Things to Know Camels carrying cargo

Often long trips are made through the desert with lots of people. This is called a caravan.

An oasis is a watering hole in the middle of the desert.

The Desert night sky is clear and full of stars...

How many triangles can you count in this one?

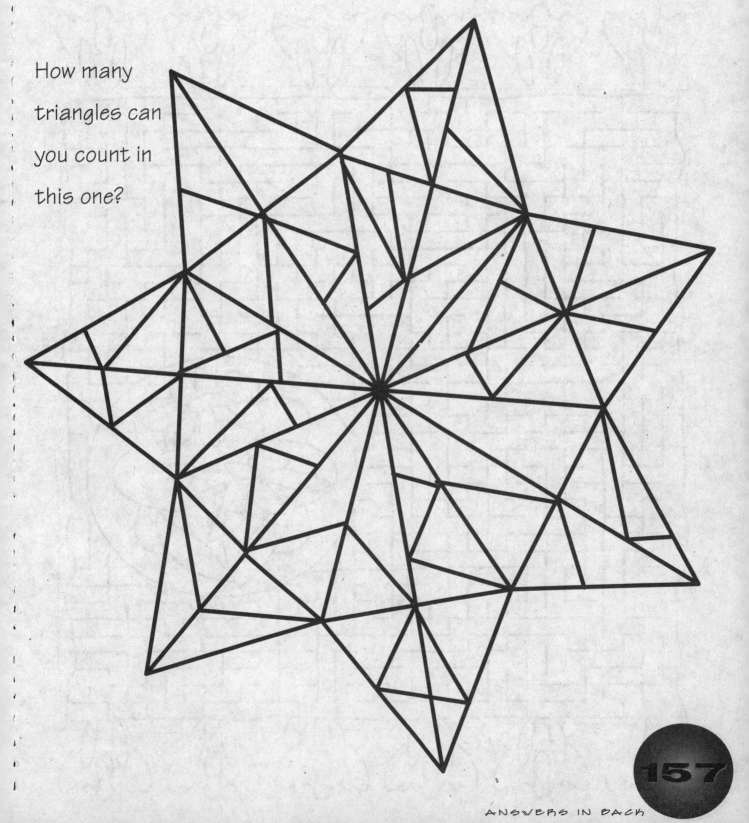

157

Abraham's servant gave Rebekah beautifully embroidered cloth.

Find your way through the maze.

Start

End

ANSWERS IN BACK

Help the ram get out ot the thicket.

Find your way through the maze.

It pleases God when we obey Him.

How do we obey God?
Match the picture with the right sentence.

When I help my mom and dad,
I am obeying God.

When I pray,
I am obeying God.

When I help my friends,
I am obeying God.

When I love others and do not fight,
I am obeying God.

When I help others who are sick or lonely,
I am obeying God.

Can you write some other ways
that you obey God?

_____

_____

_____

_____

_____

ANSWERS IN BACK

North, south, east, or west: where will Abram stop to rest?

Help Abram get to the land of Canaan.

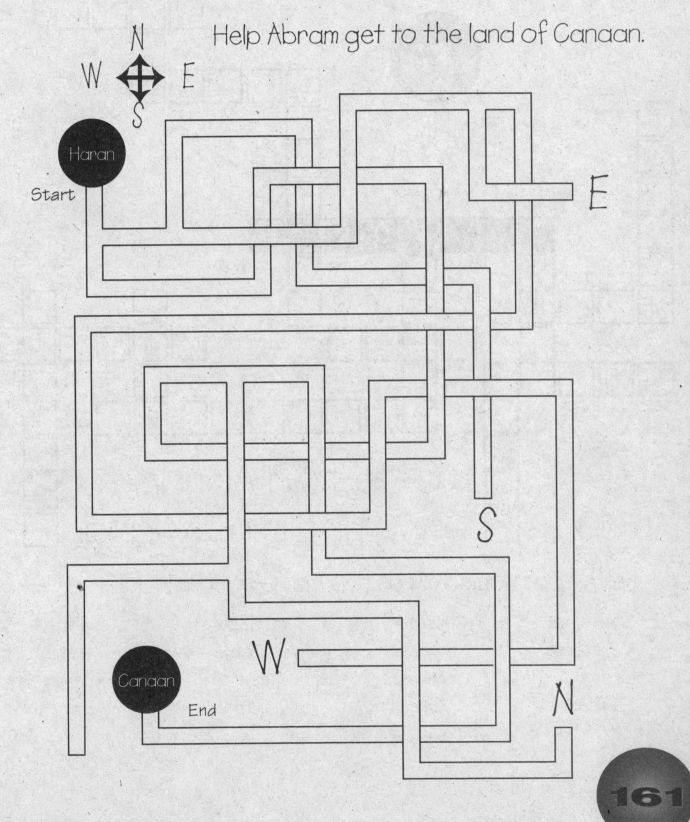

Genesis 12•1-3

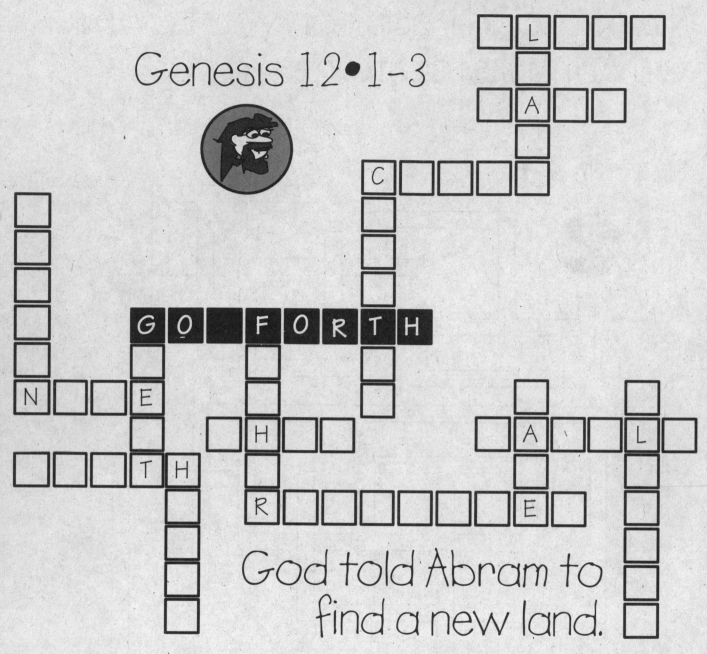

God told Abram to find a new land.

Below are some words found in God's instruction.

Country	Land	Bless	House
Relatives	Show	Name	Nation
Leave	Make	Curse	Blessed
Father	Great	Family	Earth

ANSWERS IN BACK

What did God tell Abram to take with him on his journey?

Unscramble the words below to find out!

1. fWie aSiar _____

2. pwheeN otL _____

3. vsrntSeas _____

4. lodG _____

5. lerivS _____

6. nTtse _____

7. hepSe _____

8. tlaCte _____

9. nkyoseD _____

163

ANSWERS IN BACK

In old times people had to use the sun, moon, and stars to help direct them when they traveled.

If God Told Abram to travel SOUTH, which way would he go?

ANSWERS IN BACK

Abram needs to feed his flock...

...but the ground is full of rock!

Green is the color animals like best. After they eat they can rest.

165

God told Abram to look to the heavens and count the stars.

This was to show Abram God's promise of multiplying his family, generation to generation.

ANSWERS IN BACK

Connect the stars...

...to hear what God would say to you!

3
2
1

7
5
13
6
4
14
17
19
20
21
22
12
15
23
24
8
11
10
25
9
16
18
28
26
27
32
33
39
40
34
29
44
41
31
37
35
43
36
30
42

167

Can you guess what I am?

Clues are in God's promises to Abraham!

What am I?

3. If I were an old man you might think it was my snore: the pounding of waves on the...

1. I shine brightly in the sky. When people draw me I have points of 5...

4. I am what all plants need. Large or small I'm called a...

2. I touch the ocean, I touch the land, I'm zillions of tiny rocks, called...

5. Add, subtract, divide: the one word missing is...

ANSWERS IN BACK

Isaac and Rebekah had twin boys named Esau & Jacob.

The name Esau means "hairy" and Jacob means "heel-catcher."

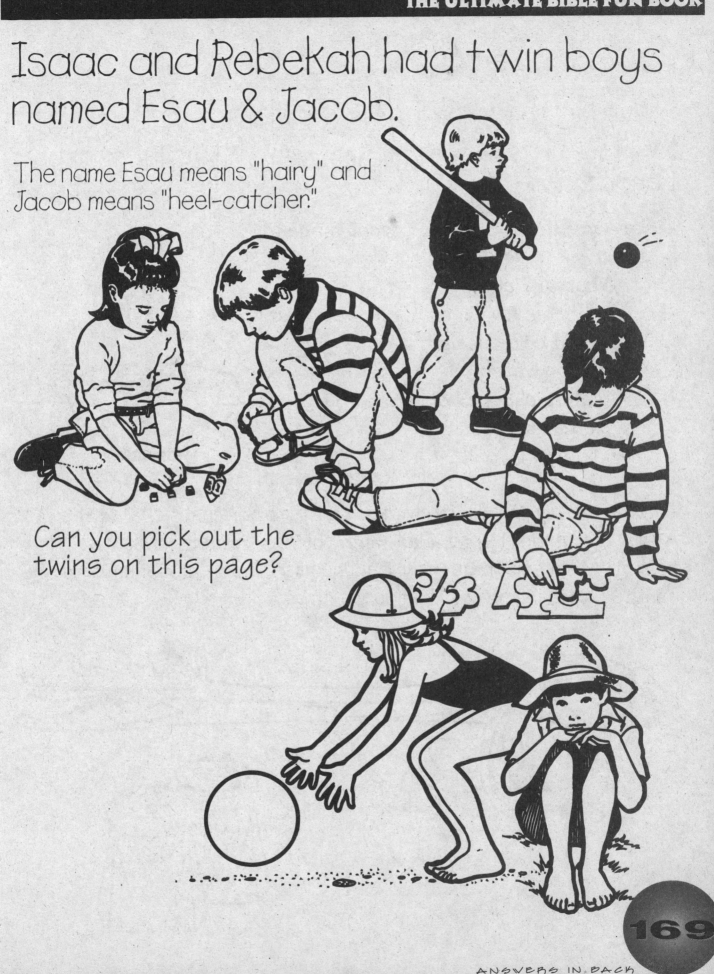

Can you pick out the twins on this page?

169

Genesis 25•29-34

Esau sold Jacob his birthright for a bowl of lentil soup.

Lentil Soup

Make some Lentil Soup like Jacob made for Esau...

- 1 cup dry lentils
- 1/4 lb meat (Jacob used goat meat)
- 1/2 cup diced celery
- 4 cups water
- 1/2 cup chopped onion
- 1/4 tsp pepper
- 1 tsp garlic salt

Rinse and sort lentils. Brown the meat and drain off the excess fat. Add water and bring to a boil. Add the remaining ingredients, bring to a boil, and stir frequently. Reduce heat, cover, and simmer for 60 minutes, stirring every 15 minutes or so.

Garlic Salt Pepper

Genesis 28•10-19

Jacob has a dream of a ladder...

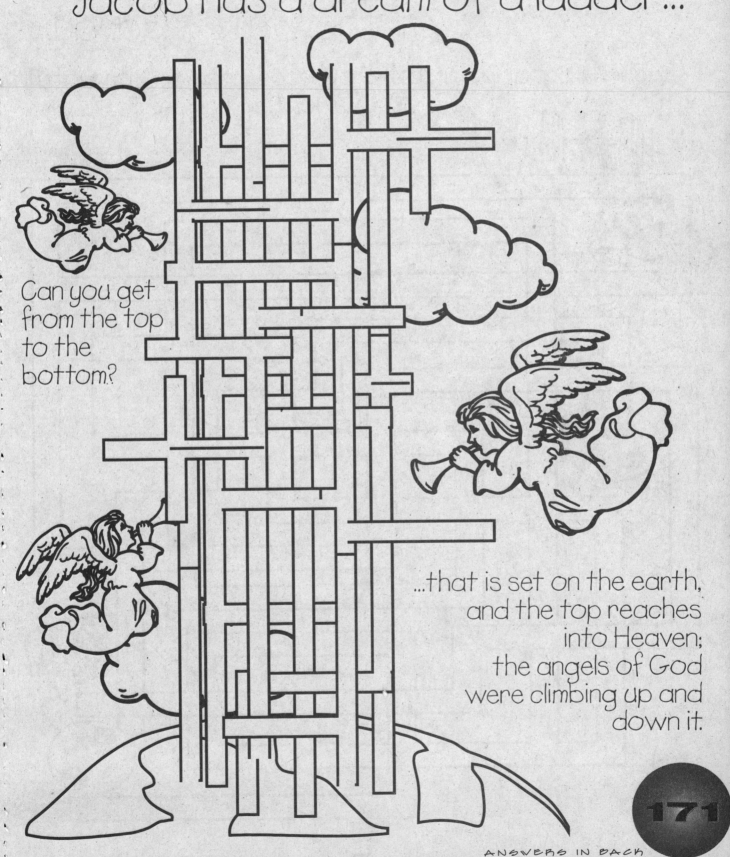

Can you get from the top to the bottom?

...that is set on the earth, and the top reaches into Heaven; the angels of God were climbing up and down it.

171

Genesis 29•1-14

Jacob meets Rachel at the well of Haran...

Rachel is bringing her father's sheep to the well for water. Can you help her get to Jacob?

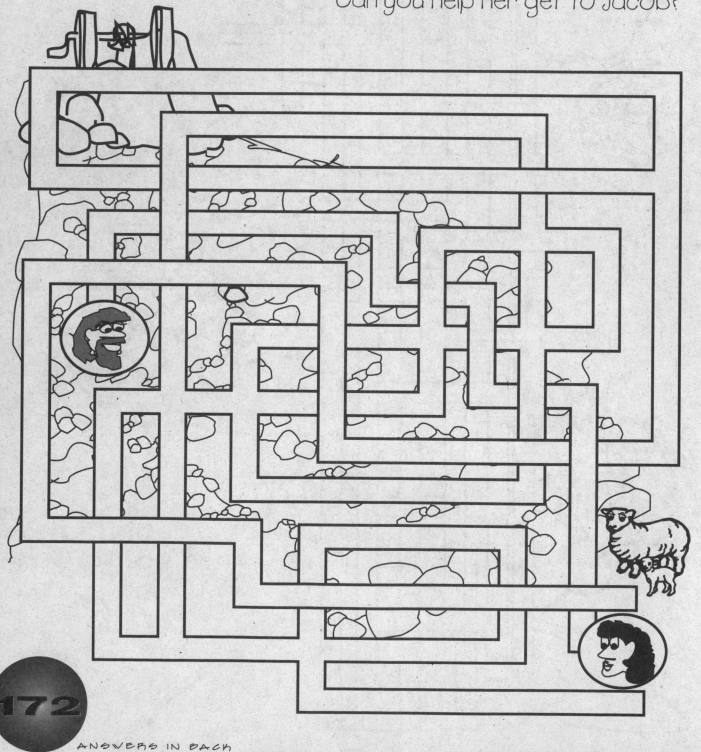

172

ANSWERS IN BACK

Genesis 29•13

Jacob goes with Rachel to meet her dad, Laban.

To marry Rachel, Jacob must feed and care for Laban's flocks for 7 years.

Jacob has favor with God and God blesses the flock with strength and numbers. How many sheep, lambs and goats do you see?

173

Genesis 31•1-20
After Laban tricked Jacob into marrying Leah...

...he allowed Jacob to take Rachel as his wife for another 7 years of labor. After that, Jacob contracted to leave with the Speckled and spotted sheep, brown sheep, amd speclked and spotted goats.

Can you help Jacob by coloring the animals so that he can take them?

How many of each should Jacob have?

174

Genesis 31•17
Jacob, Leah, and Rachel, with all their children and herds, leave Laban.

Connect the dots and you will find out what type of animal they rode on to travel this very long distance.

175

Help Jacob, Leah, and Rachel find their way through the desert to Canaan.

End

Start

ANSWERS IN BACK

Genesis 32•24-28
Jacob wrestles with an angel through the night.

He will not let the angel go until he blesses Jacob. With the blessing the Lord God changed Jacob's name to 'Israel.'

Israel means "contender with God."

How many words can you make from:

CONTENDER WITH GOD

GREEN	

177

All of these people are in Jacob's family.

Guess their names using the code!

A ✡
B ✝
C ✢
D ✣
E ✦
F ✧
G ★
H ☆
I ✪
J ☆
K ★
L ☆
M ✫
N ✬
O ☆
P ✶
Q ✷
R ✳
S ✴
T ✵
U ✶
V ✷
W ✸
X ✹
Y ✺
Z ✻

☆✦✡✡✣   is the father of ☉✡✣✝✦✝   .

Jacob has a big brother named ✢✦✡☆   , whom

Jacob and his mother, ✢✣✝✢✡☆✦★   , tricked

into giving Jacob his birthright as the firstborn.

Jacob wants to marry Rachel, but is tricked by ✦✦☆✝☆✦

          , Leah's father, into marrying ✦✣☆✡★   first.

Two weeks after Jacob marries Leah he is then allowed by

Laban to marry ✦☆☆✣★✣✡   .

Jacob and Leah have lots of children. The boys are

✢✣✦✝✣✝☆   , ✦☆★✣✝☆   , ★✣✦☆   ,

☉✦✢✝☆★   , ☆✦✢☆✣★☆✦   , and

✦✣✝✦★✦☆   . They also have one daughter.

Her name is ✢☆☆☆✡★   .

Jacob and Rachel do not have as many children. They

have two boys, ☉✦✦✣☆★   and

✝✣☆✦☉☆★☆☆   .

Jacob's Family History

How many sons did Jacob have altogether?

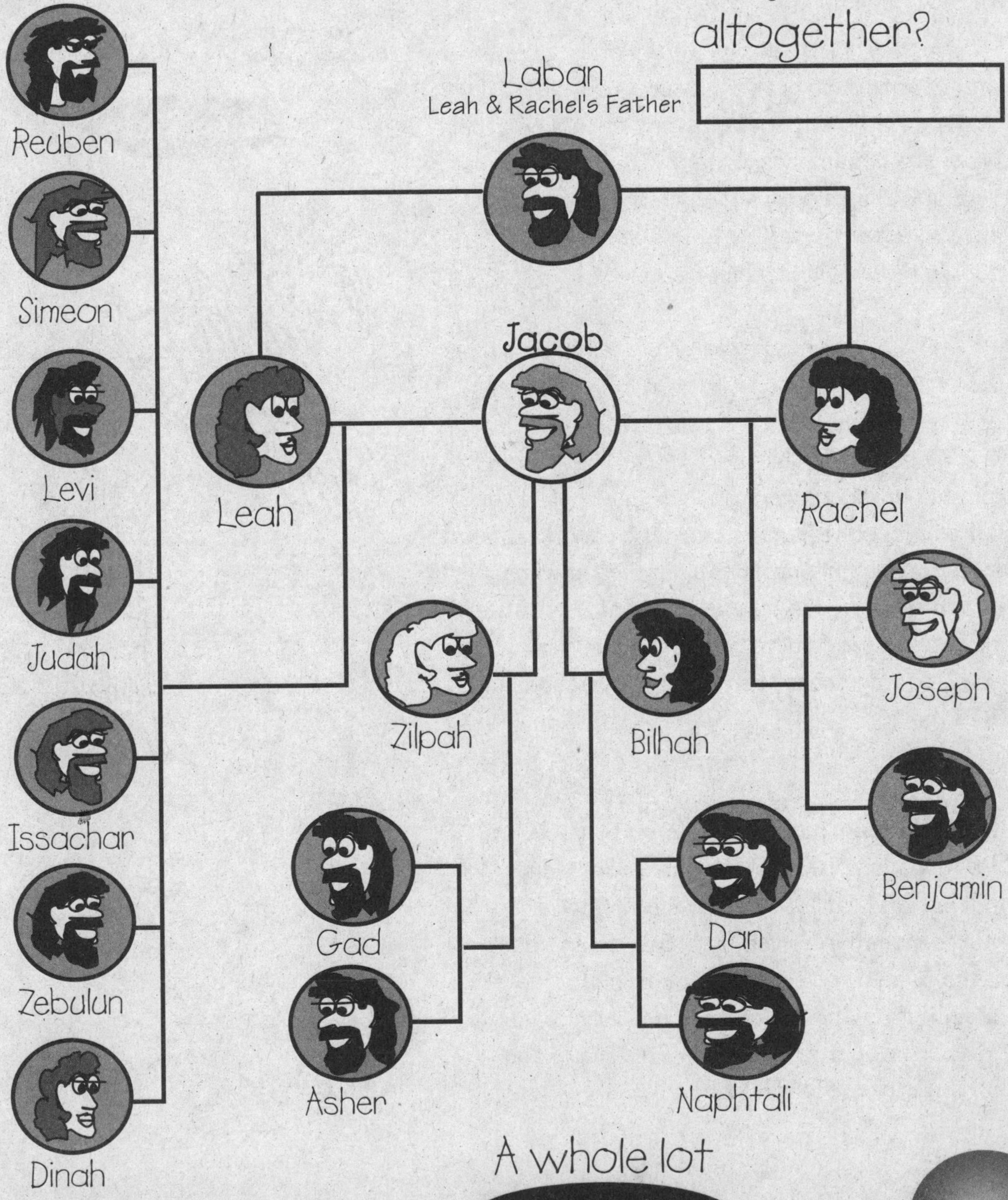

Reuben

Simeon

Levi

Judah

Issachar

Zebulun

Dinah

Laban
Leah & Rachel's Father

Jacob

Leah

Rachel

Zilpah

Bilhah

Joseph

Gad

Dan

Benjamin

Asher

Naphtali

A whole lot

More to Come

179

Joseph was one...

... of twelve sons born to Jacob. He was Jacob's favorite son.

Joseph's Story

BibleTells

One day Jacob made a coat of very bright and beautiful colors for Joseph. Because Joseph was his father's favorite son, the other brothers became very angry. They were jealous because they, too, wanted their father's special attention. They hated Joseph and couldn't even talk to him nicely.

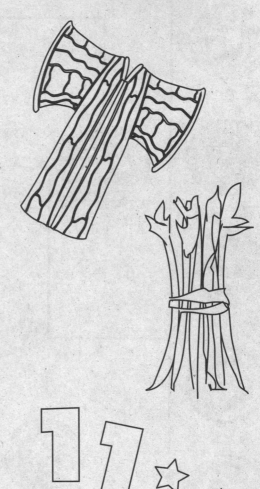

One day Joseph had a dream and he told his brother's. They hated him even more after he told them the dream. He asked them to listen and he began to tell them that in his dream he and his brothers were gathering wheat in the fields. Joseph's bundle of wheat stood tall and straight, but his brother's bundles of wheat bowed down to his bundle of wheat. After his brother's heard this they asked him if he was going to reign over them, and they hated him even more.

Then Joseph told them of another dream where the sun, moon, and eleven stars bowed down to him. The sun and moon represented his mother and father and the eleven stars represented his eleven brothers. Even Joseph's father was upset over this dream and asked Joseph if he and his mother and all his brothers would bow to him? This made the brothers even more jealous.

All the brothers...

...went out to pasture their father's flocks in a nearby place called Shechem.

Jacob sent Joseph to find out how his brothers were and to report back. When Joseph reached Shechem he found out that his brothers had moved on to Dothan. He then went there to find his brothers. They saw him coming as he was approaching the place where his brothers were feeding the flocks. They began to plot to kill him because they hated him so badly.

Reuben, the oldest brother, felt some responsibility in keeping Joseph safe. He suggested they hide Joseph in an old, dried-up well and not kill him. So the brothers did this. In the meantime, some Ishmaelites were traveling across the desert in a caravan carrying lots of spices and balm and myrrh. The brothers decided to sell Joseph to the Ishmaelites as a slave for twenty pieces of silver. Later they took a goat, killed it, spread the blood over Joseph's coat of colors, and returned it to Jacob saying that a wild animal had attacked and killed Joseph.

His father, Jacob, was very upset. In those days when people were in mourning they would tear their clothes and rub ashes on themselves, so Jacob did this and wept for Joseph.

Joseph's Story

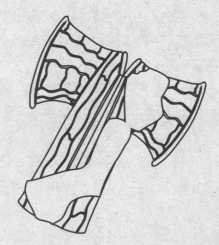

Meanwhile...

... the Ishmaelites arrived in Egypt and sold Joseph to Potiphar, an Egyptian officer of Pharaoh the king. Because God's blessing was on Joseph, Potiphar's household prospered. Potiphar was so happy that he let Joseph be in charge of everything. The only problem was Potiphar's wife really liked Joseph and wanted him for herself. Joseph had honor towards his master and would not betray him. This made the wife angry and she tricked Joseph one day when they were in the house alone. She grabbed him by his coat and begged him to be with her. Joseph fled, leaving his coat behind. Potiphar's wife accused Joseph of attacking her and said "Look he even left his coat behind." This made Potiphar very angry but he did not know he was believing a lie. He had Joseph thrown in jail as punishment for his conduct.

When Joseph was in jail he met two other of Pharaoh's servants: a butler and a baker. They both had dreams and asked Joseph to interpret the dreams for them. Joseph said the butler's dream meant he would be released from jail in three days and be back in the good graces of the king. The other dream was not so good because it meant the baker was going to be killed. Joseph's interpretations came true.

He remained in jail for two more years.

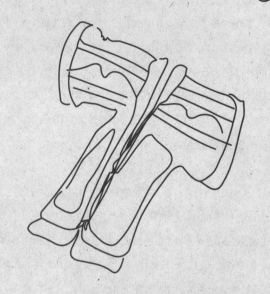

Joseph's Story

BibleTells

Then one day...

... Pharaoh had a dream and no one could interpret it.

The butler, who was in jail with Joseph, remembered that Joseph could interpret dreams. He told the king and the king released Joseph from jail so he could interpret the dream. The king said to him " I heard that you can interpret dreams when they are told to you." Joseph said that God did the interpretations through him. In Pharaoh's dream he saw seven fat cows come out of the Nile River and begin eating the grass that was all around. Then seven thin cows came and ate up the seven fat cows, but they remained thin. He had another dream that was like this one but in it; seven ears of thin corn swallowed up seven ears of fat corn.

Joseph told the king that these dreams were a warning from God about what he was about to do in Egypt. There would be seven years of abundance and then seven years of famine. Joseph also said that Pharaoh should put someone in charge of the land to make sure that one fifth of all the produce was stored so they would have plenty when the famine came.. Pharaoh said "Where will I find a man with such wisdom to organize this?"

Joseph's Story

BibleTells

He then realized...

... that the person he was looking for was right in front of him. He appointed Joseph to be second in command of the land and to carry out the plan of saving grain for the famine which was coming. Pharaoh gave Joseph his ring with the king's symbol on it and a gold necklace and dressed him in fine linens and gave him authority as if he were the king.

Joseph's Story

The seven years of abundance had ended and the famine began to spread. It even hit Canaan where Joseph's family was. Jacob, Joseph's father, sent his ten sons to get grain in Egypt because the people in Canaan were hungry too. When they arrived, they approached the governor, which was Joseph, and asked if they could have grain for their family. Joseph recognized them immediately but they did not recognize Joseph. As they were bowing to Joseph, he accused them of being spies. They said "No, we are not spies." They began to tell Joseph that they were twelve brothers, the youngest of whom was at home with their father and another one of whom was dead. Joseph told them to go back to Canaan and get their youngest brother and bring him back as proof that what they were saying was true. But before they went back he put them in jail for three days.

When he let them out on the third day he filled their bags with wheat to take back with them and secretly placed the silver they brought with them in the bags of wheat.

BibleTells

Joseph also...

...decided to keep one of the brothers to insure they would return. He tied up Simeon and put him in jail until the brothers returned.

When the brothers were on their way back to Canaan they stopped to rest and eat some food that Joseph had provided for them. When they looked in their bags they saw that the silver had been returned to them and they couldn't figure out what was going on.

Joseph's Story

They continued back home and when they arrived they told their father Jacob all that had happened. Jacob did not want them to take Benjamin back because he loved him so much and he thought he would lose him just like he lost Joseph. The grain began to run out and Jacob told his sons to go back to Egypt and buy more grain and to take the finest things that Canaan had to offer to this person of authority.

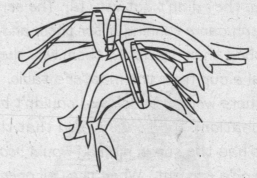

So they took Benjamin, along with precious goods such as honey, balm, spices, myrrh, pistachio nuts and almonds, and plenty of silver to buy the grain with. When the brothers arrived in Egypt they were invited to have dinner with Joseph. This made the brothers very nervous because they thought they would be in trouble for taking the silver they brought the first time back home with them.

Now that you've read Joseph's Story

Can you answer

these questions about Joseph's life?

1. How many brothers did Joseph have?

2. What did Jacob, Joseph's father, give Joseph that caused his brothers to become very angry?

3. Joseph had two dreams. What did the bundles of wheat do?

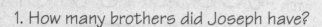

4. How many stars were in the second dream?

5. What did the sun, moon, and the stars represent in Joseph's dream?

6. When Joseph went out to check on his brothers, what were they doing?

7. Were did the brothers put Joseph before they sold him?

8. What did Joseph's brothers do to his coat? Why?

188

ANSWERS IN BACK

9. Why was Joseph put into jail?

10. Who did Joseph meet while he was in jail?

11. Whose dreams did Joseph interpret, causing his release from prison?

12. What were the two objects in the dreams?

13. What did the dreams mean?

14. What did Pharaoh give Joseph when he put him in charge?

15. When the famine overtook the land, who came to Egypt for grain?

16. What did Joseph request of his brothers?

17. What did the servant put in one of the bags?

18. Whose bag was he instructed to put it in?

19. Why did Joseph's brothers not recognize him?

20. When Joseph lets his brothers know who he is, what did they all do?

21. At the end of the story, why does Joseph send his brothers back to Canaan?

189

Genesis 37•3

Draw the other half of Joseph's coat and color it in.

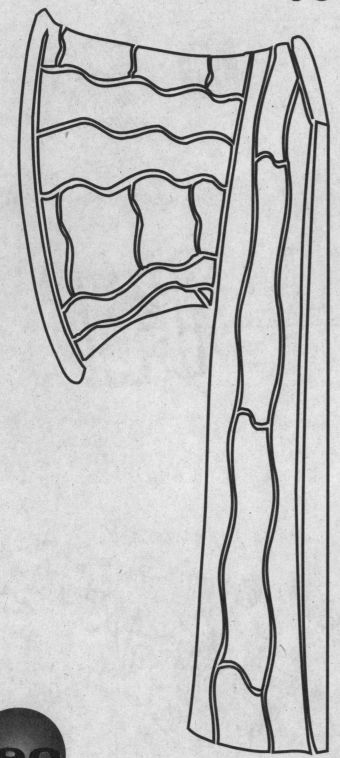

Can you find these colors in the puzzle below?

Cyan
Bone
Ruby
Red
Green
Purple
Blue
Gold
Silver
Orange
Violet
Yellow
Pink
Gray
Taupe
Amber
Teal
Mauve
Olive
Brown
Wine
Plum

```
B R O W N S C Y A N
O U C K N I P G Z X
N B P Y E L L O W A
E Y U G T V U L V M
D E R B I E M D N B
M A P O O R A N G E
Y B L U E A U L S R
N E E R G E V I L O
T A U P E D E N I W
```

191

You can color clothing like Joseph's coat, using batik.

What you will need:

- Light-colored fabric (you may want to batik a t-shirt to wear or a square from an old sheet to hang in front of a window)
- Pencil, old paint brushes
- Newspaper or brown paper sacks
- Melted crayon mixed with paraffin
- Old muffin tray
- Warming tray or electric skillet
- Iron

1. Draw a pattern or design on your fabric with pencil. Your design should totally cover the space.
2. Place fabric on several layers of newspaper.
3. Separate crayons by color. Melt peeled crayons and paraffin in muffin tin in electric skillet on low.
4. USE CAUTION WITH MELTED CRAYONS AND ELECTRIC CORDS.
5. Paint the melted crayon mixture onto the fabric until it soaks all the way through the fabric. (If it doesn't seem to be soaking through, paint the opposite side of the fabric too.)
   HINT: The brightest colors give the best results. Colors tend to lighten.
6. When cool, remove any left-over wax. Place brown paper sacks on both sides of fabric. Using a warm iron (make sure the iron does not touch the wax directly), iron over the paper sacks from both sides to melt the wax. The wax will transfer to the brown paper sacks. You may need to repeat the process with a second round of clean paper sacks.

Genesis 37•3

Jacob makes a coat of many colors for Joseph.

Color Key
1 - blue
2 - green
3 - purple
4 - yellow
5 - red
6 - orange

ANSWERS IN BACK

Know your colors!

Color the objects using the colors listed.
Then draw a line from the color to the matching picture.

- Green

- Orange

- Red

- Yellow

- Purple

- Pink

- Blue

ANSWERS IN BACK

The Letter "e" is common in each of the colors from the last page...

...except 1. Which color does not have the letter "e" in it?
Can you fill in the missing letters for all the other colors?

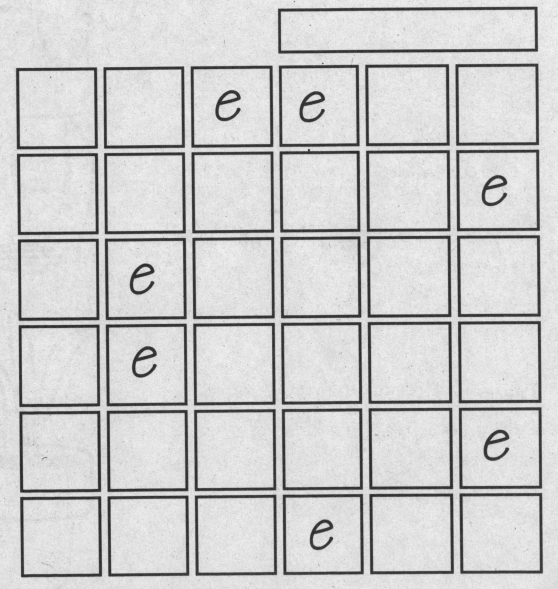

195

Colorful

1. If you go around WEARING ROSE-COLORED GLASSES it means...
    a. you had juice for breakfast.
    b. you think everything in the world is fine.
    c. you are watching a 3-D movie.

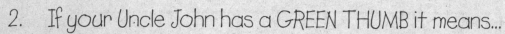

2. If your Uncle John has a GREEN THUMB it means...
    a. he is rich.
    b. he is not feeling well.
    c. he can grow plants well.

3. If your sister is GREEN WITH ENVY it means...
    a. she is jealous.
    b. she is lucky.
    c. she is hungry.

4. If your mom is SEEING RED it means...
    a. she is wearing rose-colored glasses.
    b. she is angry.
    c. she is from Russia.

ANSWERS IN BACK

Language

5. If your doctor says you're IN THE PINK it means...
   a. you are cooked medium rare.
   b. you are quite well.
   c. you are out of breath.

6. If your dad says this is a RED-LETTER DAY it means...
   a. you did poorly on your report card.
   b. something important is going to happen.
   c. today is your birthday.

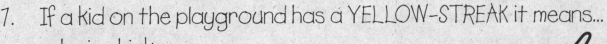

7. If a kid on the playground has a YELLOW-STREAK it means...
   a. he is chicken.
   b. his hair is blond.
   c. he has been painting.

8. If your friend is FEELING BLUE it means...
   a. she is sleepy.
   b. she is listening to music.
   c. she is sad.

ANSWERS IN BACK

Joseph has two dreams.

In the first dream, Joseph and his brothers are all working in the field on the harvest. They are tying grain into bundles. Joseph's bundle stands upright and all of his brother's bundles stand up and bow down in honor of Joseph.

When Joseph shared this dream with his brothers they became angry and jealous and said, "Do you think you are going to rule over us?"

In the second dream, the sun and the moon and the stars bowed down to Joseph. This dream not only made Joseph's brothers angry but also made his father angry, for he could not believe a time would come when they would all bow down to Joseph.

Cool•Things to Know

What is a dream? While you are sleeping you have pictures in your mind that you sometimes remember when you wake up. Sometimes dreams come from God. He uses them to help show his plan for a person's life. .

198

Sun, Moon, and Stars
Get a glimpse of Joseph's dream!

What you need:

- paper plate
- black paint
- something to cut holes
- Flashlight

1. Take a paper plate and cut out a sun, moon, and stars.

2. Paint the plate black so that light will only shine through the cuts you've made.

3. Go into a dark room, turn on the flashlight, point toward the plate, and watch the show on your ceiling.

Genesis 39•1-5

Because Joseph's brothers are so angry and jealous, they decide to sell Joseph into slavery.

God turns this to good and causes Joseph to become a great man in Egypt.

Potiphar, the captain of the royal guards, was Joseph's owner. He gave responsibility for all household matters to Joseph.

God had favor on Joseph and all that he touched prospered.

Joseph has Control of Potiphar's household

Joseph would have been very good with numbers. See if you can figure out these addition blocks.

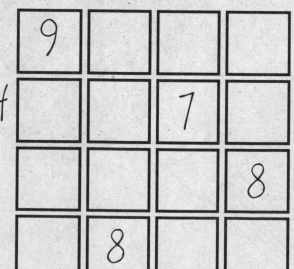

200

Joseph lived in Potiphar's house.

What are some of the things he might have seen when he looked out his window?

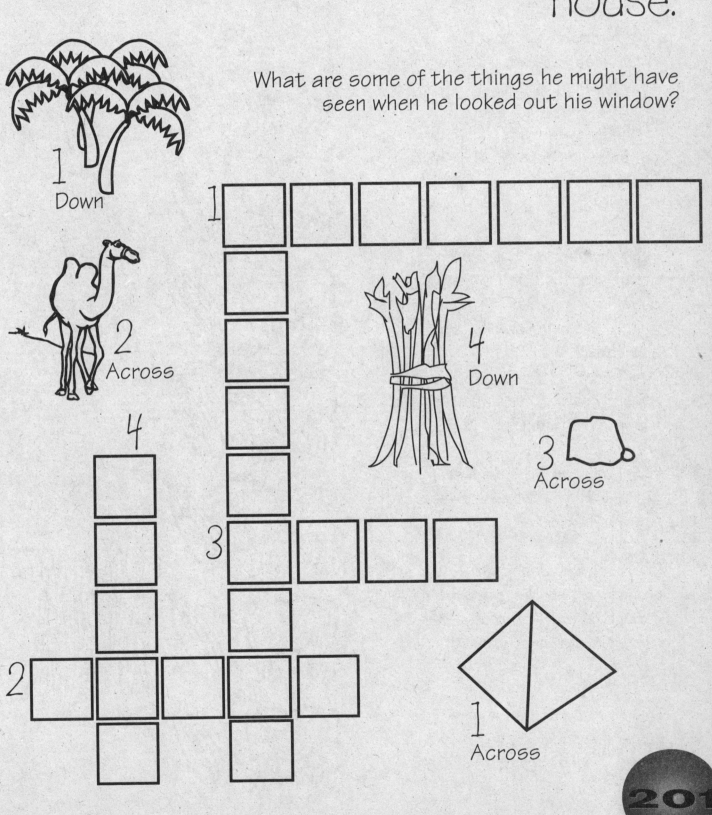

1 Down

2 Across

4 Down

4

3 Across

3

2

1 Across

201

Genesis 41•1-40
Pharaoh's dreams.

The Pharaoh has two different dreams and Joseph tells him what they mean.

In the first dream the king saw 7 cows feeding in the field, then 7 sickly looking cows came and swallowed them up.

Then the pharaoh had a second dream like the first. Instead of cows he dreamed of corn on a stalk with 7 ears being swallowed up by 7 sick ears.

Joseph got the interpretation of the dreams from God.

For seven years there will be great plenty in Egypt, followed by seven years of famine.

Pharaoh picks Joseph to set up a program for storing extra grain during the years of plenty. Then in the years of famine they will still have food.

This gives Joseph great power. He is made second only to Pharaoh in all of Egypt.

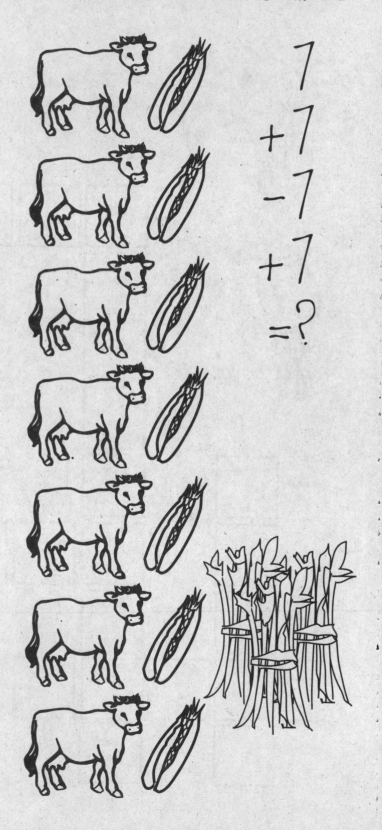

$$7$$
$$+7$$
$$-7$$
$$+7$$
$$=?$$

202

Pharaoh's dreams

After Joseph interpreted Pharaoh's dreams, he was so grateful he adorned Joseph with jewelry.

Make some fun edible jewelry

You will need:
- Licorice Strings
- Small pretzels
- Cereal in Shapes that have holes
- Candy with holes

1. Thread the licorice through the pretzels, cereal, and candy. Tie ends in a knot and you've made a candy necklace or bracelet!

2. Use small strands of licorice and wrap or tie in knots to form a ring.

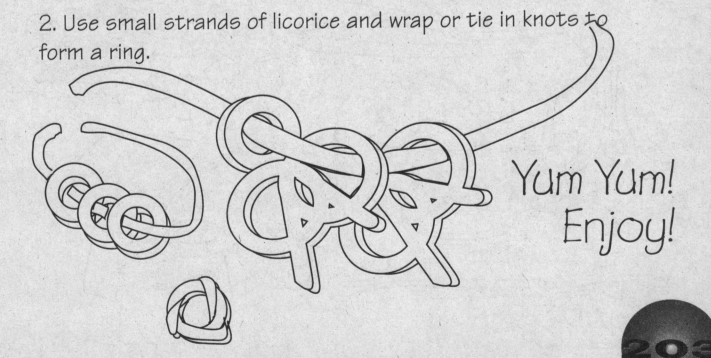

Yum Yum!
Enjoy!

Joseph stored grain for the famine God spoke of in Pharaoh's dreams.

Circle all the foods below that are made of grains.

204

Joseph had a very special dinner for his brothers called a feast.

Circle the words in the puzzle below that tell you what you might find at an Egyptian feast!

W	P	I	N	P	S	P	I	P	H	X	A
P	O	M	E	G	R	A	N	A	T	E	S
A	O	L	I	V	E	S	S	E	T	A	D
G	P	F	P	X	B	W	H	H	E	P	N
Z	P	G	P	O	M	S	N	O	I	N	O
P	N	P	O	Q	U	A	P	N	E	Z	M
G	A	R	L	I	C	P	D	E	I	G	L
P	X	I	W	E	U	U	P	Y	O	P	A
I	P	O	P	E	C	Q	H	G	P	W	E
Z	L	E	E	K	S	T	U	N	L	A	W

cucumbers   garlic   walnuts
duck   olives   dates
leeks   onions   honey
pomegranates   figs   almonds

205

In times of the Bible, spices were very precious.

Caravans would carry them through the region.
Try this delicious combination of spices to make a
"HOT TEA" for those cold days.

Hot Spice Tea

- 1 3oz package instant lemonade
- 2 cups instant orange juice mix
- 2 cups sugar
- 1 cup instant tea
- 1 tbl. cinnamon powder
- 1 tbl. ground cloves

Mix all ingredients together and keep in an airtight container.

When you're ready for that cup of spice tea,
Mix 2 tsp of mixture to 1 cup of boiling water.

ANSWERS IN BACK

Joseph hid his cup in his brother's bag of grain.

See if you can find it below

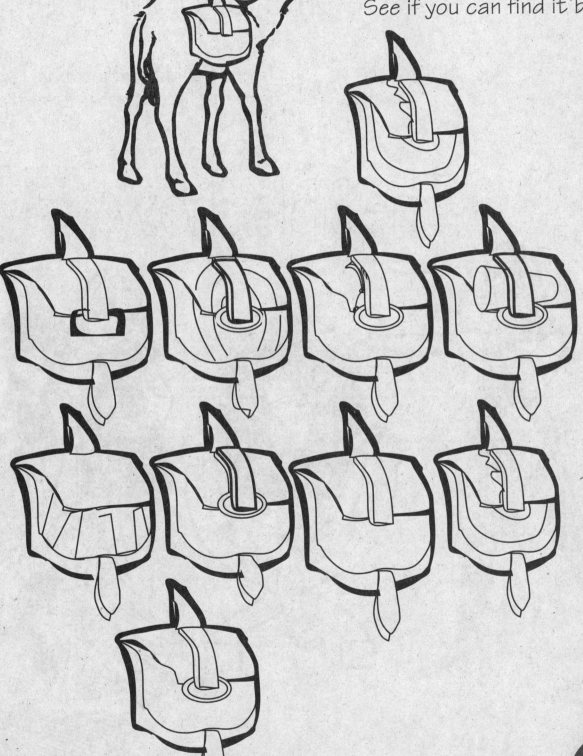

207

Bible Fun
Have a "TALK SHOW" with some of your friends.

Assign Bible characters to your friends and then interview them.
See how well they remember their Bible stories.

The Bible Show

Joseph is no longer a slave in Egypt, but a ruler in the land of the pyramids.

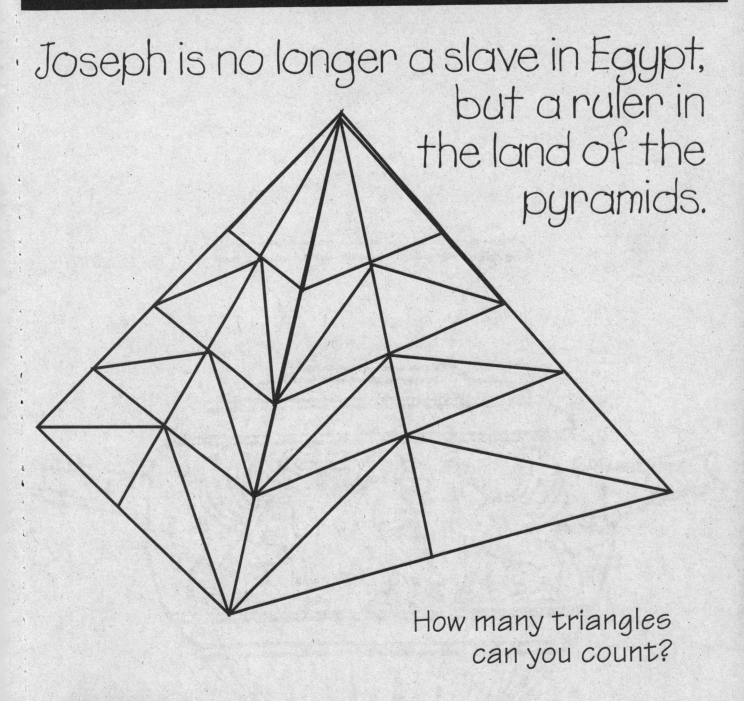

How many triangles can you count?

Cool•Things to Know

The Pyramids in Egypt were built over 4,000 years ago. They served as tombs for the pharaohs.

211

Many years after...

...Joseph died, a new king arose over Egypt. He did not know of Joseph and all the good he had done for Egypt. The King only saw how the Israelites outnumbered the Egyptians both in people and in strength and he was afraid of them.

Moses' Story

Because of his fear he decided to make life very hard for the Israelite people. He forced them to make bricks and build stone cities. The more the Egyptians tried to put hardships upon the Israelites, the more the Israelites multiplied and expanded. This made the Egyptians very angry. They made the Israelites' lives bitter with all kinds of hard work.

One day Pharaoh decided that all Hebrew baby boys should die. He commanded that they be thrown into the river. Only the baby girls could live. One baby boy's mother loved him so much that she refused throw him in the river. She kept him hidden for as long as she could. When this baby boy was too big to hide, she decided to place him in a basket that was made to float in the river. She had his big sister follow along, hiding in the bushes, while the basket floated down the river.

At this very same time Pharaoh's daughter came to the river to bathe. She came across the floating basket and found the baby boy! She was so pleased with the baby that she decided to keep him. She named him 'Moses' which means "I drew him out of the water."

Baby Moses...

...was hidden from Pharaoh. Some other things are also hidden! Can you find all 10?

Baby Moses

Pharaoh's Daughter

Mouse

Frog

Crown

Shepherd's staff

Grasshopper

Cup

Bricks

Pyramid

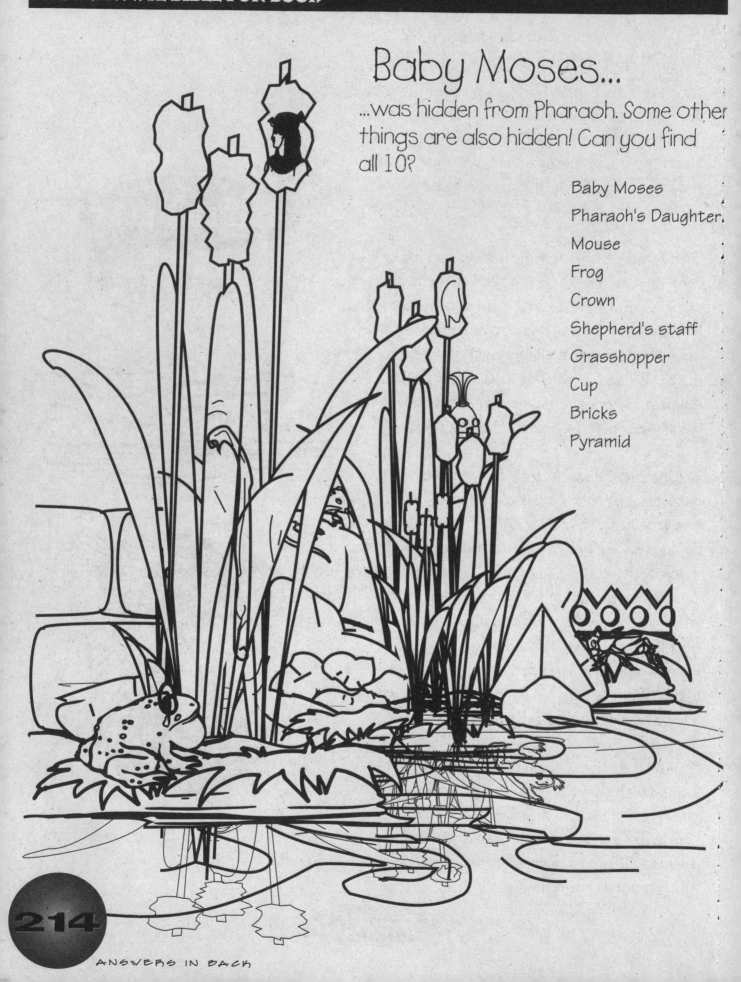

ANSWERS IN BACK

Moses' Story

Start

Baby Moses...

...was too big to hide, so his mom decided to place him in a basket that was made to float in the river.

Can you help baby Moses float down the river?

End

215

One day, after...

...Moses was grown, he saw an Egyptian beating up one of his Hebrew brothers. This made Moses very angry and he killed the Egyptian. Knowing he had done wrong, and being afraid of Pharaoh, Moses fled to Midian where he lived for nearly forty years. While in Midian he married Zipporah and had a son named Gershom.

During this time, Pharaoh died and the Israelites kept crying out to God to free them from their bondage in Egypt. God heard them and remembered His promises to Abraham, Isaac, and Jacob.

One of Moses' jobs was to take care of the Flock. He would move them from the back to the west side of the wilderness. One day while moving the flock, he came upon Sinai, the mountain of God. He could see a bush on fire, yet it was not burning up. As he moved closer to it, God called to him and said, "Moses Moses!" Moses answered, "Here I am." God told him to remove his shoes because he was on holy ground. Then He told Moses, "I am the God of your father, the God of Abraham, the God of Isaac, and the God of Jacob." Moses hid his face because he was very afraid to look at God.

Moses' Story

216

BibleTells

Help Moses Reach the burning bush!

End

Start

217

God told Moses...

...that He had heard the cries of the Israelites in Egypt and that Moses was to go back to Egypt and set them free. Moses asked God what he should say to the Israelites and who he should say sent him. God said to Moses, "I AM WHO I AM and WHAT I AM and I WILL BE WHAT I WILL BE; Tell them I AM sent you."

But God knew that the new Pharaoh would not let the people go unless God stretched out his hand and did mighty wonders to make the Pharaoh believe. So God told Moses, "I will give my people favor and respect in the sight of the Egyptians and you will not leave Egypt empty handed."

Moses still did not believe that he could be the man God wanted to use to set the Israelites free from the Egyptians. God told Moses to throw his shepherd's stick on the ground, and it became a snake. This scared Moses and he ran from it. But God told Moses to reach down and pick the snake up by the tail. As he did, it became a shepherd's stick again. God told Moses to use this as a sign that God had sent him. God also told Moses to put his hand inside his coat and take it out. When he did this, his hand was covered with a disease called leprosy. God told Moses to put his hand back in his coat and pull it out. This time his hand was healed of the leprosy. This was the second sign God gave Moses to use as proof that God had sent him.

"Help!!!"

"Help!!"

"Help!"

Moses' Story

218

BibleTells

In Exodus 3•14
God said to Moses

"I AM WHO I AM and WHAT I AM, and
I WILL BE WHAT I WILL BE."

We use many names for God. Here are some examples below.
Can you unscramble all these names? Do you have a name for God?

God	dolr odg	_____
God Almighty	odg mgythila	_____
Living God	l ma	_____
Heavenly Father	dgo fo sohst	_____
Lord God	vngiil dgo	_____
I AM	eoahvhj	_____
Jehovah	dgo fo evaenh	_____
King Eternal	aelynveh htfare	_____
Most High God	ihytgm odg	_____
God of Hosts	dgo	_____
Father	mgthyila odg	_____
Holy One of Israel	leusoja	_____
Mighty God	tralnee odg	_____
Almighty God	lyho eon fo reilsa	_____
Jealous	gikn treanle	_____
Father of Light	somt gihh dgo	_____
Everlasting God	vratngislee dgo	_____
Eternal God	ehfrat fo ihgtl	_____
God of Heaven	cenniat fo asdy	_____
Ancient of Days	tharfh	_____

219

As a third ...

...sign, God told Moses to take some water from the Nile river and pour it upon the dry land, and that the water would become as blood on the dry land. Then Moses said to God, "I am a man slow of speech and have a strange voice." God told Moses to go and that He would teach him what to say. But Moses was still afraid to go. God said, "Bring Aaron your brother. I know he can speak well. I will be with your mouth and with his mouth, and will teach you what you shall do. He shall speak for you to the people, acting as a mouthpiece for you, and you shall be as God to him."

Moses obeyed God and took his wife and his sons, and set them on donkeys to return to Egypt. Along the way Moses met Aaron and told Aaron all that God had said. When Moses and Aaron got to Egypt they gathered all of the elders of the Israelites together and Aaron told them these things from God.

All the people believed! They bowed their heads and worshiped God!

Next, Moses and Aaron went to the Pharaoh, and said, "Thus says the Lord, the God of Israel, 'Let My people go, that they may hold a feast to Me in the wilderness.'" Pharaoh said, "Why should I obey your Lord and let Israel go? I do not know this Lord and I will not let Israel go." Then Pharaoh commanded that the work be increased upon the Israelites.

Moses' Story

BibleTells

In the Book of Exodus God had a message for Pharaoh...
...to be delivered by Moses.

Using the words listed fill in the boxes, one letter in each. When all the letters are in the right place, a message will appear.

- Egypt
- Israelites
- Egyptians
- Hardships
- Pharaoh
- Baby
- Boy
- Daughter
- Plagues
- Moses
- Death
- Freedom
- Gave

221

Moses cried out ...

...to God and said, "Since I came to Pharaoh to speak in Your name, he has done evil to this people, neither have You delivered Your people." God said to Moses, "Now you will see what I will do to Pharaoh. Because of my strong hand, he will let my people go; he will drive them out of his land. Now go and tell the Israelites that I am the Lord, and I will bring them out from under the burdens of the Egyptians, and I will free them from their bondage, and I will rescue them with an out- stretched arm."

Moses and Aaron went back to Pharaoh and did as the Lord had commanded. Aaron threw down the shepherd's stick before Pharaoh and his servants, and it became a snake. Pharaoh did not believe this was an act of God because his own wizards turned their sticks into snakes. Aaron's stick swallowed up all of the other sticks that had turned into snakes, but Pharaoh still did not believe.

The next day God told Moses and Aaron, "Go to the river and wait for Pharaoh. When he comes to the river, take the shepherd's stick and hit the water of the river. The water will turn to blood and all the fish in the river will die." Once again the Pharaoh's heart was made hard and he did not believe God's sign.

Moses' Story

222

BibleTells

In Exodus when God sent Moses to Pharaoh...

...to ask him to let God's people go, Pharaoh would not let them go.

Because of the hardness of Pharaoh's heart, God sent 10 plagues.

1. Strike the water of the Nile, and it will be changed into ____.

2. Stretch out your hand over streams and ponds and make ____ jump everywhere.

3. Stretch out your staff and strike the dust of the ground and the dust will become a ____.

4. God sent swarms of ____ upon all the Egyptians.

5. A terrible plague on your ____ in the fields: cattle, horses, donkeys, and camels.

6. Take handfuls of soot from a furnace and toss it into the air in the presence of Pharaoh. Festering ____ will break out on men and animals of Egypt.

7. Stretch out your hand toward the sky so that ____ will fall over Egypt.

8. Stretch out your hand over Egypt so that ____ will swarm over the land and devour everything growing.

9. Stretch out your hand toward the sky so that ____ will spread over Egypt.

10. At midnight the Lord struck down all the ____ in Egypt.

223

God continued ...

...to instruct Moses and Aaron. Several more times God sent signs as proof to Pharaoh that He was commanding him to let Israel go. But each time, Pharaoh's heart was made hard and he did not believe.

Moses' Story

The last sign that God commanded was for every firstborn son to die. But God provided a way for those who loved Him to protect their sons. This is called Passover, as God passed over the homes of the Israelites who obeyed Him and did as He commanded.

The Israelites obeyed God and took a sheep or goat without spot, a one year old male, keeping it in their home for four days. On the fourth day they prepared it for dinner, taking the blood and putting it on the two side posts and on the top of the door of their house. With the meat they ate unleavened bread, and bitter herbs. Anything left over they burned in the fire. While they ate they were dressed for a journey, ready to leave at any minute.

While they ate the Passover meal, God passed over and no plague came upon them. God's judgment came against the Egyptians' firstborn, both man and beast, and against all the gods of Egypt. Then Pharaoh believed and let God's people go.

BibleTells

Exodus 12•1-11

T S F R R S
E V O S A P
E S F O S A I P
R

God told the Israelites to have a special
meal once a year on the same day.
This meal helps them to remember
how God saved their ancestors
when they were slaves in Egypt.

Follow the paths to find the
answer!

Cool•Things to Know

Did you know that God set this celebration
to be in the first month of the new year
for the Israelites?

225

"Wilderness"

Moses led Israel out of Egypt when Pharaoh finally let them go.

The Israelites wandered through the wilderness for 40 years. Help them to find a message by picking up letters along the way. Only one path has the right letters.

226

"Red Sea"

By the time Moses got to the Red Sea, Pharaoh realized what he had done and went after them!

Start

End

The Israelites had to cross the sea to get away from Pharaoh. God instructed Moses to lift his rod and divide the waters of the sea so that the people could walk on dry ground.

Start on the WHITE square and then go to the BLACK square touching it. Then go WHITE, BLACK, WHITE, and so forth. (Do not go corner to corner)

Cool•Things to Know

Did you know that God first knocked off the wheels of the Egyptians' chariots before the Red Sea flowed back together?

227

"Brain Power"
Question & Answers

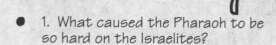

Match the right answer
with the question...

Pour it upon dry land ●

Go back to Egypt and set the
Israelites free ●

Sinai ●

Killed ●

Fear ●

To keep him from dying ●

Freedom from bondage ●

I am Who I am and What I am and
I Will Be What I Will Be ●

Turned into Blood ●

Moses' Sister ●

The Flocks ●

Snake ●

Aaron ●

Pharaoh's daughter ●

Burning Bush ●

Leprosy ●

...by drawing a
line between
the dots!   Ten ●

Passover ●

● 1. What caused the Pharaoh to be
so hard on the Israelites?

● 2. Why did Moses' mother put him in a
basket to float down the river?

● 3. Who did Moses' mother send to follow the
basket down the river?

● 4. Who found the basket and kept the baby Moses?

● 5. What did Moses do that was wrong and resulted
in his running away from Egypt?

● 6. After Moses left Egypt, the Israelites kept
crying out to God for what?

● 7. When Moses fled to Midian and married Zipporah
he took care of what?

● 8. What did Moses see on the mountain of God?

● 9. What is this mountain called?

● 10. When Moses spoke to God, who did
God say He was?

● 11. What did God ask Moses to do?

● 12. God caused Moses' shepherd stick to turn into
something. What was it?

● 13. God also caused Moses' hand to get
a disease called_____.

● 14. What did God tell Moses to do with the water
from the Nile River?

● 15. What happened to the water when Moses
obeyed God?

● 16. What was Moses' brother's name?

● 17. How many plagues did God send upon Egypt
before Pharaoh let God's people go?

● 18. At the last plague, God provided a way to
protect the firstborn of those who
loved God. What was this called?

228

ANSWERS IN BACK

"The 10 Commandments"
God's law for His people

God spoke the law to Moses and wrote the tablets with his finger.

Have no other gods before me.

Do not worship idols.

Do not speak God's name disrespectfully.

Keep the Sabbath day holy.

Respect and love your parents.

Do not commit murder.

Love your husband or wife and be faithful to them.

Do not take things from others.

Do not lie.

Do not long to have other people's things.

What are some of the ways you obey God's Commands? Can you list at least six?

229

"The Tabernacle"
A place to worship God in the desert.
Exodus 25

The Lord asked Moses to build a tabernacle. He tells Moses to take an offering from all the Israelites and ask them to give of their gold, silver, bronze; blue, purple and scarlet yarn and fine linen; goat hair; ram skins dyed red; acacia wood; olive oil and spices; and onyx stones and other gems.

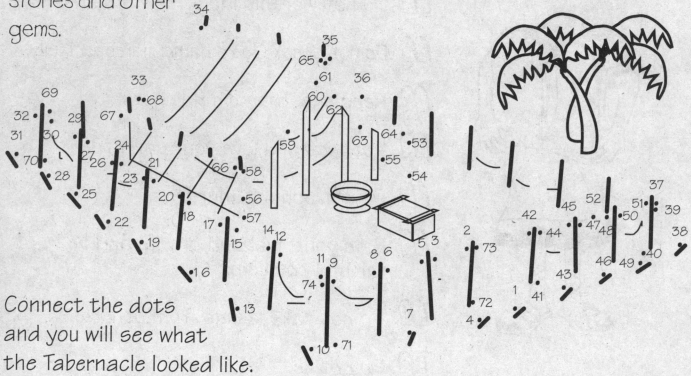

Connect the dots and you will see what the Tabernacle looked like.

Cool·Things to Know

Did you know that all the precious items used to build the tabernacle were given to the Hebrews by the Egyptians? You can read about this in Exodus 12•35-36.

Moses lived
to be very old!

Moses lived long, but not as long as his ancestors. Why do you think that is?

Can you guess Moses' age?

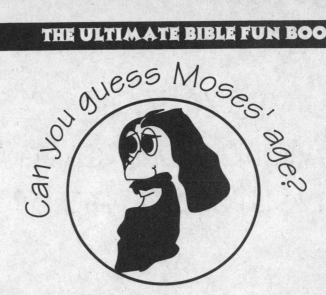

Do the math and find out how old Moses lived to be.

Add 50 and 49 together

$$50$$
$$+49$$
$$---$$

Take that number and add 139

$$+139$$
$$----$$

Take this number and subtract 50

$$-50$$
$$--$$

Take your number and add 20

$$+20$$
$$---$$

Take this number and subtract 100

$$---$$
$$-100$$
$$----$$

Now add 12

$$---$$
$$+12$$
$$---$$

How old was Moses?

Cool·Things to Know

There have been many great prophets since Moses, but Moses was the last prophet to have a very special face to face relationship with God. God gave Moses many special miraculous signs and wonders to do while he was in Egypt. All of these helped in getting Pharaoh to let God's people go. If you want to read about this, read Deuteronomy 34.

231

"Mezuzah"
Make your own Mezuzah!
Deuteronomy 6•4-9 and 11•13-21

Cool•Things to Know

What is a Mezuzah? Did you know that in the Old Testament God's people would write scriptures on paper and put them in a box? They would then attach the box to the doorframe of their house. As they came in and out of the house they would touch the box and be reminded of God's word.

Love the Lord your God with all your heart and with all your soul and with all your strength
Deuteronomy 6:5

The Lord lives! Praise be to my Rock! Exalted be God my Savior!
Psalm 18:46

Make your own Mezuzah out of a shoe box. Fill it with all of your favorite scriptures. Keep it someplace very special where you can enjoy opening it and reading how much God Loves you!

"Deuteronomy 33"
Before Moses died he blessed the tribes of Israel.

Below are listed the names of the twelve tribes.

Can you find all the names in the boxes below?
Circle them or color them in.

J	B	E	N	J	A	M	I	N	H	M
U	O	M	A	G	R	A	R	A	I	A
D	O	L	D	V	E	A	S	A	Z	N
A	P	F	A	S	H	E	R	H	E	A
H	P	G	G	C	M	H	E	O	B	S
P	N	P	A	Q	P	A	U	N	U	S
G	A	S	L	E	C	P	B	E	L	E
P	S	I	M	E	O	N	E	Y	U	H
I	L	A	T	H	P	A	N	G	N	W

Asher   Benjamin   Dan   Ephraim   Gad   Issachar
Judah   Manasseh   Naphtali   Reuben   Simeon   Zebulun

"Basketful of Blessings"

In the basket, unscramble the words to discover a multitude of blessings Moses enjoyed through his life!

DCTOEUAIN

_____

MLIFYA   DOFO

_____   _____

RTERHOB

_____

SRFEDIN

_____

VLEO

REOMDEF _____

234

"Pillar of Smoke"

By day the Lord went before the children of Israel in a pillar of cloud.

Start

End

Cool•Things to Know

Exodus 13•21 also says that God watched over them by night from a pillar of fire.

235

"Scramble"

The scrambled message below reads
God said, "Let my people go,."

There is one letter missing.
Can you find which one?

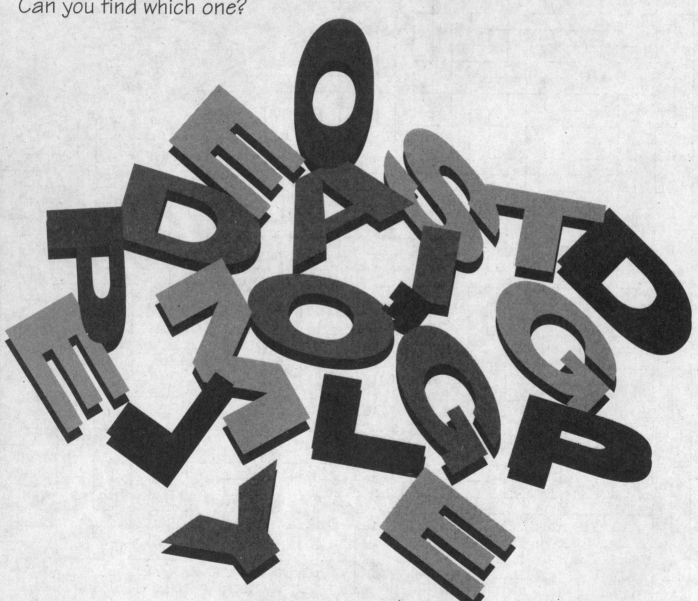

GOD SAID, "LET MY PEOPLE GO."

236

ANSWERS IN BACK

"God is Everywhere"

By day the Lord was there in a pillar of cloud. By night the Lord was there in a pillar of fire. When they where hungry, God brought manna from Heaven.

How many times can you find God hidden in the puzzle? Look every direction you can.

G O D O G D O G
O D O G O D G O
D O G D D G O D
D G O D G O D O
G O O O D O O G
D D G D D O G O
G O D D O G O D
O G O D G O D O
D D G G O D O G
G D O G D G O D
O D G G D O G O
D O G O D G O D
G G O D D D O D
G O D D D O G G
O D D O G O O D
D O G G O D O G

ANSWERS IN BACK

"Manna from Heaven"

Every day God's people would go out and gather Manna in the morning. In the evening the Lord brought Quail.

End

Start

238

Exodus 16•2-13

Long ago in a...

...country called Moab, there lived a king named Balak. Balak was very afraid for his country because the tribes of Israel were getting close to his land and he did not want them to come in and take the land from his people. The Israelites had just conquered the Amorites and Balak was afraid that this was going to happen to him too. Balak sent his messengers to a man whose reputation was that if he cursed a people they would really be cursed and if he blessed a people they would really be blessed. This man's name was Balaam. The messengers told him that King Balak wanted him to come and curse the Israelites so he could defeat them in battle. Balaam asked the messengers to stay the night. The next day he would give them the answer from the Lord.

That night God spoke to Balaam and told him not to curse the people of Israel because He had blessed them. When everyone woke up the next morning Balaam told them that God had told him not to go back with them and that they needed to go without him. The messengers went back to Balak and told him that Balaam had refused to come with them. Balak sent more messengers to try to persuade Balaam to come and curse the Israelites, but Balaam told them again that even if Balak offered his house full of gold and silver he could not go against the word of the Lord his God. Again that night God spoke to Balaam and told him, "Since these men have come again, go with them, but do only what I tell you."

Balaam and the Donkey

BIBLE TELLS

BIBLE TELLS

235

So the next day...

...Balaam saddled his donkey and started out on his way to Moab. Along the way, an angel of the Lord stood with a sword in front of the path of the donkey. When the donkey saw the angel of the Lord standing in the road, she turned off the road into a field. Because Balaam could not see the angel, he became very angry that his donkey was going the wrong way. He was so angry that he began to beat his donkey to get her on the path again. Then the angel of the Lord appeared again. This time the donkey was heading for the vineyard between two walls. When the donkey saw the angel, she pushed up against one of the walls and crushed Balaam's foot. This too made Balaam very angry, and he began to hit his donkey again. Then the angel of the Lord moved up the road and stood in a very narrow place where the donkey had no room to go either right or left. When she saw the angel of the Lord, she lay down with Balaam still riding her. This made Balaam furious and he began to beat the donkey harder than before. Then the Lord opened the mouth of the donkey and she began to speak."What have I done to you that you would hit me these three times?" Balaam, being surprised, answered back and said,"You have embarrassed me and if I had a sword I would kill you right now!" Then the donkey answered back and said "Am I not the donkey you have ridden on your whole life, and have I ever done anything like this to you?" Balaam replied,"No". Then the Lord opened his eyes and he saw the angel of the Lord standing there with his sword drawn. Balaam bowed all the way to the ground.

Balaam and the Donkey

240

ANSWERS IN BACK

Numbers 22

Balaam
and the Donkey

What did Balaam's donkey see that Balaam did not see?

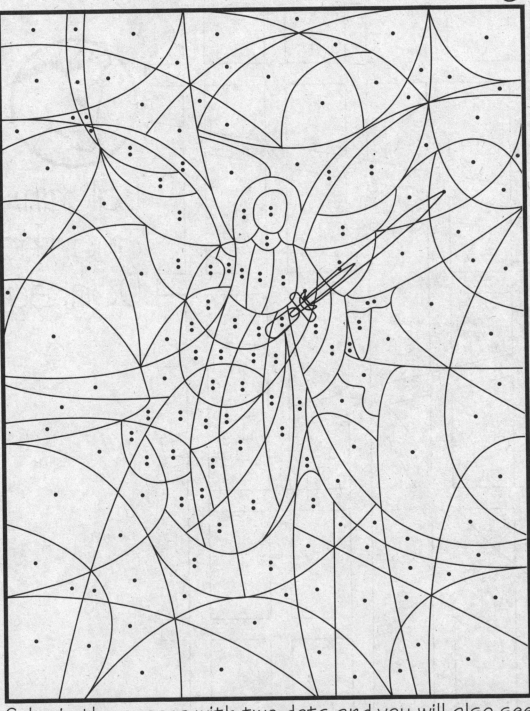

Color in the spaces with two dots and you will also see!

"Donkey Maze"

Numbers 22:23 The donkey sees the angel of the Lord standing in the road.

Balaam's donkey takes the wrong path to get away from the angel of the Lord. Help her to find a path where Balaam can see the Angel.

Start

Balaam and the Donkey

242

End

The angel said...

..."I have come here to come against you because your path is a reckless one. Your donkey saw me these three times and turned away. If she had not turned away, I would certainly have killed you by now, and I would have spared her." Balaam then said, "I have sinned," and asked for forgiveness. Then the angel said "Go with the men, but speak only what I tell you."

When Balaam arrived in Moab, he told Balak "I must only speak what God puts in my mouth." The next morning Balak took him into the mountains. They made altars to God three different times. Each time they went higher and higher on the mountain, and each time Balaam blessed the Israelites. This made Balak very angry and he told Balaam he would have given him riches if he had cursed his enemies, but since he blessed them, he must leave with nothing. Balaam once again told Balak that he could not cursed what God has blessed, and Balaam returned to his home and Balak went his own way.

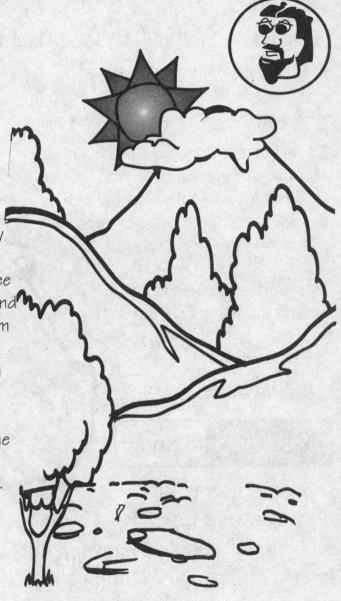

Balaam and the Donkey

"Donkey Talk"

Numbers 22:28 The Lord opened the donkey's mouth, and she talked to Balaam...

Create your own talking donkey.
All you need:
• 1 Brass Brad • 1 popsicle stick • glue

1. Cut out the donkey below. You may want to glue it to cardboard.
2. Attach the mouth with the brad.
3. Glue the popsicle stick to the back of the mouth peice.

By moving the popsicle stick up and down you can make your donkey talk, just like Balaam's.

Push the brad through the circles on the donkey's face!

Cool·Things to Know

Did you know that donkeys were used by all kinds of people-even very important people? During this time if a King rode a donkey it meant he was coming in peace.

"Speaking Blessing"

Numbers 23•11 Balak wanted Balaam to curse the Israelites, but instead Balaam blessed them. What did God say to Balaam to keep him from speaking curses?

Balaam and the Donkey

By using multiplication you can figure out the code and solve the answer below.

4 x 4 = _____ (T)   6 x 9 = _____ (C)   4 x 6 = _____ (Y)
6 x 8 = _____ (A)   7 x 8 = _____ (P)   12 x 3 = _____ (M)
8 x 4 = _____ (B)   3 x 6 = _____ (R)   5 x 3 = _____ (U)
3 x 7 = _____ (G)   3 x 3 = _____ (O)   4 x 15 = _____ (D)
9 x 9 = _____ (H)   7 x 4 = _____ (N)   8 x 9 = _____ (S)
6 x 7 = _____ (E)   4 x 3 = _____ (I)   8 x 12 = _____ (L)

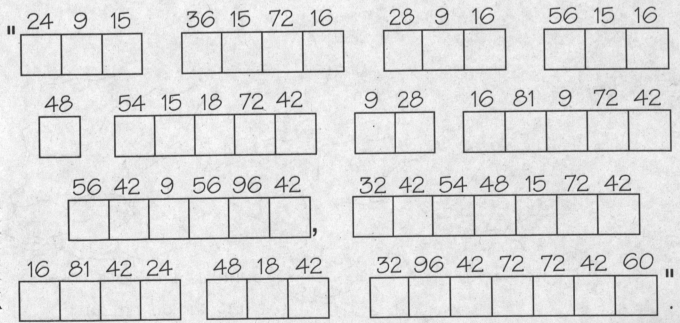

" 24 9 15   36 15 72 16   28 9 16   56 15 16

48   54 15 18 72 42   9 28   16 81 9 72 42

56 42 9 56 96 42 ,   32 42 54 48 15 72 42

16 81 42 24   48 18 42   32 96 42 72 72 42 60 " .

"Jericho"

The Walls of Jericho came falling down!

The City of Jericho sat on top of a hill. The walls of the city were so big that many of the people who lived in Jericho built their homes in the wall.

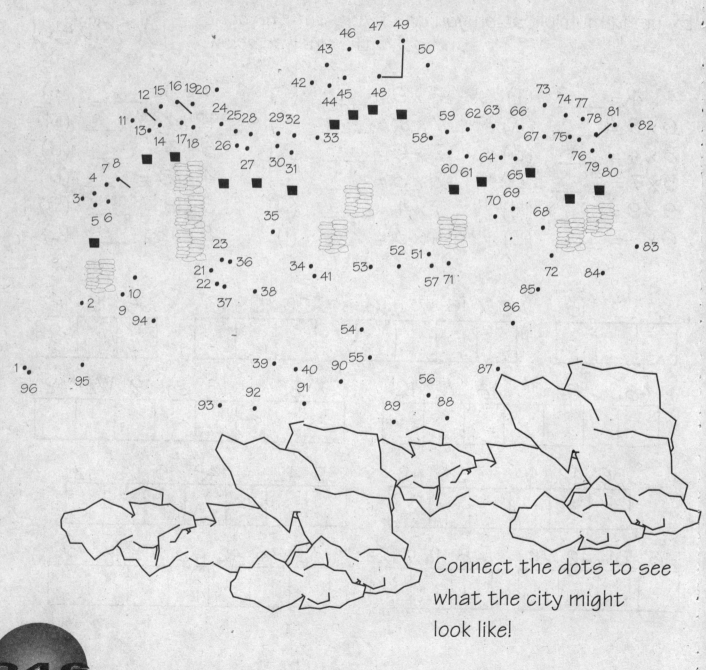

Connect the dots to see what the city might look like!

"Joshua 5&6"
The Walls of Jericho came falling down!

God told Joshua to march around the city walls
with his army one time a day for six days.
While they marched, seven priests carried horns in
front of the ark of the covenant. On the seventh day they
marched around the city walls seven times and the priests
blew on the trumpets. When the people heard the loud
blast of the horns they shouted very loudly.
Then the walls of Jericho came falling down!

Walls of Jericho

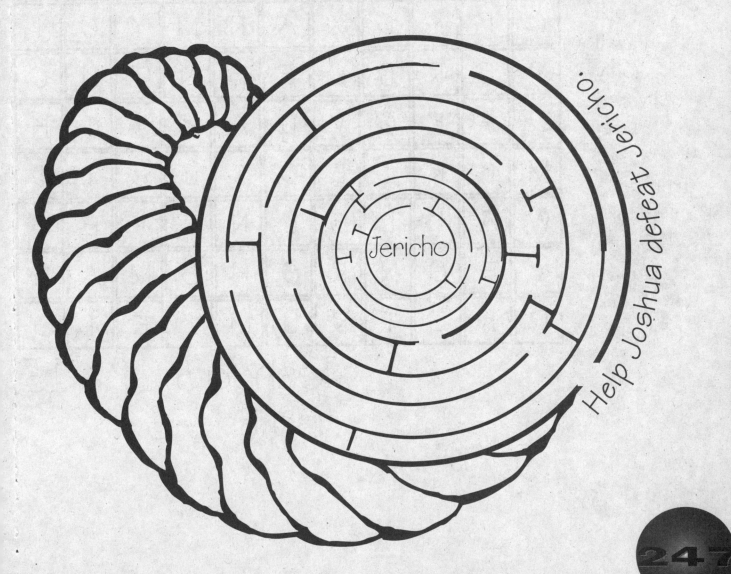

Help Joshua defeat Jericho.

Jericho

247

Walls of Jericho

"Joshua obeyed..."

...the instructions God gave him, and the walls of Jericho came falling down.

Fall
Jericho
Sword
Army
Lord
Wall
City
Delivered
King
March
Trumpets
Ram's Horn
Seven
Shout
Ark
Priests

F	A	L	L	P	K	I	N	G	H	J
A	O	M	E	S	W	O	R	D	S	E
L	R	L	I	H	E	S	E	E	H	R
O	P	K	C	X	A	R	M	Y	O	I
R	P	R	P	O	E	S	N	T	U	C
D	A	P	O	V	U	A	P	I	T	H
M	P	R	I	E	S	T	S	C	I	O
W	A	L	L	S	U	N	E	V	E	S
I	E	O	N	R	O	H	S	M	A	R
D	L	E	T	R	U	M	P	E	T	S

Joshua 5: 13 - 15
and 6:1 - 5

248

"Jericho"

Find these hidden items in the walls of Jericho...

Sword
Angel
Sandals
King's crown
Ram's horn
Silver coin
Gold Cup

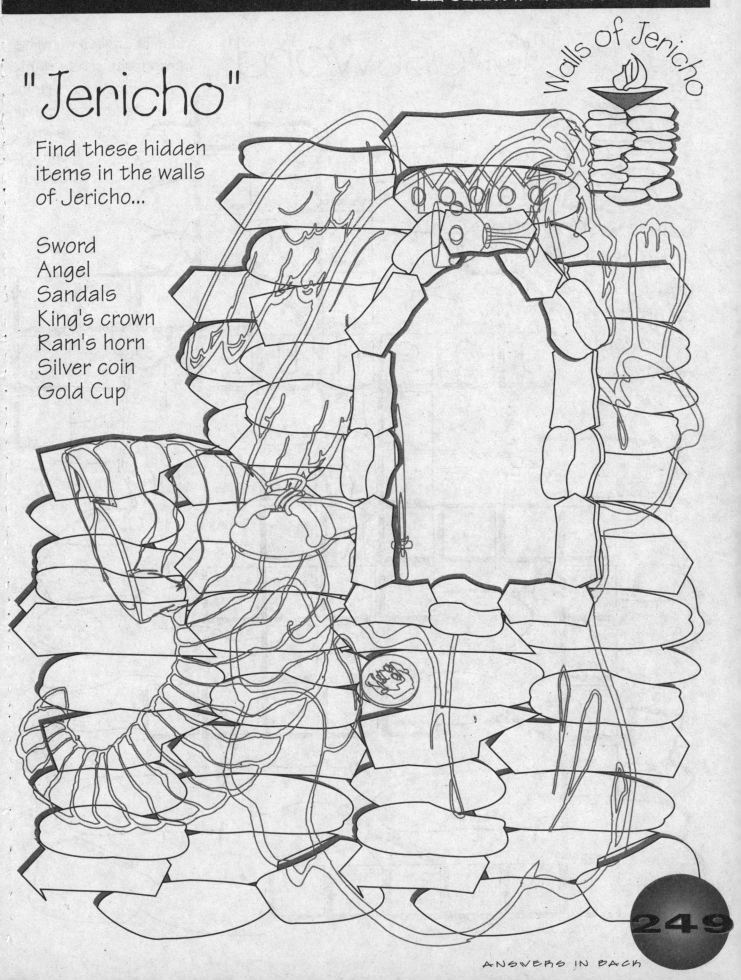

Walls of Jericho

249

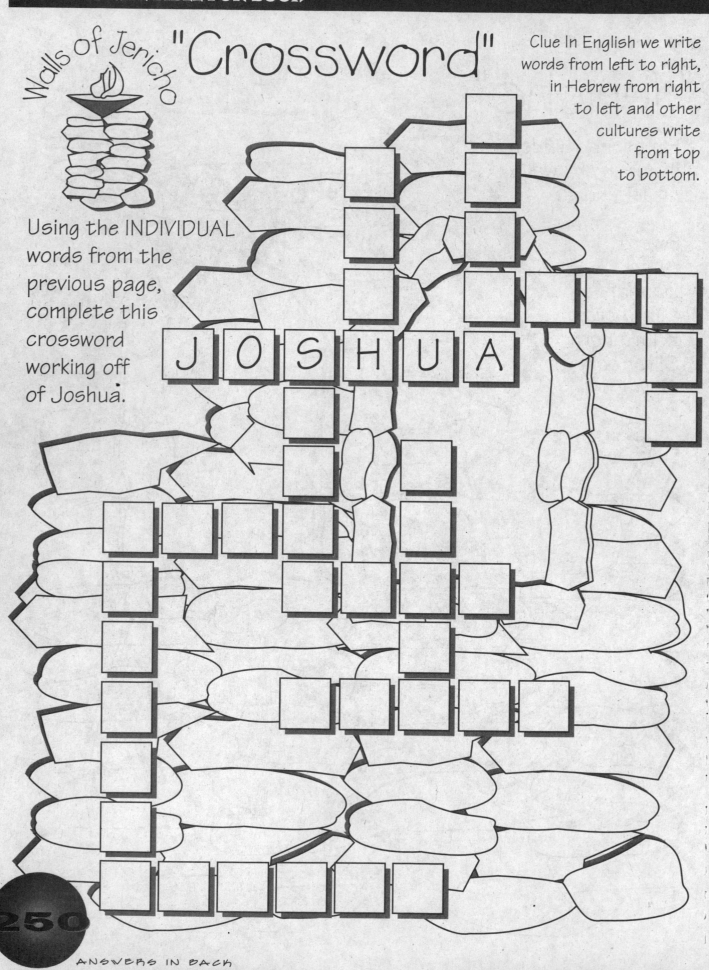

Walls of Jericho "Crossword"

Clue In English we write words from left to right, in Hebrew from right to left and other cultures write from top to bottom.

Using the INDIVIDUAL words from the previous page, complete this crossword working off of Joshua.

J O S H U A

250

A Jewish man...

...named Manoah and his wife Zorah did not have any children. One day an angel of the Lord appeared to them and told them that they were going to have a son. The angel told them that Zorah must not drink any wine or eat any unclean thing while she was pregnant, and that they must never cut the boy's hair because he was going to be set apart for God from birth. The angel said that the boy would one day begin the deliverance of Israel from the hands of its enemies, the Philistines.

Zorah gave birth to a boy and named him Samson. Samson was faithful to God from the time he was born and God gave him awesome physical strength. One day, Samson even killed a lion with his bare hands. Another time he killed 1000 men all by himself.

Samson met and fell in love with a woman named Delilah. Delilah said, "Tell me the secret of your great strength and how you can be tied up and stopped." Delilah was one of the Philistine people, the enemies of Israel. She wanted to find out Samson's weakness so she could tell the Philistines and they could defeat Samson.

BibleTells

Samson

For a long time...

... Samson would not tell Delilah the real reason he was so strong. Finally she convinced him to tell her. He told her that the secret to his strength was that his hair had never been cut since his birth. He said that if his head was shaved, his strength would leave him and he would become as weak as any other man.

Delilah went and told the rulers of the Philistines and they sent someone to shave off Samson's hair while he was asleep. When he woke up, Samson realized that his strength was gone. The Philistines took him as their prisoner. While Samson was in prison, his hair began to grow back.

One day the Philistines were having a big celebration and they brought Samson out of prison to make him perform for them. Samson asked God to give him special strength just one more time so he could defeat his enemies. Samson put his arms out toward the two main columns on which the Philistine temple stood. Then he pushed with all his might and down came the temple on top of all his enemies.

BIBLE TELLS

Samson

ANSWERS IN BACK

"Samson's" Super Human Hair

Samson was very strong.

Connect the dots to discover what is hidden in his hair.

Cool·Things to Know

Did you know that a man who made a special "Nazirite" vow to God had to let his hair grow? This vow was one of separation to the Lord. The Nazirite also had to follow several other rules. You can read about this in Numbers 6.

253

"Hair Maze-ing"

Samson's hair was very, very long.

How long will it take you to get through this hairy maze?

254

 "Samson Scramble"
The scrambled message below reads
"Samson's hair makes him very strong."

Oops! There's one letter missing.
Can you find which one?

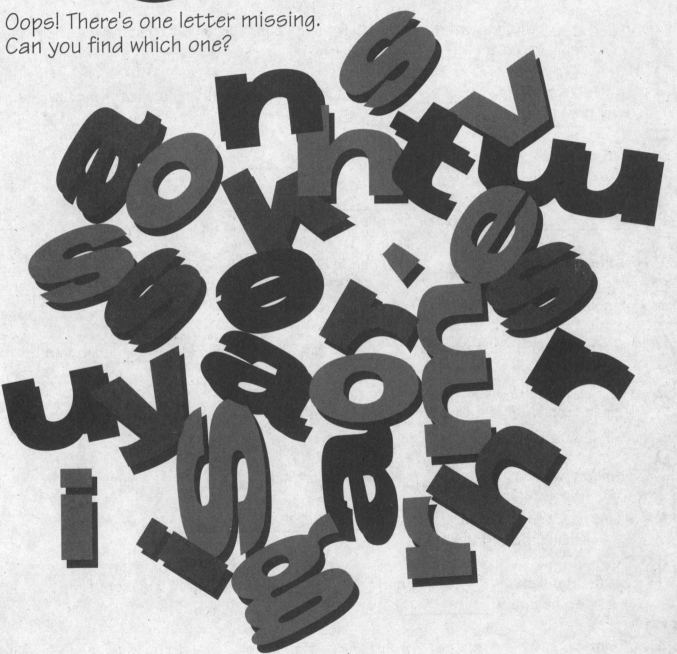

ANSWERS IN BACK

What do you remember?
Using the Samson story, fill in the blanks to these sentences.

1. An _____ of the Lord appeared to Samson's mother and father, telling them they were going to have a _____ .

2. Samson's mother, _____ , could not drink wine or eat any unclean thing while she was pregnant.

3. They were also told never to ____ Samson's _____ .

4. Samson would one day begin the _____ of Israel from the _____ , their enemies.

5. Samson was very _____ because his hair had never been cut.

6. Samson fell in love with _____ , a Philistine.

7. Samson said if his head was _____ his strength would _____ him and he would become as _____ as any man.

8. Delilah told the Philistine rulers and they shaved Samson's hair while he was _____ .

9. Samson was put in _____ by the Philistines.

10. One day the Philistines were having a big _____ , and brought Samson to it.

11. Samson asked _____ to give him _____ strength just one more time so he could _____ his enemies.

12. Samson put his arms out toward the two main _____ on which the Philistine _____ stood.

13. Samson pushed the columns over with all his _____ and the temple came _____ .

Samson

The Philistines...

... and the Israelites lined up for battle against each other. The Philistine army stood on one hill and the Israelite army stood on another hill with a valley in between them.

The champion of the Philistines was a man named Goliath who was over 9 feet tall. He wore a bronze helmet on his head and a coat of scale armor. He carried a spear with a huge iron point.

Goliath shouted to the army of Israel, "Why do you come out and line up for battle? Choose a man and have him come and fight me. If he kills me, we will become your servants. But if I kill him, you will become our servants. I defy the army of Israel to give me a man and let us fight each other." When they heard these words, King Saul and all the Israelites were very afraid.

Now David's three oldest brothers were in the Israelite army and stayed at the camp near the battle line. Meanwhile, David was tending his father's sheep out in the field. One day, David's father sent David to take some bread to his brothers at the army camp and to bring back a report about how they were doing. David did what his father asked and went to see how his brothers were doing. When David reached the camp, the Israelites were just going out to take their battle positions. Israel and the Philistines lined up facing each other. David ran up to talk to his brothers, but as he did, Goliath shouted his usual challenge and David heard it. When the Israelites heard it, they all ran from Goliath in great fear.

BIBLE TELLS

David and Goliath

STORY PAGE 1

1 Samuel 17

David and Goliath

1 Samuel 17•17

David needs to bring bread to his three brothers. Can you help match the bread to the brother?

"David's father sent David to take some bread to his brothers at the army camp and to bring back a report."

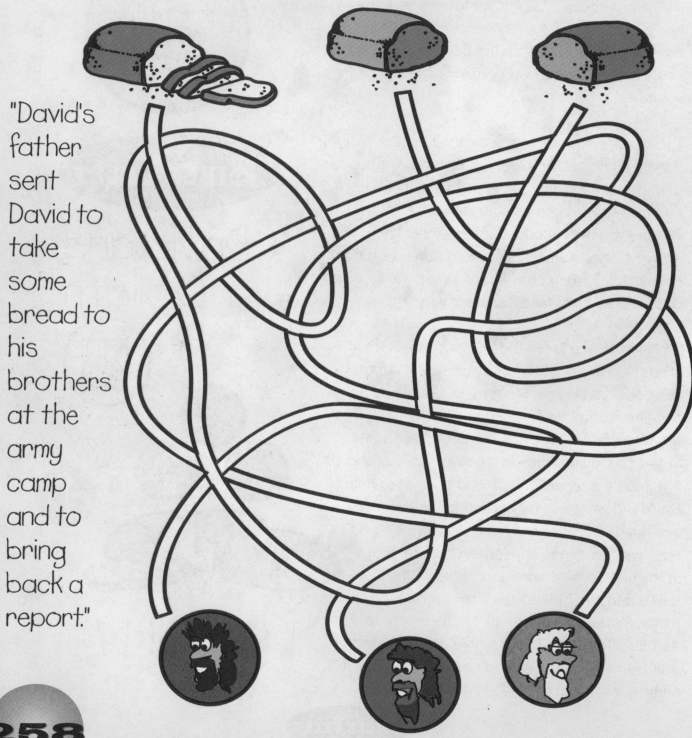

258

Now King Saul...

... had promised that he would give great wealth and other good things to the man who defeated Goliath. But no one in the Israelite army was brave enough to fight Goliath. David said to King Saul, "This Philistine is defying the army of the living God. Do not be afraid; I will go and fight him." David told King Saul that God had helped him kill both a lion and a bear while David was protecting his father's sheep. David said, "God will protect me from Goliath." So King Saul let David fight Goliath.

King Saul wanted David to wear a coat of armor, but David refused because he wasn't used to wearing armor. Instead, he took his sling with him and chose 5 smooth stones from a nearby stream. Then David approached Goliath.

When Goliath saw David coming toward him and realized that David was only a boy, Goliath was mad. But David said to Goliath, "You came against me with your sword and spear, but I come against you in the name of the Lord Almighty, the God of the army of Israel. I will strike you down and then the whole world will know that there is a God in Israel and that it is not by sword or spear that the Lord saves; for the battle is the Lord's."

Then David took a stone and slung it at Goliath. The stone struck Goliath right in his forehead and Goliath fell down and died. Therefore David beat Goliath, the Philistine champion, with only a stone and a sling, because the Lord his God was with him.

David and Goliath

STORY PAGE
2

David and Goliath

Follow each step to see David's answer!

David went into battle against Goliath, a

PHILISTINE

The "P" needs to leave; make it an "S."

We have too many "I's;" remove the first and the last.

Now the "H" is all wrong; move it between "S" and "T."

The "N" needs help getting between "I" and "S."

The "E" needs to change to the letter after "F" in the alphabet.

Oh my! We forgot the "O" between "H" and "T."

You are almost there, but the "G" needs to move between "N" and "S."

Now we are sure you can see where a space needs to be.

But David said to King Saul, "This Philistine is defying the army of the living God. Do not be afraid; I will go and fight him."

ANSWERS IN BACK

David...

1. Do you know what Goliath wore into battle?

2. Do you know what King Saul wanted David to wear in his fight with Goliath?

3. Why was David so sure of himself?

4. David believed the battled belonged to whom?

Unscramble the words for your answers. Then circle as many question numbers as you think apply.

1 • 2 • 3 • 4	EORBZN EMHLTE
1 • 2 • 3 • 4	ZOBENR ORRMA
1 • 2 • 3 • 4	OZBERN DEHLIS
1 • 2 • 3 • 4	APRES
1 • 2 • 3 • 4	RWDOS
1 • 2 • 3 • 4	RHDSDPEH FTFAS
1 • 2 • 3 • 4	TOSHOM EOSSNT
1 • 2 • 3 • 4	NLGIS OSTH
1 • 2 • 3 • 4	DGO

If you need help you can look in your Bible at 1 Samuel 17•5-7, 38-40, 47

...and Goliath

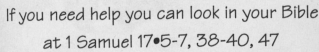

261

David and Goliath

"David has faith in God"

is what this message is supposed to read. But one of those Philistines ran off with one of my letters. I don't know which one it was. Can you help me find it?

1 Samuel 17•45-47

262

"Hide & Find"

In this drawing of shapes 6 items are hidden.

Can you find them?

sword

shield

shepherd
staff

spear

five
smooth
stones

sling
shot

263

"Sling Shot"

David and Goliath

This sling shot is just for fun • USE ONLY COTTON BALLS!

Make your own, like David's...

You will need:
- 2 12" pieces of string
- A piece of fabric 2" long by 1" wide
- Lots of cotton balls

How to make:
Punch two holes in the fabric, one on each end. Tie the strings through the holes.

Now you have a sling shot!

Put a cotton ball into the fabric. Holding the end of each string in one hand, swing it around and around. Once you have it swinging really well, let one string go. The cotton ball should go flying across the room.

When you get really good at this, cut out Goliath and pretend you're David!

Cut along dotted line and glue to a piece of cardboard to stand.

264

After David...

... killed Goliath, King Saul kept all of his promises and from that day on kept David with him. Jonathan, who was King Saul's son, became very good friends with David. Jonathan once even took off his robe and gave it to David, along with his tunic, his sword, his bow, and his belt.

David became very successful and always accomplished whatever Saul sent him to do. Saul trusted him so much that he gave David his own high rank in the army. When he did this, it made everyone very happy because they all liked David very much. One time when they were returning home from a battle, the women came out from all the towns of Israel to meet King Saul. They were joyful with singing, dancing, and playing instruments. As they danced, they sang: "Saul has slain his thousands, and David his tens of thousands."

When Saul heard this song it made him very angry and he became jealous of David. He was afraid David would one day take his kingdom away. So from that day forward Saul did not trust David and he looked for ways to kill David.

Saul was also afraid of David because he knew that the Lord was with David and no longer with him. Saul decided to send David away. He gave David command over a thousand men in his army and sent him off to battle their enemies.

BIBLETELLS

David and King Saul

STORY PAGE 1

1 Samuel 18•1-13

BIBLETELLS

265

In everything...

...David did he had great success because God was with him. Saul saw how successful David was, and this made him even more afraid of David. Because David was so successful in all his battles, all Israel and Judah loved him, which made it even more difficult on King Saul.

Saul decided to let David marry his daughter Merab as a way to try to keep David loyal to him. But David did not feel it was right for him to become the king's son-in-law. So Merab was not married to David, she was married to someone else instead. Saul had another daughter, Michal, who was in love with David. When she told her father, he was very pleased and arranged for her to marry David. But David still did not feel worthy to be the son-in-law to the king. Then the king said the only price he wanted for the bride was a hundred dead Philistines, to take revenge on his enemies. He did this in hope that David would also be killed by the Philistines.

David was pleased to hear that the king wanted the hundred Philistines because he could do this in battle against the Philistines. He took his army right out and they killed two hundred Philistines. As King Saul had promised he gave David his daughter Michal to marry. But now he was even more afraid as he knew his daughter loved David and that God was still with David.

BibleTells

David and King Saul

STORY PAGE
2

David and King Saul

1. What did Saul keep when David killed Goliath?

2. What was the first item Jonathan gave David?

3. Saul sent David on many tasks and each time David was very _____.

4. Who came out to meet King Saul and David after the battle?

5. The women sang a song that made Saul very mad and _____.

6. Who was with David that caused him to be so successful?

7. Who was the king's daughter that married David?

8. Jonathan and David were good _____.

9. David's wife did something to help David escape during the night. What was it?

10. David had opportunities to kill King Saul but would not do it. He did cut something off of Saul's robe. What was it?

11. David would not kill King Saul because he was God's _____.

1 Samuel 18

Saul was so...

...upset that he even told his son Jonathan to try to kill David. But Jonathan was good friends with David and would not do it. He even warned David that Saul wanted him dead. The next day Jonathan spoke to his father, saying, "Do not do wrong to David; he has not done anything wrong against you, and he has benefited you greatly. He took his own life in his hands when he killed the Philistine. God has won a great victory for Israel, and you saw it and were glad. Why would you want to kill an innocent man like David, and without cause?" Saul listened to Jonathan and said, "Before the Lord I say, 'David will not be put to death.'" Then Jonathan reunited Saul and David and their relationship was restored.

Shortly after, David went off to war and was more successful than before. Once again Saul got very angry and wanted to kill David. He sent men to watch David's house and kill him. But Michal, David's wife, warned him, and he escaped during the night.

From this time on David went into hiding. Saul continued to pursue David and tried to kill him several times. David even had an opportunity to kill Saul, but would not do it. He did cut off the hem of Saul's robe to show Saul that he could have killed him. But David would not kill Saul because the Lord had told him not to, as he was the Lord's anointed.

David and King Saul

STORY PAGE
3

David and King Saul

Help David get away from King Saul!

Start

End

269

David  and King Saul

What did the women sing that made King Saul so jealous of David?

Using the information on the opposite page, find each letter by moving in the given direction, always beginning at the ⭐ symbol. The first one is done for you.

1 Samuel 18•7

| S | | | |

1. South 2 East 2
2. West 2
3. West 1
4. South 1 West 1
5. South 2 East 1
6. East 3
7. South 2 West 1
8. West 3
9. North 2 East 2
10. East 2 South 1
11. East 3 North 1
12. North 1
3. West 1 North 1
14. West 3 North 1
15. North 2 West 2

15. North 2 West 2
16. South 2 West 2
17. East 3 South 1
18. North 2 West 1
19. West 2 North 1
20. East 2
21. South 2
22. South 1 East 1
23. North 1 East 1
24. West 3

25. West 2 South 1
26. East 3
27. East 1
28. East 3 North 1
29. North 1 East 1
30. South 1
31. North 1 West 3
32. South 2 East 2
33. South 2 West 2
34. North 1 East 2

35. South 1 East 1
36. West 2 North 2
37 East 1 North 2
38. South 1 West 3
39. North 2
40. South 2 East 1
41. North 2 West 1
42. West 1
43. West 1 South 2
44. West 2
45. North 1
46. South 1 West 2
47. East 2

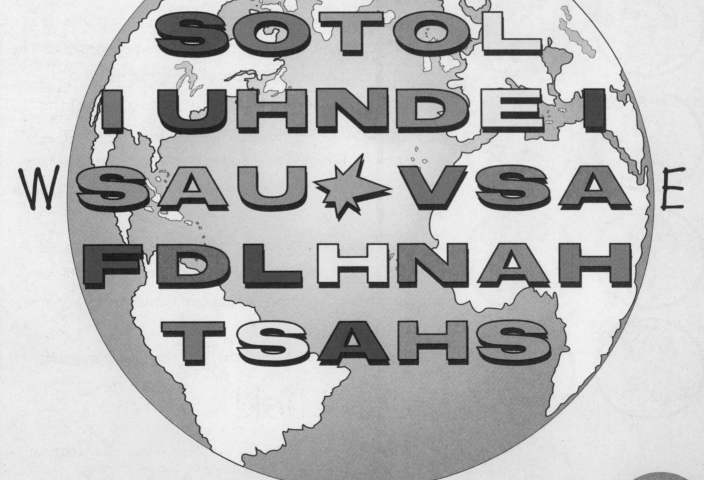

BibleTells "Checkers"

Help David become King

- Play BibleTells Checkers!
- First, cut out the playing pieces. You might want to glue them to cardboard first.
- Then, turn the page to the game board.

Rules:

1. Place your pieces on the black squares on your side of the board. Have your opponent place his/her pieces on the other side of the board on the green squares.

2. Take turns moving one space at a time toward the other side (you can only move diagonally forward on your same color). The object is to jump your opponent's piece and to take it off the board while you try to get to his/her side.

3. If you get one of your pieces to the other side that is called a "KING" and is "crowned" with one of your pieces that has been captured (a king can move diagonally in any direction).

4. Take turns moving until there is only one player left.

Good Luck!

CAUTION: Cut out these pieces after you have worked the activity on the page before!

272

David becomes...
...King over Judah and Israel

David asked the Lord, "Shall I go up to one of the towns of Judah?" The Lord said, "Go up." David then asked, "Where shall I go?" "To Hebron," said the Lord. David obeyed the Lord and took his family and all the men who were with him and their families up to Hebron. While in Hebron the men of Judah came to David and anointed him King over the tribe of Judah.

Before David was made king of Judah, King Saul and his son Jonathan had been killed in battle. Saul's son, Ish-Bosheth, was made king over Gilead, Ashuri, Jezreel, Ephraim, Benjamin, and all of Israel. But the people of Judah followed David. This caused war between the people of David and Ish-Bosheth.

One of the battles happened in Gibeon. They decided to have some of the young men fight hand to hand: twelve men from Ish-Bosheth's army and twelve from David's army. They fought until all twenty four of the men were dead. Then both armies fought. By the end of that day only nineteen of David's men were found missing but three hundred and sixty Benjamites were killed. After this battle the war between Ish-Bosheth and David lasted a very long time. All the while David grew stronger and stronger and Ish-Bosheth grew weaker and weaker.

BIBLETELLS
King David

STORY PAGE 1

2 Samuel 2•2-5

BIBLE TELLS

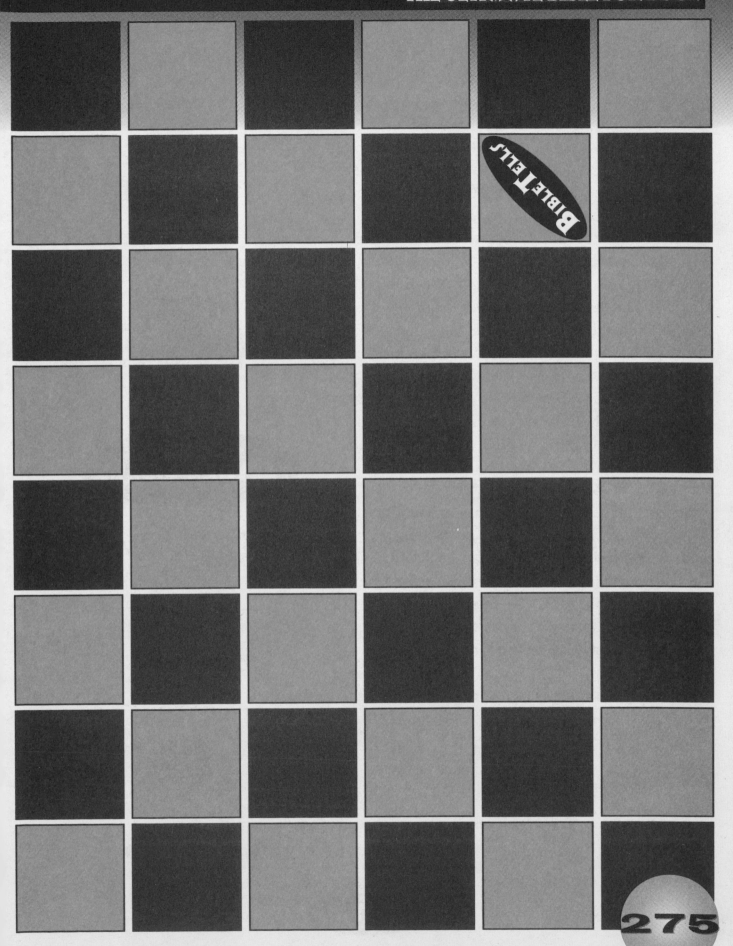

BIBLE Tells

Abner, who...

...served Ish-Bosheth, sent a messenger to David, saying, "Whose land is it? Make an agreement with me, and I will help bring all Israel over to you." So David made an agreement with Abner and then sent Abner away. When one of David's men found out that Abner had been sent away, he pursued him and had him killed. David wept over this because he was a just man and knew this was not right. Once Ish-Bosheth heard that Abner was dead, he became afraid and all Israel became alarmed. During the night, two of Ish-Bosheth's men came into his home and killed him. They then took the news to David. To their surprise this did not please David, and he had them put to death for killing Ish-Bosheth, an innocent man.

After Ish-Bosheth was killed, all the tribes of Israel came to David and said, "We want you as our king. You are part of us; you have led Israel in her battles and the Lord said, 'You will shepherd the people of Israel, and you will become their king.'" When all the elders of Israel came to David, he made an agreement with them and became the King over all of Israel. David was thirty years old when this happened. David was king over Judah for seven years and six months and over Israel and Judah for thirty three years-a total of forty years.

King David

STORY PAGE 2

2 Samuel 5•1--5

David becomes King over Judah & Israel

2 Samuel 5

Start

End

Use the Maze to help David lead all the people to Hebron.

ANSWERS IN BACK

"Unscramble"
David becomes King over Judah

2 Samuel 2

Can you unscramble the names of these people that Ish-Bosheth was made king over? If you need help you can find the answers in the story you just read.

ALGDEI

RHAIUS

ERELEZJ

IRPMAHE

IANBNMJE

ERILAS

IADVD ASW NKGI

EVRO AUHDJ

"Agreement"
David becomes King over Judah and Israel

David makes an agreement with all of the elders of Israel to be their king.

What is an agreement?

• It means everyone involved in a situation comes to an understanding on how to handle the situation.

• This can be done both in writing and by talking.

• Write an agreement with your Mom and/or Dad for doing your chores.

• Work out something in your agreement that you would like to get for doing your chores. Once it is written, have everyone sign it as a promise to fulfill their part.

• This is also called a contract.

• CONTRACT •

This is an official agreement between the undersigned. You: _____,

agree that if I _____

_____

_____,

then you will give me _____

_____

_____

for my efforts.

_____ _____

Undersigned, print your name here!　Date

_____

Sign your name here!

_____ _____

Other person, print your name here!　Date

_____

Sign your name here!

David reigned
for many years as king!

David was king in Hebron and in Jerusalem.

Do the math to get the answer.

Can you guess how many years?

Add 190 and 220 together

$$190$$
$$+220$$
$$\underline{}$$

Take this number and divide it by 2

$$\underline{-\ -\ -}$$

$$2\overline{\smash{)}}$$
$$\underline{-\ -\ -}$$

Take this number and subtract 80

$$-80$$
$$\underline{-\ -\ -}$$

Take your number and multiply by 3

$$\underline{-\ -\ -}$$
$$\times 3$$

Take this number and divide it by 3

$$3\overline{\smash{)}}$$
$$\underline{-\ -\ -}$$

Take this number and subtract 85

$$\underline{-\ -\ -}$$
$$-85$$

How long did King David reign?

$$\underline{-\ -\ -}$$

280

David brought...

...together over 30,000 men of Israel to move the ark of God, which is called by the name of the Lord of hosts, who sits enthroned above the cherubim. The ark, being the greatest symbol of Israel's faith, contained the stone tablets of the Ten Commandments. During King Saul's reign the ark had been neglected and placed in a private shrine in the town of Kirjath-jearim. David thought if he could move the ark to the City of David it would help revitalize the kingdom of Israel.

They made a new cart and set the ark on it for moving. The people guiding the cart were Uzzah and Ahio. While the ark was being moved, David and the tribes of Israel were celebrating with all their might before the Lord with songs, lyres, harps, tambourines, castanets, and cymbals. While moving the ark, the oxen stumbled. Uzzah, thinking the ark might fall, reached up and touched the ark. At that very moment when Uzzah touched the ark, the very power of God came upon him and he died. David was very upset by this and said "How can the ark of the Lord ever come to me?" He decided not to move the ark to the City of David as planned and moved it to the house of Obed-Edom, the Gittite, where it stayed for three months. During those three months Obed-Edom was very blessed by the Lord!

2 Samuel 6

BIBLE TELLS

King David brings the Ark of the Covenant to Jerusalem

BIBLE TELLS

STORY PAGE 1

281

BibleTells

When David...

...heard how blessed Obed-Edom was, he decided to move the ark to the City of David. This time David made sure to follow all of the rules concerning moving the ark. The ark cannot be moved in man's way; it must be moved in God's way! This time after the ark was moved six steps, they stopped and sacrificed a bull and calf to the Lord. David wore clothes of the priests and danced before the ark with all of his strength, and the tribes of Israel brought up the ark with shouting and with the sound of the trumpet.

When the ark was brought into the City of David, they set it in its place inside the tent which David had put up just for it. Once again, David offered burnt offerings and peace offerings before the Lord and blessed all the people in the name of the Lord of hosts. He also gave the people bread, meat, and a raisin cake, and then they all went to their homes.

King David brings the Ark of the Covenant to Jerusalem

2 Samuel 6

STORY PAGE

2

BibleTells

All these men of Israel look the same...

King David brings the Ark of the Covenant to Jerusalem

...but two are an exact match. Can you circle which two?

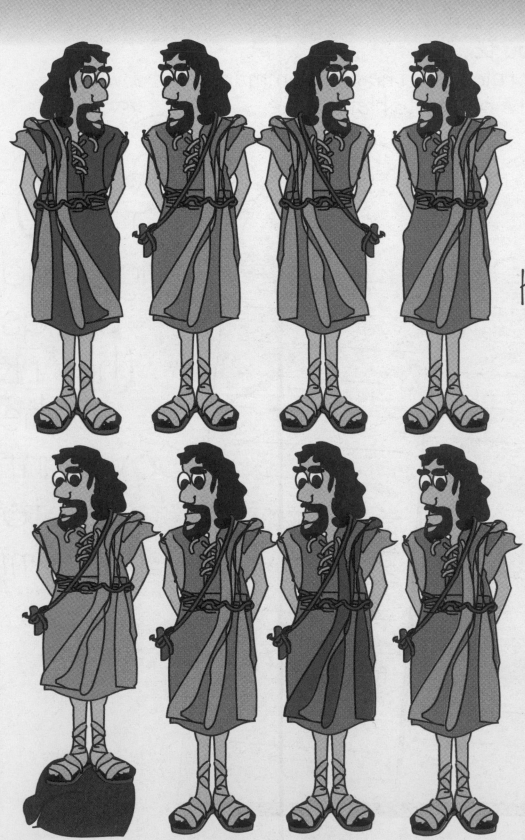

283

ANSWERS IN BACK

By reading this story...

... we find out that the Ten Commandments are inside the ark.

If God told you to
write ten new rules for the Ten Commandments, what
would you write on the tablets?

1._____
_____
_____
2._____
_____
_____
3._____
_____
_____
4._____
_____
_____
5._____
_____
_____

6._____
_____
_____
7._____
_____
_____
8._____
_____
_____
9._____
_____
_____
10._____
_____
_____

King David
brings
the Ark
of the
Covenant
to
Jerusalem

"Kirjath-jearim"
is a very funny name for a town!

This is where King Saul kept the Ark during his reign.

How many words can you spell from the letters in
K I R J A T H - J E A R I M ?

King David
brings
the Ark
of the
Covenant
to
Jerusalem

285

"What's Wrong"
2 Samuel 6

David brought the ark to the City of David in hopes that it would prosper the kingdom of Israel. The picture below shows a very prosperous city today.

CAN YOU FIND: a backward hat • triangle • musical note • coat hanger • funny face • mailbox • open book • screwdriver • butterfly

ANSWERS IN BACK

David brings the Ark to Jerusalem

• marshmallow • donut • slipper • baseball • saw • log
• yo-yo • flower • rabbit • pencil • comb • and a fish.

287

"What's Wrong"
2 Samuel 6:5

While the ark was being moved, David and the tribes of Israel were celebrating with all their might before the Lord with songs, lyres, harps, tambourines, castanets, and cymbals.

These people are playing instruments, but what's wrong here? Can you find at least 10 things that are wrong in this group of musicians? (wrong colors are not an answer)

ANSWERS IN BACK

King David brings the Ark of the Covenant to Jerusalem

They brought the ark of the Lord and set it in its place inside the tent that David had put up just for it.

• Start

End •

2 Samuel 6:17

285

ANSWERS IN BACK

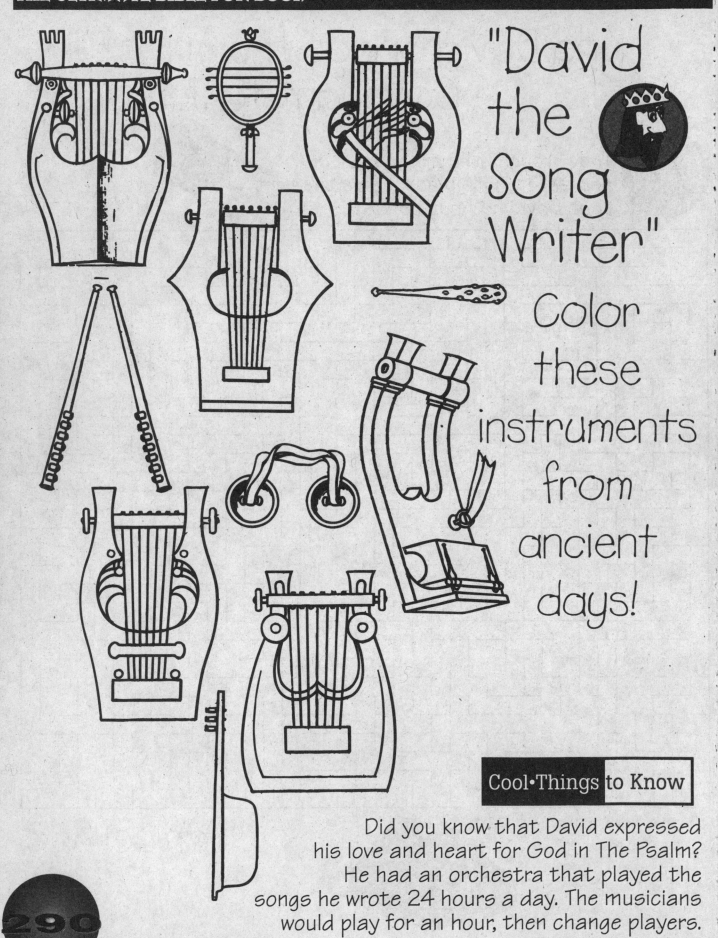

"David the Song Writer"

Color these instruments from ancient days!

Cool·Things to Know

Did you know that David expressed his love and heart for God in The Psalm? He had an orchestra that played the songs he wrote 24 hours a day. The musicians would play for an hour, then change players.

When you read Psalms, remember that they are songs!

David's wife...

...Bathsheba came before the king and requested that he fulfill the promise he made to her. David replied to this request by saying, "As surely as the Lord lives, who has delivered me out of every trouble, I will surely carry out today what I swore to you by the Lord, the God of Israel: Solomon your son shall be king after me, and he will sit on my throne in my palace." Bathsheba was very happy and said, "May my lord King David live forever!"

Then David called before him Zadok the priest, Nathan the prophet, and Benaiah, son of Jehoiada. He said to them, "Take your lord's servants with you and set Solomon my son on my own mule and take him down to Gihon. There, have Zadok the priest and Nathan the prophet anoint him king over Israel. Blow the trumpet and shout, 'Long live King Solomon!' Then you are to go up with him, and he is to come and sit on my throne and reign in my place. I have appointed him ruler over Israel and Judah."

When David knew his life was ending he spoke to Solomon his son and said, "I am about to go the way of all the earth. Be strong, show yourself a man, and observe what the Lord your God requires; walk in His ways and keep His decrees and commands, His laws and requirements written on the commandments, so that you will prosper in all you do and wherever you go. The Lord will then keep His promise to me; if your descendants watch how they live, walk in faith before me with all their heart and soul, you will never fail to have a man on the throne of Israel.'"

Then David rested with his fathers and was buried in the City of David. Solomon sat on the throne of his father David, and his rule was firmly established.

BIBLE TELLS

David Makes Solomon King

1 Kings 1•28-2•12

David Makes Solomon King

See if you can solve this crossword puzzle by using the "David makes Solomon King" story.

1 Kings 1•30

1. Who was David's wife that came and made a request?

2. David made this son the one to follow in his footsteps as king.

3. David called these 3 people to him so they could go and anoint Solomon King.
Who were they?
3a = Priest
3b = Prophet
3c = Son of Jehoiada

4. What did David have Solomon ride on?

5. What instrument were they to blow?

6. What did the new king sit on?

7. David instructed Solomon to walk in the ways of God. If Solomon would do this then God would keep His _____ to David.

8. When David died, Solomon's rule was firmly _____.

ANSWERS IN BACK

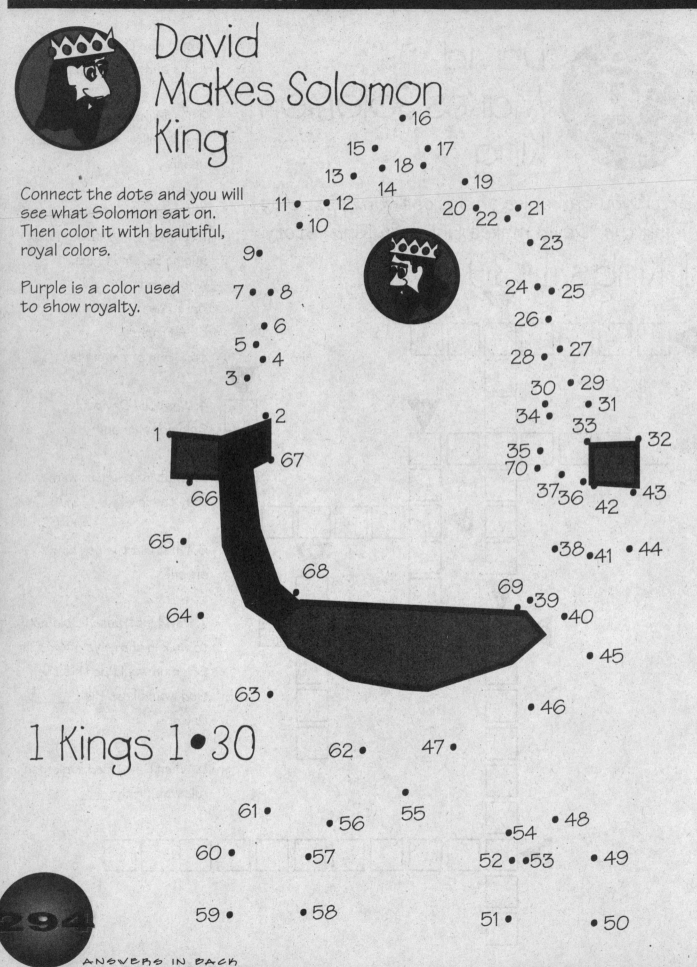

David Makes Solomon King

Connect the dots and you will see what Solomon sat on. Then color it with beautiful, royal colors.

Purple is a color used to show royalty.

1 Kings 1•30

294

David Makes Solomon King

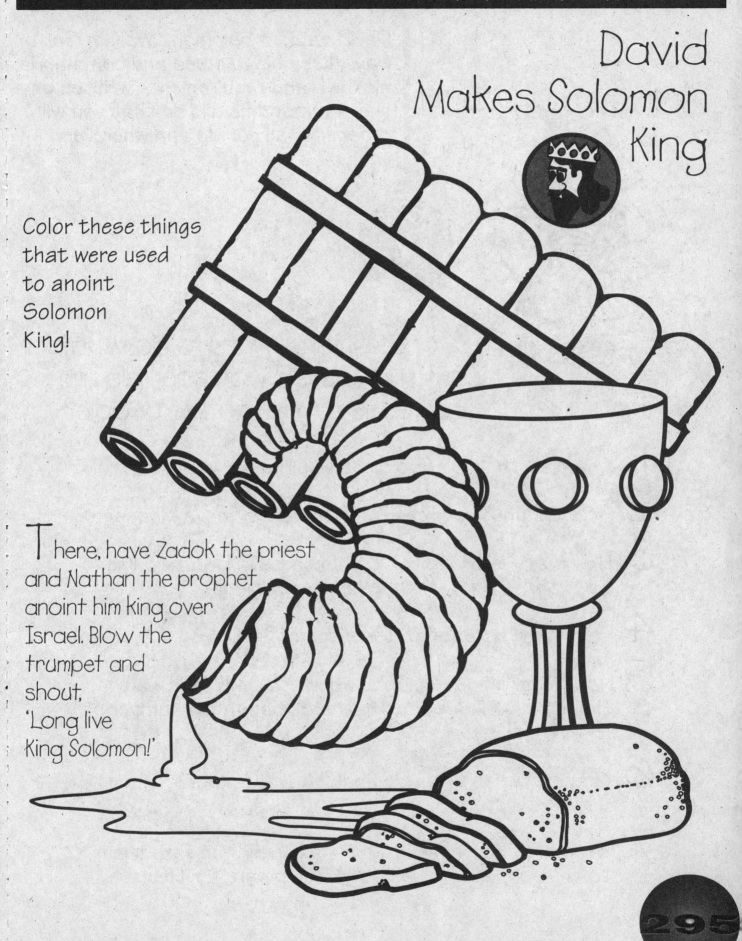

Color these things that were used to anoint Solomon King!

There, have Zadok the priest and Nathan the prophet anoint him king over Israel. Blow the trumpet and shout, 'Long live King Solomon!'

David Makes Solomon King

David said to Solomon, "Walk in God's ways, keep his decrees and commands, his laws and requirements written on the commandments, so that you will prosper in all you do and wherever you go."

Solomon wants to do what David has asked. Can you help him find something he needs to give to the people?

1. Start at the place Solomon would sit.

2. Go east until you reach the items God gave Moses.

3. How many laws are written on these? Now go to the spot that has the same number of items.

4. From here, go east to the place of worship.

5. Now follow the path. Stop when you find the item that Solomon would wear on his head. Count the number of jewels in this item.

6. Go northwest until you find the same number of a different item.

7. These are the items Solomon is looking for. Take them to the people so Solomon can help care for them.

King Solomon

North
West ✦ East
South

297

"Solomon Asks God for Wisdom"

BibleTells

King Solomon

1 Kings 3•4

STORY PAGE
1

Solomon showed...

...his love for the Lord by walking according to the ways of his father David. He was still making sacrifices in the high places because a temple had not yet been built for the Name of the Lord. He went to the high places to make a sacrifice and the Lord appeared to Solomon during the night in a dream. God said, "Ask for whatever you want me to give you." Solomon said, "You have shown great kindness to your servant, my father David, because he was faithful to you and pure and upright in heart. You have continued this great kindness to him and have given him a son to sit on his throne to this very day. Now, O Lord my God, you have made your servant king in place of my father David. But I am only a little child and do not know how to carry out my duties. Your servant is here among the people you have chosen, a great people, too numerous to count or number. Please give your servant a discerning heart to rule your people and to know between right and wrong. For who is able to rule this great people of yours?"

Solomon Asks God for Wisdom
1 Kings 3•6-11

See if you can find and circle all of them!

W	R	O	N	G	E	L	S	K	A
D	I	D	U	T	I	E	S	I	N
I	N	S	H	E	A	R	T	N	R
S	E	M	D	D	I	V	A	D	I
C	S	O	L	O	M	O	N	N	G
E	S	G	I	A	M	Z	A	E	H
R	E	L	H	H	E	R	T	S	T
N	L	Z	C	L	G	E	I	S	H
M	B	Z	P	E	M	H	O	F	R
E	D	M	A	A	U	T	N	Z	O
N	E	R	F	E	M	A	S	I	N
T	S	A	C	R	I	F	I	C	E

Solomon
Wisdom
David
Father
Throne
Child
Duties
Right
Wrong
Discernment
Bless
Kindness
Fame
Nations
Heart
Sacrifice
Temple

All of the words listed
come from the story "Solomon
asks God for wisdom."

299

When the...

...Lord heard these words He was very pleased with Solomon and said, "Since you have asked for this and not for long life or wealth for yourself, and have not asked for the death of your enemies but for discernment of right and wrong, I will bless you. I will give you a wise and discerning heart, so that there will never have been anyone like you nor will there ever be. I will also bless you with those things you did not ask for, both riches and honor. In your lifetime you will have no equal among kings. Keep my ways and obey my requirements and commands as David your father did and I will give you a long life."

God gave Solomon wisdom and very great insight and understanding as measureless as the sand on the seashore. Solomon's wisdom was greater than the wisdom of all the men of the east and greater than all the wisdom of Egypt. His fame spread to all the surrounding nations. He spoke three thousand proverbs and his songs numbered a thousand five. He described plant life, from the cedars of Lebanon to the hyssop that grows out of walls. He also taught about animals and birds, reptiles and fish. Men of all nations came to listen to Solomon's wisdom, sent by all the kings of the world who had heard of his wisdom.

King Solomon

1 Kings 3•10-14

STORY PAGE
2

King Solomon

Solomon asked God for wisdom and was well-known for being a fair king thoughout the land.

(A)	L	G	H	P	W	F
B	C	U	B	H	Q	T
K	P	D	P	W	N	V
W	E	P	O	Z	J	H
M	D	F	R	H	I	Q
A	B	D	G	C	J	P
W	E	I	Z	Y	K	F
G	A	E	N	L	X	W
D	M	O	D	M	V	A
O	P	L	K	S	J	U
N	X	Q	R	L	T	Z

How wise are you? Put on your thinking cap for this one.

Start at the top with 'A.' Move up, down, right, left, or diagonally to the nearest 'B.' Continue with 'C' and so forth until you have found the entire alphabet.

King Solomon

Start

End

This maze looks hard, but if you think ahead
you'll whip right through it.

Start at the black circle at the top and jump onto the maze.
You may make 1 more jump to and from a grey circle intersection.
You may go under a road that looks like it follows through.
You may crossover grey lines.

"King Solomon's wisdom"

Solomon was always solving problems for all kinds of people. Can you solve how many boxes are in the one big box?

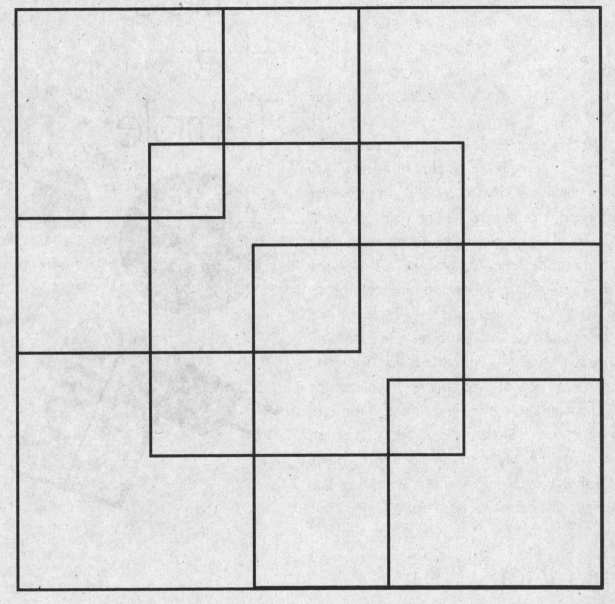

ANSWERS IN BACK

BIBLE TELLS

There was a...

...king named Hiram who lived in Tyre. He was very good friends with David. When he heard that Solomon was made king after his father David, he wanted Solomon to know he would be his friend too and help him in any way he could. So he sent Solomon a message letting him know he was a friend he could count on.

When Solomon received the message he sent a reply back to Hiram saying, "My father always wanted to build a temple for the Lord, but due to all the wars he could not get the temple built. As for me, I have been blessed by God with peace on every side. I have no adversaries or problems to deal with. Now I will build the temple for the Name of the Lord my God, as the Lord told my father David when he said, 'Your son whom I will put on the throne in your place will build the temple for my name.' "You can help me by ordering that cedars of Lebanon be cut for me. My men will work with yours, and I will pay you for your men, whatever the cost. You have the best men trained for cutting timber."

1 Kings 5•17

King Solomon builds the Temple

STORY PAGE
1

BIBLE TELLS

Solomon needs...

...some of these from this forest to build the temple. But before he can cut them down they have to be cleared of all the objects that don't belong!

CAN YOU FIND: a piece of pizza • fish • nail • rocket • saw
pair of scissors • 2 arrow heads • pencil • ice cream cone • log

305

When Hiram...

...received this message he was very pleased and worshipped God for the wise son He had given David. Hiram sent another message back to Solomon saying, "I will gladly provide you with the cedar and pine logs, along with all the men you need. I will have my men haul the wood down from Lebanon to the sea, and I will float them in rafts by sea to the place you want them. All I would like for you to do to repay me is to provide food for my royal household."

Solomon and Hiram made an agreement and so each set out to fulfill his part. Hiram supplied all the cedar and pine logs needed. Solomon gave Hiram one hundred twenty five thousand bushels of wheat and one hundred fifteen thousand gallons of pressed olive oil. Solomon continued to do this for Hiram year after year. Once again this showed all the people what great wisdom Solomon had.

Solomon also had to get laborers from all of Israel - a total of thirty thousand men! He would send them off to Lebanon in shifts of ten thousand men a month. There they would work with Hiram's men in preparing the wood. They would work in Lebanon for one month and then be home for two months. He also had seventy thousand carriers and eighty thousand stone cutters in the hills, as well as thirty-three hundred foremen who supervised the project and directed the workmen.

King Solomon builds the Temple

STORY PAGE 2

1 Kings 5•8

"Calendar of the Bible"

The foundation of the temple of the Lord was laid in the fourth year, in the month of Ziv and was finished in the eleventh year, in the month of Bul, the eighth month.

It took a total of seven years to build.

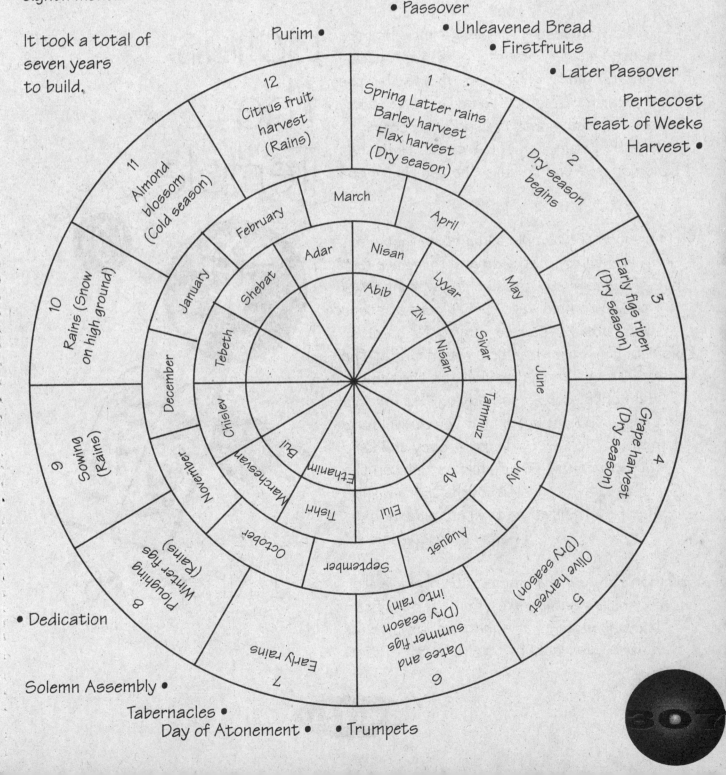

• Passover
• Unleavened Bread
• Firstfruits
• Later Passover

Purim •

Pentecost
Feast of Weeks
Harvest •

12 Citrus fruit harvest (Rains)

1 Spring Latter rains Barley harvest Flax harvest (Dry season)

2 Dry season begins

11 Almond blossom (Cold season)

3 Early figs ripen (Dry season)

10 Rains (Snow on high ground)

4 Grape harvest (Dry season)

9 Sowing (Rains)

5 Olive harvest (Dry season)

8 Ploughing Winter figs (Rains)

6 Dates and summer figs (Dry season into rain)

7 Early rains

March, February, January, December, November, October, September, August, July, June, May, April

Adar, Shebat, Tebeth, Chislev, Marchesvan, Tishri, Elul, Ab, Tammuz, Sivar, Iyyar, Nisan

Abib, Ziv, Nisan, Bul, Ethanim

• Dedication

Solemn Assembly •
Tabernacles •
Day of Atonement •   • Trumpets

At Solomon's...

...orders they removed from the quarry large blocks of quality stone to provide a foundation of dressed stone for the temple. All of the men used were greatly skilled craftsmen and they came from Solomon, Hiram, and the men of Gebal.

It had been a very long time since the Israelites had left Egypt. To be exact, it was four hundred and eighty years. It was also the fourth year for Solomon to be king over Israel. It was also the month called Ziv according to the Hebrew calendar. This was the time that Solomon started to build the temple for the Lord.

He wanted the temple to be built ninety feet long and thirty feet wide and forty-five feet high. He designed it so nothing was inserted into the temple walls. Only blocks of stone were cut at the rock quarry. No hammer, chisel, or any other iron tool was heard at the temple site. When all was done on the temple, God spoke to Solomon saying, "As for this temple you are building, if you do all I have commanded, follow my decrees, obey and keep my commands, I will fulfill through you the promise I gave to David your father. I will live among the Israelites and will not abandon my people Israel."

Solomon finished the inside of the temple with cedar paneling and planks of pine for the floor. He created an inner sanctuary from cedar boards. This would be the Most Holy Place.

King Solomon builds the Temple

STORY PAGE

3

1 Kings 5•6

BibleTells

"It Adds Up"
Solomon Builds the Lord's Temple

All these numbers are written with words in the story,"Solomon Builds the Lords Temple." Can you write them using numbers? When you're done add them up to see one really big number!

Four hundred eighty years | 480

Fourth year

Ninety feet long

Thirty feet wide

Forty-five feet high

One hundred twenty-five thousand bushels of wheat

One hundred fifteen thousand gallons of pressed olive oil

Thirty thousand men

Ten thousand

Seventy thousand carriers

Eighty thousand stone cutters

Thirty-three hundred foremen

ANSWERS IN BACK

The inside of...

...the temple had carvings of gourds and open flowers. Everything was covered with cedar; no stone was to be seen. Then Solomon covered the inside of the temple with pure gold. He extended gold chains across the front of the inner sanctuary, which was also overlaid with gold. He also made two cherubim out of olive wood, then overlaid them with gold. They were so big that they touched wing tip to wing tip in the middle of the inner sanctuary and wing tip to wall. The doors were made of wood and carved with decorations and overlaid with gold.

Solomon also made all the furnishings that were in the Lord's temple: golden altar, golden table for the showbread, the ten lampstands of pure gold, the gold floral work and lamps and tongs, the pure gold basins, wick trimmers, sprinkling bowls, dishes and censers, and the gold sockets for the doors of the innermost room, the Most Holy Place, and also the doors of the main hall of the temple.

When all the work King Solomon had done for the temple of the Lord was finished, he had the elders of Israel and the priests bring the ark from the City of David to the temple. When the priests put the ark in the Most Holy Place and withdrew from there, a cloud filled the temple of the Lord.

King Solomon builds the Temple

1 Kings 6

STORY PAGE
4

The priests could not perform their service because of the cloud, for the glory of the Lord filled His temple. Then Solomon said, "The Lord has said that He would dwell in a dark cloud. I have indeed built a magnificent temple for the Lord, a place He will dwell in forever." Then Solomon turned around and blessed all the people.

310

King Solomon builds the Temple

1 Kings 7•48-50

Solomon also made all the furnishings that were in the Lord's temple: golden altar, golden table for the showbread, the ten lampstands of pure gold, the gold floral work and lamps and tongs, the pure gold basins, wick trimmers, sprinkling bowls, dishes and censers, and the gold sockets for the doors of the innermost room, the Most Holy Place, and also the doors of the main hall of the temple.

What am I? Match the items with the correct description:

Lampstands •

Tongs •

Basins •

Sprinkling bowls •

Altar •

Censers •

Wick trimmers •

Showbread •

• I am a raised platform on which the sacrifices unto the Lord were performed.

• I get to be made out of fine flour and set out for the Lord's Sabbath.

• Pressed olive oil is placed on me for constant burning before the Lord.

• I get to be used for grasping items.

• I hold liquid and can be used for washing hands.

• I get to cut the cord that burns in the olive oil.

• I am a container in which the incense is burned.

• I hold liquid and am used for sprinkling the liquid in the tabernacle.

ANSWERS IN BACK

Solomon Builds the Lord's Temple
1 Kings 6

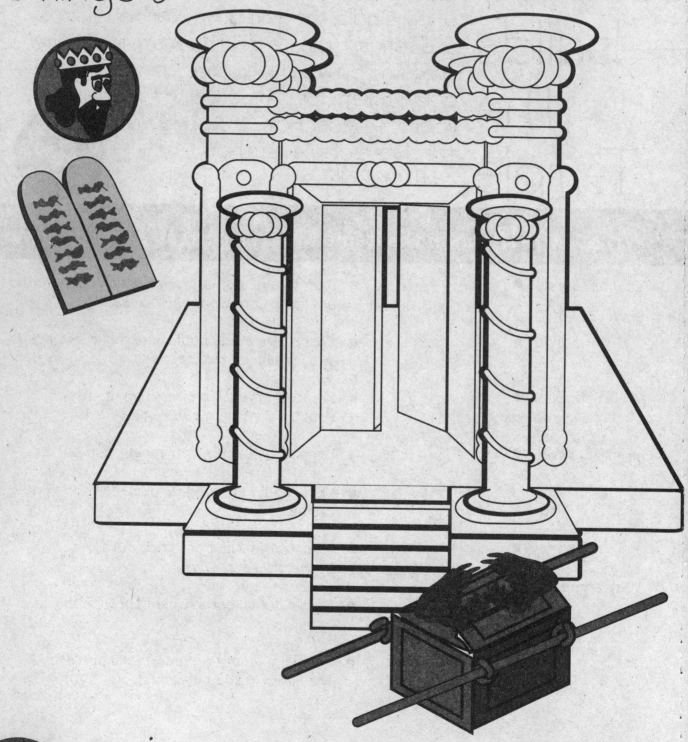

Solomon Builds the Lord's Temple

1 Kings 6:11 - 13

When all was done on the temple, God spoke to Solomon saying, "As for this temple you are building, if you do all I have commanded, follow my decrees, obey and keep my commands, I will fulfill through you the promise I gave to David your father..."

To find what the promise is, solve this puzzle. The secret decoder is "F" means go forward, "B" go backward. Start with "I."

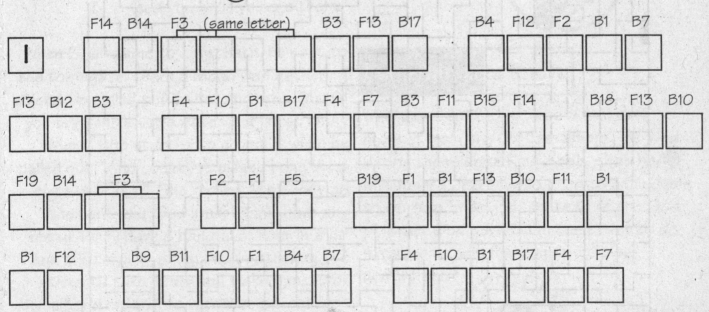

A B C D E F G H Ⓘ J K L M N O P Q R S T U V W X Y Z

ANSWERS IN BACK

Then Elijah...

...told her, "Do not be afraid. Go home and do as you had planned. But first make a small cake of bread from what you have and bring it to me, then go back and make food for yourself and your son. For if you do this the God of Israel says, 'The jar of flour will not become empty and the jug of oil will not run dry until the day the Lord returns the rain to this land.'"

She went home and did as Elijah told her. From that day on, every day she would make bread to feed Elijah and her family. Each day she would have flour and oil as God had promised through Elijah.

One day the widow came to Elijah and said, "What do you have against me you man of God? My son is very sick. Did you come to remind me of my sin and kill my son?" Elijah said, "Give me your son." He took her son to where he was staying and laid him on his bed. Then Elijah cried out to God and stretched himself out on the boy three times and said, "O Lord my God, let this boy's life return to him!"

God heard the cries of Elijah and healed the boy. Then Elijah brought the boy back to his mother and she said, "Now I know that you are a man of God and that the word of the Lord you speak is truth."

Three years had gone by without rain and God spoke to Elijah saying, "Go before Ahab and I will send rain on the land."

Elijah & Elisha STORY PAGE 2

BibleTells

Elijah & Elisha

All of these words have to do with the miracles Elijah performed.
Can you find them in the puzzle?

C	R	I	E	D	O	U	T	T
Z	A	P	G	W	A	T	E	R
X	T	N	I	A	T	P	A	C
U	L	Z	Z	N	P	O	W	H
S	A	C	R	I	F	I	C	E
O	R	S	Z	Q	L	L	Z	A
N	A	W	I	D	O	W	T	L
V	I	U	Z	Q	U	J	Z	E
K	N	Z	F	I	R	E	Q	D

Rain
Widow
Son
Healed
Oil
Flour
Altar
Sacrifice
Fire
Water
Cried Out
Captain

1 Kings 17-19 & 2 Kings 1 & 2

317

When Ahab saw...

...Elijah, he said, "Is that you, you troubler of Israel?" Elijah said, "I have not made trouble for Israel, but you and your father's family have. You have gone away from the things of God and followed false gods. Bring all the people from Israel and meet me on Mount Carmel. Also bring the four hundred fifty prophets of the false gods and the four hundred prophets of false gods who eat at Jezebel's table." Then Ahab did as Elijah had said.

Then Elijah spoke to all the people, saying, "How long will you not take a stand? If the Lord is God, follow Him; but if you believe these false gods are God, follow them." Not a person would speak in response.

Then Elijah said, "I am the only one of the Lord's prophets left, but the false gods have four hundred fifty prophets. Bring two bulls and we will sacrifice them, you unto your gods and me unto the Lord God. We will not set fire to them. You will call upon your god and I will call upon the name of the Lord. The god who answers by fire, He is God."

Everyone liked this idea and agreed. The prophets of the false gods called on the name of their god from morning till noon. But there was no response; no one answered. At noon Elijah began to tease them, saying that their god was too busy, or traveling, or maybe sleeping. This made them shout even louder in hopes that their god would hear them. By evening there was still no answer.

Elijah & Elisha

STORY PAGE 3

312

"Word Sramble"

Ravens	•	• AIEHJL
Ahab	•	• IRNA
False-gods	•	• EAHDLE
Provoke	•	• ILO
Elijah	•	• EAHNVE
Rain	•	• HOPTEPR
Morning	•	• EJEELBZ
Bread	•	• ENAGL
Double	•	• ASLHIE
Evening	•	• ROFUL
Meat	•	• DORL
Feed	•	• DGO
Brook	•	• TOUDIC-ER
Whirlwind	•	• TUNCLSO
Widow	•	• ALRTA
Son	•	• AMTE
Healed	•	• EFDE
Oil	•	• ORKOB
Heaven	•	• NWRHDILIW
Flour	•	• OIWWD
Lord	•	• CFRAEIICS
God	•	• RFEI
Cried-Out	•	• RTEWA
Consult	•	• SEANVR
Altar	•	• BHAA
Sacrifice	•	• DGSOELF-SA
Fire	•	• GIRMNNO
Water	•	• DEBAR
Captain	•	• EBOLUD
Cloak	•	• GIEENNV
Prophet	•	• NSO
Jezebel	•	• EOOPKVR
Angel	•	• NAPCITA
Elisha	•	• KOCAL

Elijah & Elisha

All of these words are in the Elijah and Elisha story.

Can you match the unscrambled word with the scrambled word?

319

Then Elijah said...

`...to all the people, "Come here to me." They came to him and he repaired the altar of the Lord that they had ruined. Then Elijah took twelve stones, one for each tribe descended from Jacob. With these stones he built an altar in the name of the Lord. He dug a trench around it large enough to hold thirteen quarts of seed. Then he had them fill four large jars with water and pour it on the offering and on the wood. Then he told them to pour four more and then four more after that, a total of three times. The water ran down around the altar and even filled the trench.

Elijah then prayed to the Lord for all to hear. Then the fire of the Lord fell and burned up the sacrifice, the wood, the stones and the soil, and also licked up the water in the trench.

When all the people saw this they fell to the ground and cried out, "The Lord—He is God! The Lord—He is God!" Then all those that would not believe in God were killed.

Elijah then told Ahab, "Go, eat and drink, for there is the sound of heavy rain coming." Elijah then prayed to God until the sky grew black with clouds and the wind rose and a heavy rain came.

After this Elijah had to flee because Jezebel was going to kill him. He went into the mountain of God called Horeb, and there an angel came and fed him twice.

Elijah
& Elisha

STORY PAGE
4

BibleTells

Elijah
& Elisha

The ravens feed Elijah.
1 Kings 17•1-6

321

Then Elijah...

...heard the whisper of the Lord saying "What are you doing here, Elijah?" He said, "I have been very dedicated to you Lord God Almighty. The Israelites have rejected your covenant, broken down your altars, and put your prophets to death with the sword. I am the only one left, and now they are trying to kill me too."

Then the Lord told him to go back the way he had come and to go into the Desert of Damascus. Then he gave him specific things to do, one of which was to anoint Elisha, son of Shaphat, to succeed him as a prophet.

Elijah went and did the things God had told him to do. When he found Elisha, he was plowing in the field. Elijah went up to him and threw his cloak around him, which is symbolic of passing the calling of God on your life to another person. Elisha then left the field and ran after Elijah, saying, "Let me kiss my father and mother good-by and then I will come with you." When he was done he followed Elijah and became his attendant.

When Ahab had died, Elijah heard that the new king of Samaria had fallen and hurt himself very badly. The king wanted to know if he would survive his wounds or if he was going to die. So he sent a messenger off to one who consults with the false gods to see if they had the answer. Elijah stopped the messenger and told him to go back to the king and say, "This is what the Lord says: 'It is because there is no God in Israel that you are consulting with the false gods. You will not leave your bed. You will certainly die!'"

Elijah & Elisha

STORY PAGE 5

Elijah  & Elisha

Can you help the raven get through the maze to feed Elijah?

START

END

1 Kings 17:6

The ravens brought food to Elijah: bread in the morning and meat in the evening.

323

When the king...

...heard what Elijah told the messenger he wanted to know what kind of man Elijah was. They told him what Elijah looked like and he knew it was Elijah the Tishbite.

Then the king sent a captain and his fifty men to get Elijah. They found him on a hill and called for him to come down saying, "Man of God, the king says, 'Come down!'" Elijah said, "If I am a man of God, may fire come down from heaven and consume you and your fifty men!" which then happened. Then the king sent another captain and his fifty men and the same thing happened again. When the king sent a third captain and his men to Elijah, this captain pleaded with Elijah not to kill him and to come down and see the king. This time Elijah heard from the angel of the Lord, "Go down with him; do not be afraid of him." So Elijah went to see the king with the captain.

Elijah once again told the king what the Lord had said. Then the king died, according to the word of the Lord that Elijah had spoken.

Elijah and Elisha had stopped at the Jordan and Elijah took his cloak, rolled it up, and struck the water with it. The water divided to the right and to the left, and the two of them crossed over on dry ground. When they had crossed, Elijah said to Elisha, "Tell me what I can do for you before I am taken away by the Lord." "Let me inherit a double portion of your spirit," Elisha replied.

Elijah & Elisha

STORY PAGE 6

You can solve the crossword puzzle on the next page by answering these questions. (turn the page)

1. What was the name of the king who did more to provoke God than any other king before him?

2. Elijah told the king that something would stop for the next few years. What was it?

3. What came and fed Elijah while he was at the brook?

4. Elijah was told by the Lord to go see the _____ and she would feed him.

5. How many years went by without rain?

6. Elijah had the king and all the people meet him on a hill called _____.

7. How many stones did Elijah use to build the altar?

8. These stones represented twelve _____ of Israel.

9. Elijah even poured twelve jars of what on the altar?

10. What came down from the Lord and burned up the sacrifice, the wood, the stones and the soil, and also licked up all the water?

11. The Lord spoke to Elijah in a very soft voice called a _____.

12. The king sent a _____ and his fifty men and Elijah called fire down from heaven to consume them.

13. When Elijah met Elisha, he took off his _____ and placed it over Elisha.

14. What kind of portion of Elijah's spirit did Elisha want?

15. What came and separated Elijah and Elisha?

16. Then Elijah went up into heaven in a _____.

17. Elijah went up into heaven to be with ____.

Elijah
& Elisha

325

Elijah said...

... "You have asked a difficult thing. Yet if you see me when I am taken from you, it will be yours, otherwise not."

As they were walking along and talking together, suddenly a chariot of fire and horses of fire appeared and separated the two of them, and Elijah went up to heaven in a whirlwind. Elisha saw this and cried out, "My father! My father! The chariots and horsemen of Israel!" And Elisha saw him no more.

Elijah & Elisha

Cool·Things to Know

What was Elisha asking for when he said he wanted the double portion?
Elisha wanted to inherit all of Elijah's gifts as a prophet times two! God honored Elisha's desire and allowed him to perform twice as many miracles as Elijah. Elijah performed seven miracles and Elisha performed fourteen.

STORY PAGE 7

2 Kings 1 & 2

Elijah
& Elisha

Bonus Question:
What were Elijah and Elisha called?

6 5 16   13 10   17 14 4

After filling in all crossword boxes,
find out what Elijah and Elisha were called
by using the letters in grey outlined boxes. Match
the correct word number to the correct box number
to find the answer to the bonus question.

1 Kings 17–19 & 2 Kings 1 & 2

327

BIBLE TELLS

King...

...Nebuchadnezzar, the King of Babylon, made an image of gold that was 90 feet high and 9 feet wide and set it up for everyone to see. He ordered that whenever special music was played, everyone in his whole kingdom had to fall down and worship the image of gold. Otherwise they would be thrown into a fiery furnace.

Therefore, as soon as they heard the music, all the people fell down and worshiped the image of gold that the King had set up. But one day, some of the king's advisors went to the king and told him that Shadrach, Meshach, and Abednego, three of the King's officials, would not bow down and worship the image of gold. Shadrach, Meshach, and Abednego refused to worship any god but their God, the true God.

When the king heard this he was furious. He ordered that Shadrach, Meshach, and Abednego be tied up and thrown into the fiery furnace. Because he was so mad, the king ordered that the furnace be heated 7 times hotter than usual. So Shadrach, Meshach, and Abednego, firmly tied up, were thrown into the fiery furnace.

Daniel 3

Shadrach, Meshach, & Abednego

STORY PAGE

1

Shadrach, Meshach, & Abednego

King Nebuchadnezzaar said, "Look! I see four men walking around in the fire, unbound and unharmed, and the fourth looks like a son of the gods."

"Daniel 3•25"

Can you find the 4 men in the furnace and a man that looks like a son of the gods?

"Into the fiery furnace"

329

THE ULTIMATE BIBLE FUN BOOK

BibleTells

Then the King...

...leaped to his feet in amazement and asked his advisors, "weren't there 3 men that we tied up and threw into the fire?" "Yes, certainly, O king," they replied. He said, "Look! I see 4 men walking around in the fire, unbound and unharmed, and the fourth one looks like a son of the gods." The king then yelled to Shadrach, Meshach, and Abednego, "Come out here."

So Shadrach, Meshach, and Abednego came out of the fire and everyone crowded around them. They saw that the fire had not burned them at all and they didn't even smell like fire.

Then King Nebuchadnezzar said, "Praise be to the God of Shadrach, Meshach, and Abednego, who has sent his angel and rescued his faithful servants! They trusted in their God and defied the King's command and were willing to give up their lives rather than serve or worship any god except their own God. Therefore I decree that anyone who says anything against the God of Shadrach, Meshach, and Abednego must die, because no other god can save this way." Then the king gave Shadrach, Meshach, and Abednego promotions in their jobs in his kingdom.

Daniel 3

Shadrach, Meshach, & Abednego

STORY PAGE 2

BibleTells

"Into the Furnace"
Daniel 3

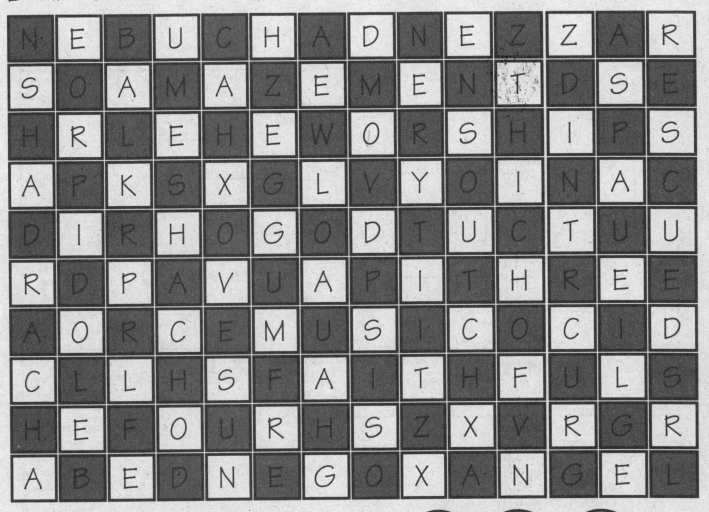

N	E	B	U	C	H	A	D	N	E	Z	Z	A	R
S	O	A	M	A	Z	E	M	E	N	T	D	S	E
H	R	L	E	H	E	W	O	R	S	H	I	P	S
A	P	K	S	X	G	L	V	Y	O	I	N	A	C
D	I	R	H	O	G	O	D	T	U	C	T	U	U
R	D	P	A	V	U	A	P	I	T	H	R	E	E
A	O	R	C	E	M	U	S	I	C	O	C	I	D
C	L	L	H	S	F	A	I	T	H	F	U	L	S
H	E	F	O	U	R	H	S	Z	X	V	R	G	R
A	B	E	D	N	E	G	O	X	A	N	G	E	L

Nebuchadnezzar   Amazement

Idol   Three

Music   Four

Worship   Angel

Shadrach   Rescued

Meshach   Faithful

Abednego   God

Shadrach, Meshach, & Abednego

Can you find all these words in the squares above and circle them?

331

"A-Mazeing Alphabet"

Work the maze, picking up letters along
the way. What did it spell?

Start •

M

H S H E

H C D A C

H C N C H A R D

A M E E

D C H D

H H A S D H

N E

A M

S A N

E B H

D S

N H

O G S N

End •

Shadrach,
Meshach, &
Abednego

E

ANSWERS IN BACK

Shadrach, Meshach, & Abednego

"NEBUCHADNEZZAR"

The king's name is very long.

It has:
2 n's
2 e's
1 b
1 c
1 h
2 a's
1 d
2 z's
1 r

How many words can you spell by using these letters?

Get started with:

Zebra

"Nebuchadnezzar"
sends a message!

May you prosper greatly!

With great joy I tell you about the wondrous signs that the Most High God has done for me.

How great are his signs. How awesome his wonders! His kingdom is eternal; His dominion endures from generation to generation.

King Nebuchadnezzar

Can you read Nebuchadnezzar's message? Hold the letter up to a mirror to see what the king says.

334

BIBLETELLS

King Belshazzar...

...was having a great banquet for his nobles. While they were all drinking and celebrating, he gave orders to bring in the gold and silver goblets that Nebuchadnezzar, his father, had taken from the temple in Jerusalem. He wanted all attending this banquet to drink from these great goblets. When the goblets were brought in, everyone took turns drinking from them. As they passed the goblets around, they praised the gods of gold, silver, bronze, iron, wood and stone.

Suddenly, King Belshazzar looked at the wall in the royal palace and saw fingers of a human hand writing on the wall. As the king watched he became very frightened - so frightened that his knees knocked together and his legs went weak.

The king called out to all his wise men who might know the meaning of this. He told them "Whoever reads this writing and tells me what it means will be clothed in purple and have a gold chain placed around his neck, and I will exalt him to the third highest ruler in the kingdom."

All the king's wise men looked upon the wall but they could not read the writing. This made King Belshazzar more terrified. Even his nobles were confused by this.

STORY PAGE 1

Writing On the Wall

Daniel 5

When the ...

...queen heard all the noise coming out of the banquet hall she went to see the king. When she found out what had happed she said, "O king, live forever! Don't be alarmed! Don't look so terrified! There is a man named Daniel in your kingdom whom the spirit of the gods is with. Your Father, King Nebuchadnezzar, found him to have insight, intelligence and wisdom and called him Belteshazzar after the name of his god. Bring Daniel here and he will be able to tell you what the writing means."

When Daniel was brought before the king, the king said, "I have heard that the spirit of the gods is in you and that you are very wise. If you can read the writing on the wall and tell me what it means, you will be clothed in purple and have a gold chain placed around your neck, and I will exalt you to the third highest ruler in this kingdom."

Daniel said to the king, "You can keep your gifts and give the rewards to someone else. I will read the writing for you and tell you what it means."

STORY PAGE
2

Writing On the Wall

Daniel 5

336

BibleTells

"The writing on the wall."

All of the these words are from the "Writing on the Wall" story. Can you find them and CIRCLE THEM?

K	I	N	G	B	E	L	S	H	A	Z	Z	A	R
S	T	E	L	B	O	G	M	N	N	T	D	A	E
H	N	L	E	H	D	W	D	R	S	H	Z	P	S
T	E	M	P	L	E	D	R	A	W	Z	R	A	W
N	E	B	O	S	D	R	A	W	E	R	Z	W	R
S	U	G	M	A	Z	Z	M	N	N	R	A	R	E
H	Q	L	E	H	E	W	D	R	I	L	I	I	S
A	P	Z	S	X	G	A	V	Y	L	E	N	T	S
S	I	Z	R	E	H	T	A	F	U	C	L	I	R
E	D	P	A	C	U	A	P	Z	T	S	R	N	E
L	O	R	U	E	M	U	Z	I	C	T	C	G	G
B	L	B	A	N	Q	U	E	T	H	F	U	L	N
O	E	F	S	I	L	V	E	R	X	I	R	G	I
N	B	G	D	D	E	N	E	T	H	G	I	R	F

Daniel 5

Belshazzar
Banquet
Nebuchadnezzar
Frightened

Silver
Goblets
Queen
Fingers

Wall
Writing
Nobles
Daniel

King
Father
Temple
Gold

Gifts
Rewards
Read

337

Daniel said...

...*"You are the son of King Nebuchadnezzar, but you his son, O Belshazzar, have not humbled yourself, and you know this. Instead, you have gone up against the Lord of heaven. You took the goblets from his temple and brought them out in honor of your celebration where you praised the gods of silver and gold, bronze, iron, wood and stone, all of which do not see, hear or understand. But you should have been honoring the God who holds your life in His hand. That is why the hand was sent to write upon your palace walls."*

Then Daniel read the writing on the wall, "MENE, MENE, TEKEL, UPARSIN," which means "Mene: God has numbered the days of your kingdom and brought it to an end; Tekel: You have been weighed upon the scales and found wanting; Peres: Your kingdom is divided and given over to the Medes and Persians."

As King Belshazzar had promised, they clothed Daniel with scarlet, put a chain of gold about his neck, and he was exalted to the third highest ruler in the kingdom.

That very same night King Belshazzar was killed by Darius the Mede, who took over the kingdom at the age of sixty-two.

STORY PAGE
3

Writing On the Wall

Daniel 5

BibleTells

In the book of Daniel, fingers wrote a message on the wall!

Writing On the Wall

Daniel 5•5

You can have fun writing with paint, but use paper instead of walls!

Baby Finger Prints

Thumb Print

Hand Print

Finger paint recipe:

• Mix paste or liquid starch 1 or 2 Tbl., Soap flakes, and food coloring in a bowl.
• Make sure to mix very well. Fill small bowls with each color...

Fun with finger paints, finger prints, and hand prints!

YOU CAN BE CREATIVE TOO!

The writing on the wall said:
"Mene, Mene, Tekel, Uparsin"

This writing is believed to have been Aramaic. The meanings to these words would have been:
• Mene - 'numbered or unit of money' • Tekel - 'weighed' • Uparsin - 'divided or half a shekel.'

You have been given by the king:
• 3 Talents
• 240 Minas
• 160 Shekels

Do you have enough money to buy the following items on your list?

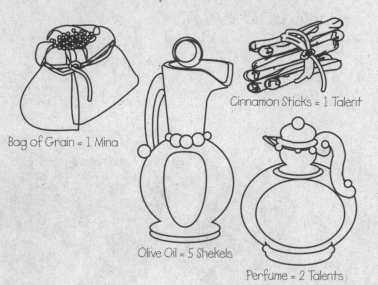

Bag of Grain = 1 Mina

Cinnamon Sticks = 1 Talent

Olive Oil = 5 Shekels

Perfume = 2 Talents

Shopping list:
1. 3 Bags of grain
2. 2 Bottles of Olive Oil
3. 5 Cinnamon Sticks
4. 1 Bottle of Perfume

Answers: Daniel 5:25

You can solve the problem using these biblical units.
• Talent = 60 Minas • Mina = 50 Shekels • Shekel = 2 Bekas • Beka = 10 Gerahs

Royal Grocery Store

ANSWERS IN BACK

BibleTells

Daniel was one...

...of the officials of King Darius. Daniel served the king so faithfully that the king wanted to place Daniel over all the other officials of the king. The other officials did not want Daniel lifted up above them in leadership, so they tried to find something wrong that Daniel had done so they could use it against him. But Daniel was so trustworthy and honest and careful in doing his job that they could not find anything bad to blame him for. They realized that they were not going to find something against Daniel unless it had to do with the law of Daniel's God. Daniel loved God and served Him very faithfully, but the king's officials did not believe in Daniel's God. So the officials came up with an evil plan. They convinced the king to issue a decree that anyone who prayed to any god or man besides the king would be thrown into the lion's den. The king put the decree in writing and sent copies of it throughout his whole kingdom.

When Daniel heard that it was against the law to pray to anyone besides King Darius, he did not stop praying to God. In fact, 3 times each day Daniel got down on his knees and prayed, giving thanks to his God, just as he had always done. It was very important to Daniel to obey the law of his God.

Daniel & the Lion's Den

STORY PAGE
1

Daniel 6

When the king's...

...officials found Daniel praying to his God, they told the king that Daniel had broken the law. When the king heard this, he was very distressed because Daniel was one of his very best men. But the law he had issued could not be taken back. So, the King had no choice but to have Daniel thrown into the lion's den. The king could not sleep that night because he was worried about Daniel. He was hoping that Daniel's God would rescue him.

First thing in the morning, the King got up and hurried to the lion's den. He called out to Daniel saying, "Daniel, has your God, whom you serve continually, been able to rescue your from the lions?" Daniel answered, "Oh King, live forever! My God sent his angel and he shut the mouths of the lions. They have not hurt me because I was found innocent in God's sight. Nor have I ever done anything wrong to you."

The King had Daniel lifted out of the lion's den and was very very happy that Daniel wasn't hurt at all. The King then ordered that the men who had falsely accused Daniel be thrown into the lion's den. The lions crushed them all.

Then King Darius issued a new decree that everyone in his kingdom must honor the God of Daniel because He is the living God who rescued and saved Daniel from the power of the lions.

Daniel & the Lion's Den

STORY PAGE
2

Daniel 6

BibleTells

Daniel & the Lion's Den

Because Daniel loved God, he was thrown into the lions' den. Help him walk out.

Daniel 6•23

BibleTells

One day...

...God spoke to Jonah and told him to go to a city called Nineveh and tell the people that God was displeased with their wicked behavior. Jonah did not like the people of Nineveh so he did not want to go. Instead, he got on a ship going the opposite direction. But God sent a storm which was so big that the ship was about to be broken up into pieces. Each of the men on the ship cried out to his own god to save them, but it didn't help. Jonah was fast asleep in the lower level of the ship and didn't even know there was a storm going on. So the captain came and woke him up, telling Jonah to call out to his god, saying "maybe your god will save us." Jonah knew that he was running away from his God and that God sent the storm because of Jonah's disobedience. So Jonah told the men to throw him overboard so that God would stop the storm. Although they didn't want to, they threw Jonah into the sea and suddenly the sea became calm. Then all the men realized that Jonah's God really was God, and they worshiped the God of Jonah.

After Jonah landed in the sea, God sent a big fish to swallow him. Jonah was in the belly of the big fish for three days and three nights. Then he cried out to God from inside the fish's belly. So God spoke to the fish and it spit Jonah out of its mouth onto dry land.

Jonah & the Big Fish!

STORY PAGE

1

Jonah 1-4

Jonah & the Big Fish!

9   10   11   22

12   23

8   21

13   20   24

25

7   31

26   30

14   19

28   29

15   18   27   32

6   17

16   36   33

34

5   35

37

4   38

3   1   40   39

2

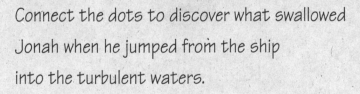

Connect the dots to discover what swallowed
Jonah when he jumped from the ship
into the turbulent waters.

Jonah 1•17

Then Jonah...

...went to the people of Nineveh and told them that God was not pleased with their behavior and that God was going to overthrow their city if they did not repent and turn from their wicked ways. All the people of Nineveh felt very bad. They turned from their wicked ways and asked God to forgive them. This made God so happy that He decided not to destroy their city.

Then Jonah was very mad at God because God had forgiven the people of Nineveh for all the bad things they had done in the past. Jonah left the city and went and made a booth to sit under. God made a plant grow up over the booth to shade Jonah's head from the sun and heat. Jonah was very grateful for the plant. But the next morning God sent a worm and a hot wind which caused the plant to die. The sun beat down on Jonah's head. He was so hot that he wanted to die.

Then God said to Jonah, "Is it right for you to be angry about the plant?" "Yes," said Jonah. But God said, "You have had pity on a plant which you did not make grow and which only lived one day. Shouldn't I have pity on all the people of the city of Nineveh and their animals?"

Jonah learned that he needed to obey God and to have mercy toward other people!

Jonah & the Big Fish!

STORY PAGE

2

Jonah 1-4

BibleTells

Jonah & the Big Fish!

God provided a great fish to swallow Jonah. He stayed in the belly of the fish three days and three nights.

Jonah 1•17

#																									
1	14	3	19	7	12	9	11	4	1	19	2	20	17	11	14	3	20	5	1	4	2	17	21	14	11
2	7	2	11	4	9	6	13	8	10	7	12	13	11	9	7	14	11	18	2	6	10	7	9	3	5
3	14	7	24	11	18	19	16	11	9	8	7	6	3	1	2	3	4	7	5	13	15	6	7	11	3
4	9	2	12	4	17	7	42	7	6	11	5	10	4	2	9	1	12	7	5	4	6	14	3	1	2
5	4	14	1	10	3	12	2	20	10	4	9	3	7	21	2	14	1	12	11	9	40	1	20	10	14
6	21	7	25	3	70	7	31	11	8	47	10	82	9	14	27	19	29	12	5	7	4	24	17	19	2
7	7	2	9	4	3	6	17	8	10	11	12	9	16	14	3	2	5	4	6	2	3	12	18	16	
8	98	7	18	11	8	14	28	9	2	8	7	78	6	4	8	3	18	21	17	11	19	8	7	2	1
9	26	2	6	1	16	9	66	46	6	16	7	6	16	36	96	11	6	14	2	7	9	46	6	61	60
10	1	4	12	20	10	8	11	1	12	13	8	10	1	17	11	6	1	9	20	77	42	12	10	1	11
11	8	7	2	9	6	11	14	7	3	10	7	12	7	3	4	5	8	9	11	17	11	6	7	5	3
12	11	9	15	7	20	3	17	6	4	15	2	19	7	9	12	1	15	4	7	6	5	19	9	4	8
13	7	11	9	19	8	40	3	21	11	1	15	4	17	16	8	27	2	42	11	17	19	9	24	43	40
14	2	13	4	7	20	14	2	17	11	22	8	12	6	4	12	8	2	14	17	47	18	20	31	14	19
15	13	1	30	2	3	4	23	6	5	3	7	43	9	11	3	8	13	10	14	2	7	30	1	0	2
16	1	10	8	7	6	9	4	2	11	8	13	6	8	17	2	19	4	8	6	12	3	16	20	18	
17	15	10	5	20	25	30	5	40	60	15	70	35	80	90	5	10	15	20	17	19	21	45	10	11	18
18	10	11	0	17	20	19	10	18	11	0	8	40	6	9	10	7	0	11	4	8	6	30	9	3	1
19	4	24	14	4	24	2	4	8	17	14	11	24	12	21	4	17	14	4	24	14	31	4	4	4	34
20	2	8	4	10	6	7	8	1	3	10	7	12	3	5	14	9	16	2	4	6	3	8	10	4	2

ROW: COLOR IN SQUARES WITH:

1 numbers greater than 10
2 odd numbers
3 even numbers
4 numbers greater than 8
5 numbers less than 5
6 numbers greater than 20
7 odd numbers
8 numbers with 8
9 numbers with 6
10 numbers with 1
11 even numbers
12 numbers greater than 10
13 numbers less than 10
14 numbers with 2
15 numbers with 3
16 odd numbers
17 numbers with 5
18 numbers with 0
19 numbers with 4
20 even numbers

Follow the directions to discover what animal taught Jonah a great lesson.

347

Jonah & the Big Fish!

By providing Jonah with the plant to shade his head and then having the worm come and eat the plant, God was teaching Jonah how to have mercy on the people of Nineveh.

In this picture can you find ten ways that people are helping others?

Jonah 3

Jonah & the Big Fish!

Follow each step to see Jonah's answer!

When Jonah did not obey God, God was

> DISPLEASED

Move the "ED" at the end to the front.

Now you can remove one "D."

Change the "AS" to an "OB."

S & E need to swap places. Make sure to use the second "E! "

That "P" is no help; it needs to leave.

Say the alphabet and when you get to "M" write the next letter in place of the "L."

You have come very far and it's not too hard. Change the "S" to the next letter in the alphabet.

Move the "OB" to the front of the line and you will find how Jonah changed his mind.

ANSWERS IN BACK

Jonah & the Big Fish

Jonah 3•10

If you lived in Nineveh you would be very thankful to Jonah for listening to God.

350

"Thanks Jonah"
My thank you letter to Jonah!

Dear Jonah,

Your friend in Nineveh

Think of something someone has done for you and write them a thankyou letter!

351

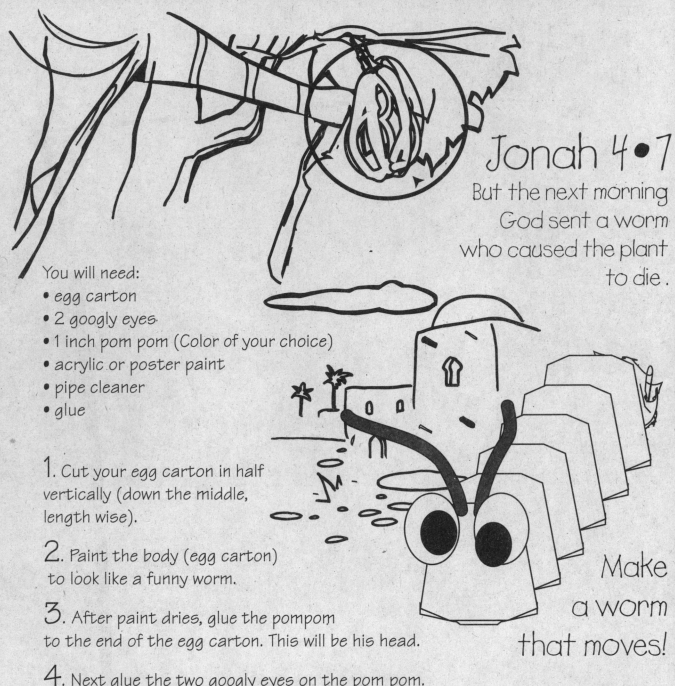

Jonah 4•7
But the next morning God sent a worm who caused the plant to die.

Make a worm that moves!

You will need:

- egg carton
- 2 googly eyes
- 1 inch pom pom (Color of your choice)
- acrylic or poster paint
- pipe cleaner
- glue

1. Cut your egg carton in half vertically (down the middle, length wise).

2. Paint the body (egg carton) to look like a funny worm.

3. After paint dries, glue the pompom to the end of the egg carton. This will be his head.

4. Next glue the two googly eyes on the pom pom.

5. Now take the pipe cleaner and make feet, antenna, or any other decorations you would like your worm to have.

Jonah & the Big Fish

In the ...

... Old Testament God made a covenant with the children of Israel. In the New Testament you will read about the "New" covenant God brings to all people. The new covenant, or promise, is about Jesus: His birth, life, death and resurrection, and how He brings hope to people all over the world.

In the city of Nazareth, in Galilee, there lived a young woman named Mary. Mary was soon to marry a young man named Joseph. One day Gabriel, an angel of the Lord, visited Mary. She was very frightened because she wasn't sure what she was seeing. The angel told her to not be afraid because he was from God and God had favor on her. Mary was still a little shocked. The angel went on to tell her that God had chosen her to have a baby and that his name would be Jesus. This would be a very special baby. He would be great, and his kingdom would last forever and ever. Mary was still surprised and questioned the angel about how she would have the baby since she was not yet married. The angel told her that the Holy Spirit would come upon her and she would conceive a child and the child would be called the Son of God. Mary bowed before the angel Gabriel and told him she would be obedient to God and that she wanted His will to be done through her. When she arose the angel had gone.

Soon after Mary had gone home her Cousin Elizabeth's son was born. Everyone thought he should be named after his father, Zachariah, but Elizabeth said "No, he will be named John."

Luke 1

The New Covenant

BibleTells

STORY PAGE 1

BibleTells

"Praise the Lord"

Connect the dots and then color the stained glass window by using the color key.

Color Key
1 - blue
2 - red
3 - green
4 - orange
5 - purple

354

The angel told Mary she would give birth to a son.

ANSWERS IN BACK

"A Child to be Born"
God sent the Angel Gabriel

Mary was very happy about her visit from Gabriel
and the special news he brought to her; she quickly wanted
to tell her cousin.

Luke 1•39-40

Can you think of any good news you've heard and wanted to share
with family and friends? Write it in spaces below.

All the neighbors...

...and relatives were surprised because there was no one in their family called John. Zachariah, John's father, was a priest in the temple. He and Elizabeth were very old and had never had children, but always wanted them very badly. He had been visited by an angel in the temple while he was burning incense to God. The angel told him his wife would have a son and he would be called John. Zachariah was so surprised, he couldn't believe what he was hearing. Zachariah questioned the angel Gabriel and asked how this could be possible since he and Elizabeth were so old. The angel told him because of his unbelief about what was spoken to him, he would not be able to speak until what the angel told him came true. When the baby was born and Elizabeth told everyone he would be called John, someone said to ask his father what the baby should be named. Because Zachariah could not speak, he asked for a writing tablet and wrote, "HIS NAME IS JOHN." Everyone was amazed that Zachariah also wanted to name him John. Immediately Zachariah began to speak, just like the angel had said. He began praising God and foretelling John's future, that he would be a great man of God and he would shed light on those who lived in darkness and he would bring knowledge of the truth to the children of Israel. What Zachariah was really saying was that John was going to tell everybody that Jesus was coming and that he was bringing hope to all.

Luke 1

His name will be Called...

BIBLE TELLS

STORY PAGE

2

"Unscramble"
Luke 1•63

Unscramble the words that Zachariah wrote on his tablet.

ISH
MNEA
SI
HJNO

Cool•Things to Know

More than likely, Zachariah wrote John's name on Papyrus. This is a material which is made from the aquatic papyrus plant found in the Nile valley in Egypt. The "paper" is made from the pith of this plant by taking strips of the pith, laying them together, soaking them, then pressing the material and drying it. This was commonly used by ancient Egyptians, Greeks, and Romans. Now you understand where our word for "paper" comes from.

357

"Off to Elizabeth's"

Help Mary get to her cousin Elizabeth's in Judea!
Remember - she is so excited about her good news she wants to get there quickly.

Start

Luke 1•39

End

358

ANSWERS IN BACK

"Good News"

Complete the dot to dot and you will see where Mary and Elizabeth shared their good news with each other.

Cool·Things to Know

In Judea and other parts of that area the houses were built from bricks made with mud or big rough stones. The houses were built with flat roofs because the people could dry things there in the sun, like fruits and vegetables and even their clothes. Sometimes if it was really hot, they would sleep on the roof.

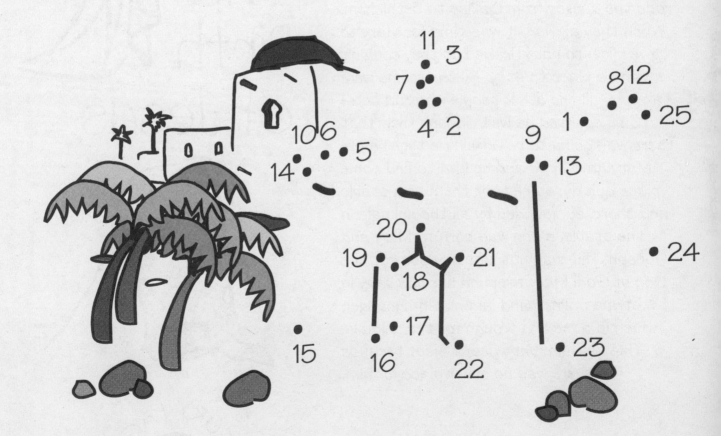

ANSWERS IN BACK

BIBLETELLS

Not too long ...

The Birth of Jesus

... after Mary and Joseph were married, Caesar Augustus ordered that everyone in the world be counted. People everywhere had to go back to their hometowns and register. Because Joseph was from Bethlehem he had to journey back there to be counted with his new wife, Mary, who was going to have her baby soon. So they loaded up the donkey with all the things they needed and Mary rode the donkey from Galilee to Bethlehem. When they arrived, it was time for Mary to give birth to baby Jesus but they couldn't find a place to stay. All the rooms were taken by all the other people who had come to be counted as well. Joseph knew that there was going to be very little time before Mary gave birth and he had to find some place quickly; so he took them to a stable and there, surrounded by all the animals in the stable, a son was born to Mary and Joseph. This was not just any son but the Son of God. Mary wrapped her new baby in strips of linen and laid him in a manger, which is a feeding trough for the animals. This is where baby Jesus slept because there was no other place for him.

Luke 2

STORY PAGE
1

"The Census"

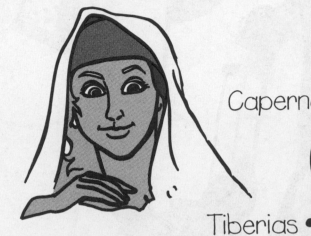

Capernaum •

The Birth of Jesus

• Bethsaida

Sea of Galilee

Tiberias •

Nazareth •

See if you can figure out these word problems.

It is 80 miles from Galilee to Bethlehem. Mary and Joseph probably walked the distance. If the trip took them 5 days, how many miles a day did they travel?

If you took an 80 mile trip today by car, and the speed limit is 65 miles per hour, how long would it take you?

Everyone went to his place of birth to register. Joseph went up from the town of Nazareth to Judea, then to Bethlehem, the town of David, because he belonged to the house and line of David.

Luke 2•3-4

361

"No Room in the Inn"

Mary and Joseph couldn't find any place to stay in
Bethlehem, so they had to go to the stable to sleep.

Luke 2:7

Cut on gray lines to make a puzzle.

"The Birth of Jesus"

Cut on gray lines to make a puzzle.

363

"A Son is Born"...

...to Mary and Joseph. This is not just any son, but the Son of God.
She wrapped him in swaddling clothes and laid him in a manger.

Luke 2•7

364

Color Mary & baby Jesus very blessed!

The Birth of Jesus

The scrambled message below, "Glory to God in the highest," is what the angels sang when Jesus was born. There is one letter missing. Can you find which one?

ANSWERS IN BACK

Although Jesus' ...

...parents were rejoicing over their new son, the angels of the Lord were rejoicing as well. That night, shepherds out in the fields tending their flocks were visited by angels. The shepherds saw a great light which frightened them and they wanted to hide. An angel appeared to them, saying, " Do not be afraid. I have come to bring you good news." The angel told them that a savior had been born in the city of David and that it was Christ the Lord, Who would bring peace on earth and promote good will to everyone. The angel told them they would know the Christ child because he would be lying in a manger with swaddling cloths wrapped around him. Suddenly the whole night sky was filled with heavenly beings singing, "Glory to God in the highest, peace on earth and good will to men!"

After the angels left the shepherds and went back into heaven, the shepherds said "Let's go into Bethlehem and see what the Lord has revealed to us." So the shepherds quickly went into town and found the baby lying in a manger just like the angel said. The shepherds were very excited and they told Mary and Joseph about the angels visiting them in the fields and telling them about the savior that was born. Everyone listening to their story was very amazed. Mary, hearing these things, held them close in her heart. The shepherds returned to the fields, praising God for what they had witnessed, and they told everyone what they had seen.

STORY PAGE

2

The Shepherds see the Star

BIBLETELLS

Luke 2

BIBLETELLS

"The Shepherds see the Star"
"Do not be afraid, I have come to bring you good news!"
Color in this picture of the wonder in the sky this shepherd boy saw.

Luke 2

"Signs in the Heavens"

How many triangles can you count in this star?

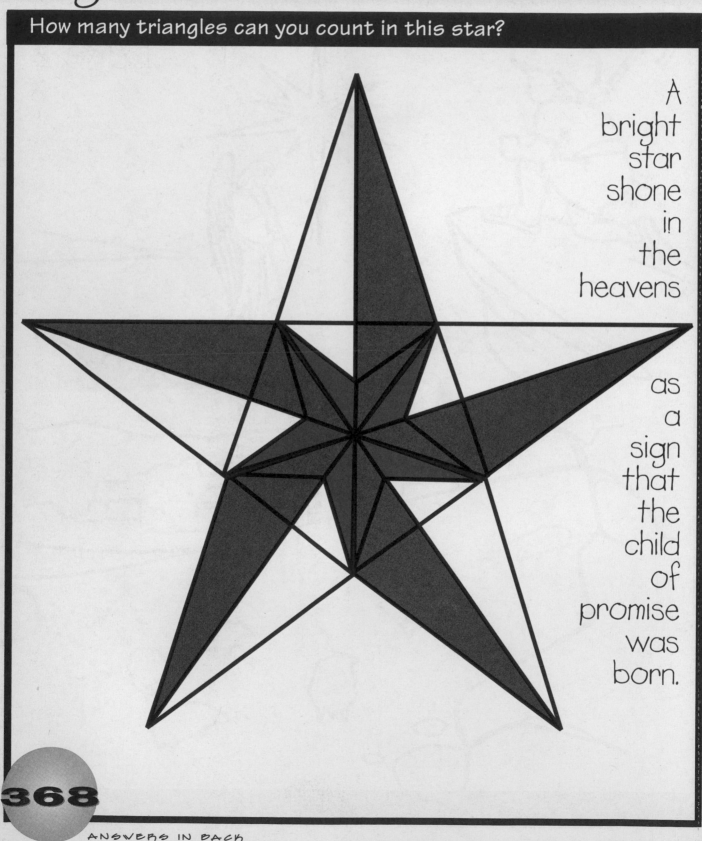

A bright star shone in the heavens

as a sign that the child of promise was born.

ANSWERS IN BACK

"Meanwhile,"
back at the manger

Luke 2•16

Name the animals that were at the manger with Mary & Joseph!

And they came with haste and found Mary and Joseph, and the babe lying in a manger.

369

"The Manger"

She gave birth to her firstborn and laid Him in a manger because there was no room in the inn.

Make your own manger scene! Look on the next page.

"The Players"

There were Joseph, Mary and Baby Jesus with all the animals, the star over head, and the shepherds from the nearby fields.

Color, cut, and paste into the manger scene.

Cool·Things to Know

Did you know that the 3 wise men did not come to the manger? They did find Mary & Joseph's house some time later.

Draw Mary, Joseph, and the shepherds as well, and add them to your scene.

371

"Manger Hair Pasta"

Make this delicious and easy pasta recipe, which symbolizes the Hay baby Jesus slept on in the Manger. You will need an adult to supervise.

Ingredients:
- 1 stick of butter (1.2 cup)
- 1/4 cup of Olive Oil or Canola Oil (Olive is better)
- 3 Large cloves of garlic, minced (Be sure to peel it first)
    or 1 Tbl. of garlic powder
- 1/4 lb of plain linguine
- 1/4 lb of spinach linguine
    (If you don't have both, one or the other will work.
- 1/2 Cup grated parmesan cheese

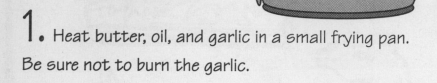

1. Heat butter, oil, and garlic in a small frying pan. Be sure not to burn the garlic.

2. When everything has melted and garlic has been sauteed, take off burner and let sit.

3. In the meantime, bring a large pot of water to a rapid boil. Cook pasta in water till done. Drain.

4. Now toss with garlic mixture, along with the Parmesan cheese. Salt and Pepper to taste!

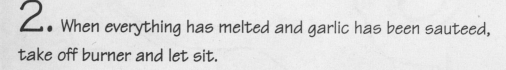

Congratulations for making a delicious dish your whole family will love!

"Animals in Stable"

You normally would find all kinds of animals at the stables. Our stable is full, boarding animals for all of the people in town, and it's feeding time!

Can you count the right number of animals we have to feed?

373

"His Name is Called"

Jesus was also called "Emmanuel," which means "God with us."

Matthew 1•23

Unscramble the names to find out their meanings.

AAMD ⬜ = Red Earth

IANBNMJE ⬜ = Son of my right hand

ENDLIA ⬜ = God is my judge

IADDV ⬜ = Loved by God

ERALIBG ⬜ = God's Hero

HJNO ⬜ = God's Mercy

EHILACM ⬜ = Who can be like God?

TBHE ⬜ = Breath of live

VEE ⬜ = Life-Giving

NNHHAA ⬜ = God's Favor

AAHRS ⬜ = Princess

ETERHS ⬜ = Star

374

ANSWERS IN BACK

"Reflections"

You'll need a mirrror to read this one. Hold it up to the mirror and you will see the very special mesasage the angels gave the shepherds.

Luke 2:10-11

I have come to bring you good tidings of great joy!

For unto you a savior is born in the city of David it is Christ the Lord!

375

"A Star in the North"

The shepherds went back to their flocks, glorifying and praising God for what they had seen and heard. Luke 2•20

Color them with wonder.

"Eye Tricks"

The shepherds thought their eyes were playing tricks on them when the agnels appeared to them.

See how yours eyes might do the same with the tricks below.

1. Which line is the longest?

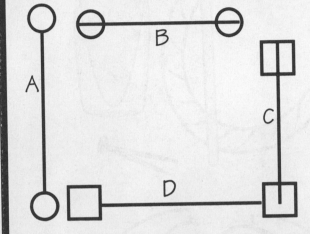

2. Which thin line is longer?

3. Which moon is larger?

377

"Paper Plate Angel"

You will need:
- Scissors
- 1 paper plate
- 1 paper fastener
- 1 pipe cleaner
- glue
- Aluminum foil

Directions:

1. Cut the paper plate in the shape below.

2. Take the pieces you cut away and attach in center of angel body with paper fastener. (You might have to poke a small hole with point of scissors.)

3. With marker, dot eyes, nose, and mouth on angel face.

4. Take the pipe cleaner and wrap around a pencil to "curl" it. Then glue on angel head for hair.

5. Cut pieces of foil in shape of wing. Glue on wing. Have fun moving her wings and pretending she can fly.

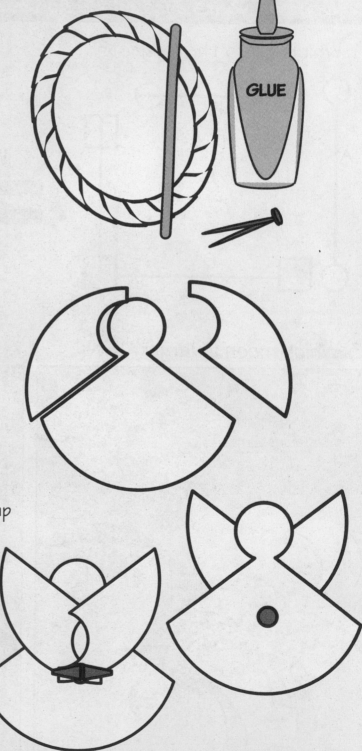

"Have Your Own Flock"
And lead it too!

Yes, you can be the shepherd of your very own flock.

- Cut out sheep below.
- Glue cotton balls on them to create their wool coats.
- Then glue 2 wooden clothes pins on back for their legs.

You'll have a blaaaaast tending sheep!

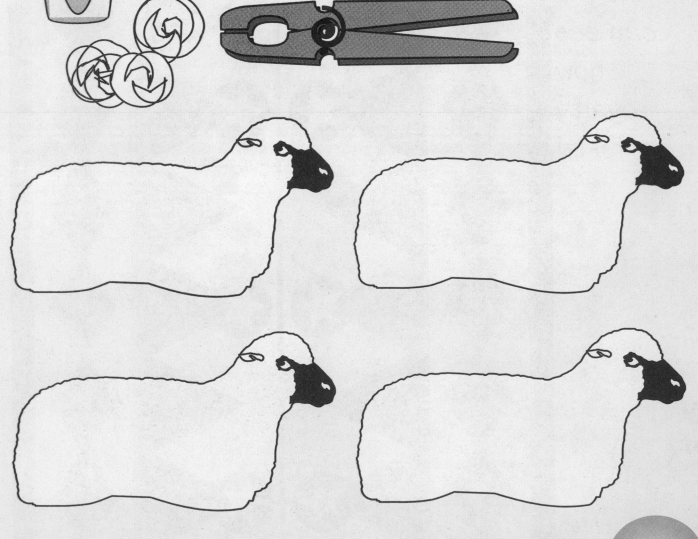

"The Crown"

The wise men told King Herod they wanted to find this new baby known as the "King of the Jews."

Matthew 2:2

Cut out the crown and glue the ends. Now you can see how royalty feels!

380

The good ...

...news of Jesus' birth was traveling fast. Three wise men from the east went to Jerusalem and asked King Herod "King of the Jews." The wise men told King Herod they had seen the star in the east and had come to worship Him. This made King Herod very jealous. In his heart he wanted to destroy baby Jesus, but he pretended to care about the baby to the wise men. He told the wise men to go to Bethlehem and find the child and to then return to him and let him know where the child was so he could worship Him also. The wise men set out for Bethlehem, led by the star they saw in the east. The star took them right to Jesus' house. When they arrived they fell down before the young child and worshiped Him. They then laid out their gifts of gold, frankincense, and myrrh before Him. The wise men were warned in a dream not to go back and tell King Herod where Jesus was because he wanted to kill baby Jesus. So they left Bethlehem and began their journey home a different way.

The Three Wise Men

BIBLETELLS

Matthew 2

STORY PAGE
1

"Bearing Gifts"

They then laid out their gifts of gold, frankincense, and myrrh before Him.

Color the Three Kings joyful they found the child!

After the ...

... wise men went away, Joseph had a dream. The angel of the Lord warned him to leave Bethlehem and take Jesus and His mother to Egypt. He would again bring a word when it was time to leave Egypt. This was to protect Jesus from King Herod who was going to hunt for Jesus and try to kill Him. Joseph took Mary and Jesus to Egypt and they stayed there until King Herod died. The angel of the Lord appeared to Joseph, releasing him and Mary and Jesus from Egypt. They traveled to Judea but were warned again by God that it was not safe. Then they headed towards Galilee and settled in Nazareth.

STORY PAGE
2

The Wise Men

Matthew 2

BibleTells

383

"Help the Wise Men"

After leaving King Herod, the 3 Wise men need to find their way to Mary and Joseph's home.

Start

End

384

"Mix & Match

Cut out rectangles. Mix and match heads, middles, and feet for a silly time.

"They Brought Gifts"

Jesus received three gifts from the wise men: Gold, Frankincense, and Myrrh.

What colors do you think these special packages should be?

Which 2 of these items match the picture on the left?

The Wise Men Came Bearing Gifts

Gold, Frankincense, and Myrrh

387

"Baby Gifts"
Matthew 2•11

Jesus received very unusual baby gifts:
Gold, Frankincense, and Myrrh.

Fill in the puzzle below to find baby gifts for today.

A   1

B   2   4 9 1 16 5 18 19

C   3

D   4

E   5   18 1 20 20 12 5

F   6

G   7

H   8   20 15 25 19

I   9

J   10

K   11   16 1 3 9 6 9 5 18

L   12

M   13

N   14   2 15 15 20 9 5 19

O   15

P   16

Q   17   2 12 1 14 11 5 20

R   18

S   19   7 15 23 14 19

T   20

U   21

V   22   3 12 15 20 8 5 19

W   23

X   24

Y   25   23 1 19 8 3 12 15 20 8 19

Z   26

2 15 20 20 12 5 19

ANSWERS IN BACK

"Luggage"

When Mary and Joseph traveled to Bethlehem from Galilee and the wise men traveled from Jerusalem to Bethlehem, did they have a suitcase for their trip?

Luke 2•4

Can you find: a fish • worm • slice of pizza • baseball banana• flower • hamburger • seashell • hammer • and an ice cream cone

389

ANSWERS IN BACK

"Who Am I"

Read the clues carefully, and write the name in the space provided.

1. I appeared to Zachariah and to Mary to tell them of their children to come.

2. I was unable to speak until my son was born.

3. I'm very old, but God blessed me and my husband Zachariah with a son.

4. I was born to tell people about the Savior. My name is_____?

5. I was not married, but the Holy Spirit blessed me with the Son of God.

6. I love Mary very much and want her to be my wife.

7. We were afraid of the bright light in the sky, but were comforted by the news from the angels.

8. We followed the star in the east to find baby Jesus to worship him.

ANSWERS IN BACK

"Test Your Counting Skills"

How many of each item or thing do you see?

391

"Celebrate"

We celebrate Jesus' birth on December 25.

It is usually very cold this time of year. Make the yummy hot cocoa mix below and sit by the fire and read the story of Jesus' birth with family and friends.

Ingredients:

- 4 cups powdered milk
- 1 1/2 cups sugar
- 3/4 to 1 cup baking cocoa
- 1 teaspoon salt
- boiling water

1. Sift powdered milk, sugar, cocoa, and salt into a large bowl. Sift several times.

2. Store in an airtight container.

How to make Hot Cocoa:

1. Combine 3 tablespoons mix in cup for each serving.

2. Add a small amount of boiling water, stirring until smooth.

3. Fill cup with boiling water and stir.

"Greeting Card"
Make a birthday card for Jesus.

Cut out the card above. Fold in half each way. Then write a greeting to Jesus.
Save it to remind you how special Jesus' birthday is!

"Birthday Party"

• God gave us the greatest

gift of all: Jesus. • That's

why we celebrate His

birth. • Invite your

friends over

and have

them

bring a gift for a less

fortunate child. • Have

fun wrapping them

at the birthday

party. • Have an adult find a local

charity that can use such gifts. • You can do this

any time of year! • Celebrate with a birthday cake

that says, "Happy Birthday Jesus!" • Enjoy

being with friends and giving to others.

HAPPY BIRTHDAY!

Happy Birthday Jesus

Have a Birthday Party for Jesus!

"Baby Jesus"

Can you solve this crossword puzzle?

Answer all the questions regarding Jesus Birth for the answers to the puzzle...

1. What do you give someone when it's their Birthday?

2. Silver & _____

3. Gift to baby Jesus that burns and smells good.

4. A stable is for?

5. Jesus was called _____ of the Jews.

6. The wise men followed a _____ in the east.

7. A _____ was Jesus' crib.

8. A gift to baby Jesus that is a sweet smelling oil.

9. Jesus' earthly father.

10. The son of God.

11. Town where Jesus was born

12. Watching their flocks at night

13. Jesus' mother

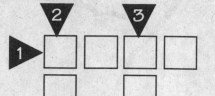

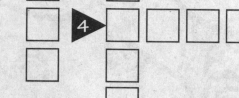

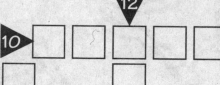
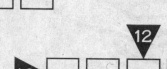
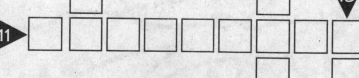
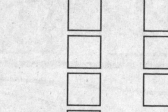
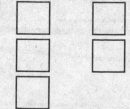

396

"What Am I?" Read the clues carefully and write the name in the space provided.

1. Zachariah was burning me in the temple when an angel appeared to him.

☐

2. My name is Gabriel. I am an _____ of the Lord.

☐

3. I am the town where Mary and Joseph lived.

☐

4. Zachariah wrote his son's name on me.

☐

5. Mary and Joseph went to this town to be counted.

☐

6. I carried Mary on the journey.

☐

7. I house the animals and also provided a place for Jesus' birth.

☐

8. Mary used strips of me to wrap baby Jesus in.

☐

9. I'm used for feeding animals, but I was the crib for Baby Jesus.

☐

10. I shone brightly in the sky over baby Jesus.

☐

ANSWERS IN BACK

BIBLE TELLS

Jesus grew up ...

...like any other boy in Galilee. Being Jewish meant he would go to the synagogue on the Sabbath, which is sundown on Friday to sundown on Saturday. On the Sabbath, or day of rest, passages are read from the Torah, which are the first five books of the Old Testament, as well as other Jewish writings. As Jesus grew older, He began to absorb the word of God. All the scholars of the temple were amazed at how much Jesus learned and how wise he was.

Jesus' family were hard working people. His earthly father, Joseph, was a carpenter. Jesus acquired this skill also. He and his father would build and repair wood related items such as furniture, tools, bowls, ladders, and so on.

As Jesus got older, people began to see more of his character. He was gentle and kind. He would heal the sick, cause blind people to see, heal the lame so they could walk, and even raise people from the dead. News got around quickly that he truly was the Son of God. Some people believed it and some didn't. Jesus would gather huge crowds wherever he went because people wanted to see these miracles. He would also preach to the people and tell them to "Repent because the kingdom of heaven is at hand."

Life of Jesus

STORY PAGE 1

Cool·Things to Know

In ancient times a zealot was a member of a Jewish group that resisted Roman rule. Zealot comes from the word zeal, which means to be very very enthusiastic regarding a goal, cause, or ideal.

BIBLE TELLS

Jesus is our "Link."

1. Brightly color these strips or links. (To make more, cut out strips of paper 3/4" wide x 5 1/2" long.)

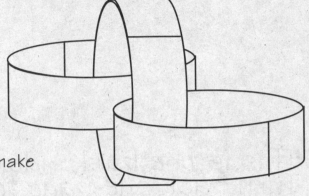

2. Cut and glue the "Links" together to make a chain.

You can decorate your room with it. Notice how each link is connected to the next.

Jesus is our "Link."

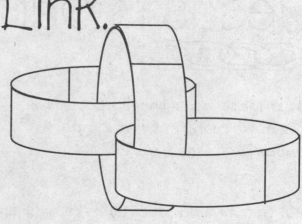

This is the back side.
Turn back one page for instructions.

Glue Here	Glue Here	Glue Here	Glue Here	Glue Here	Glue Here	Glue Here	Glue Here

"Jesus' Natural Family"

Can you find all of the names of Jesus' family members?

E	L	I	Z	A	B	E	T	H	B
M	M	A	J	E	J	A	M	E	H
A	O	R	T	O	D	X	S	A	J
R	B	Y	S	K	J	R	I	W	O
Y	I	E	L	W	K	R	A	I	S
X	P	M	N	I	A	B	V	L	E
H	E	I	O	H	J	U	D	A	S
P	L	S	C	N	B	Z	E	T	H
E	I	A	F	G	N	O	M	I	S
A	Z	A	B	E	S	E	M	A	J

Mary   James

Joseph   Joses

Elizabeth Simon

Zachariah Judas

Matthew 13•55

401

"J" is for Jesus

Can you circle all the things below that start with the letter "J"?

ANSWERS IN BACK

Luke 5•10
Jesus said: "I will make you fishers of men"

How many words can you make from the term "Fisher of Men"?

We found 14. See how many you can make.

ANSWERS IN BACK

"Rules for Living"

Jesus had so many people around him that wanted to hear him speak that he had to walk up a mountainside so he could be seen and heard.

To finish each sentence you will need to unscramble the letters on the next page. Here is a hint: use the matching letter style and you will find the answers.

1. Blessed are the poor in **S**_____, for theirs is the kingdom of **H**_____.

2. Blessed are those who **M**_____, for they shall be **C**_____.

3. Blessed are the **M**_____, for they shall inherit the **E**_____.

4. Blessed are those who **H**_____ and **T**_____ for righteousness.

5. Blessed are the **M**_____, for they shall obtain **M**_____.

6. Blessed are the pure in **H**_____, for they shall see **G**___.

7. Blessed are the **P**_____ **M**_____, for they shall be called **S**_____ of God.

8. Blessed are those who are **P**_____ for righteousness' sake, for theirs is the **K**_____ of heaven.

Matthew 5

ANSWERS IN BACK

Matthew 5
The Sermon on the Mount
"The Beatitudes"

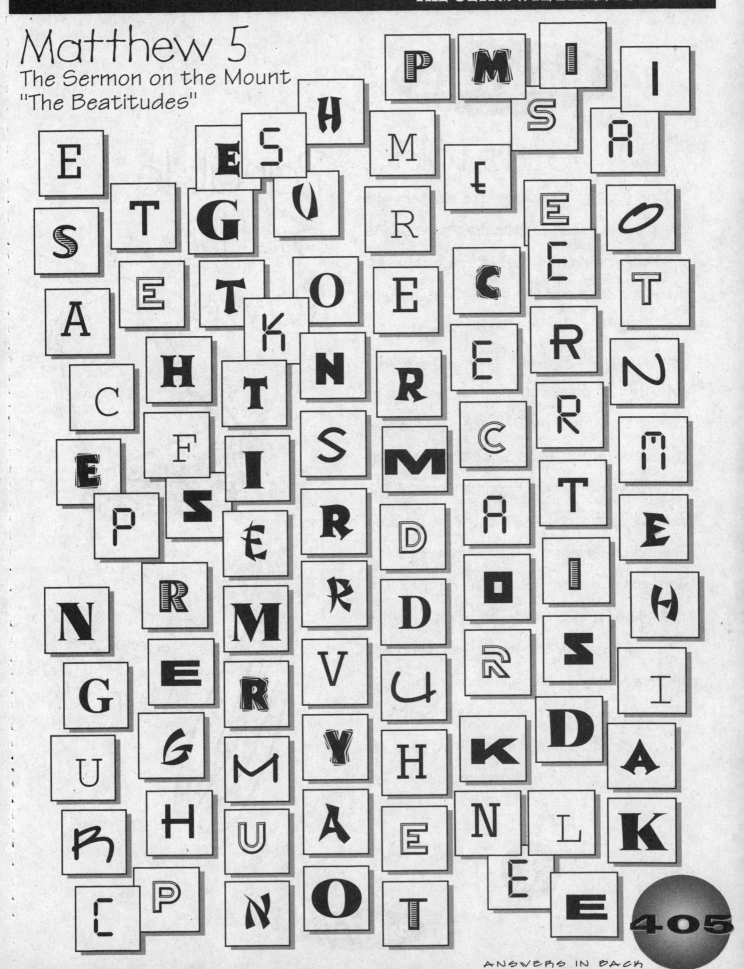

405

BIBLE TELLS

Jesus told ...

...the story of the sower (or planter) who was planting seed for the next harvest. As he was throwing handfuls of seed, some fell on the wayside and the birds came and ate it. Some fell on rocks, and because there was very little soil, the seeds grew quickly but had no place for their roots to dig in. When the sun came and beamed down on them they dried up because they were not rooted firmly in the ground. Some of the seeds fell on thorns and the thorns grew up around the seed and kept it from growing. Some of the seeds fell on the right kind of fertile soil and produced a crop that grew and grew and grew. What Jesus is really talking about is people's hearts as the soil, and the word of God as the seed. What ever condition your heart is in, that will determine how the seed grows.

Parable of the Sower

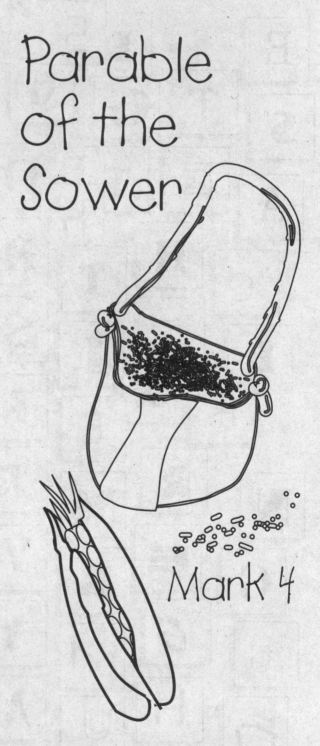

Mark 4

STORY PAGE 1

BIBLE TELLS

Parable of the Sower

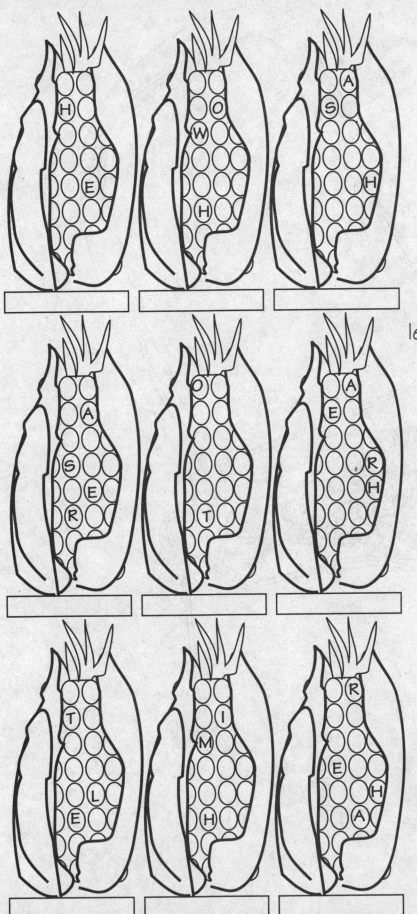

In the "ears" of corn, UNSCRAMBLE the letters you find in the kernels to find a MESSAGE!

Parable of the Sower

Color the "Sower putting the seed in the field." A sower would throw handfuls of seed from his bag out on the field.

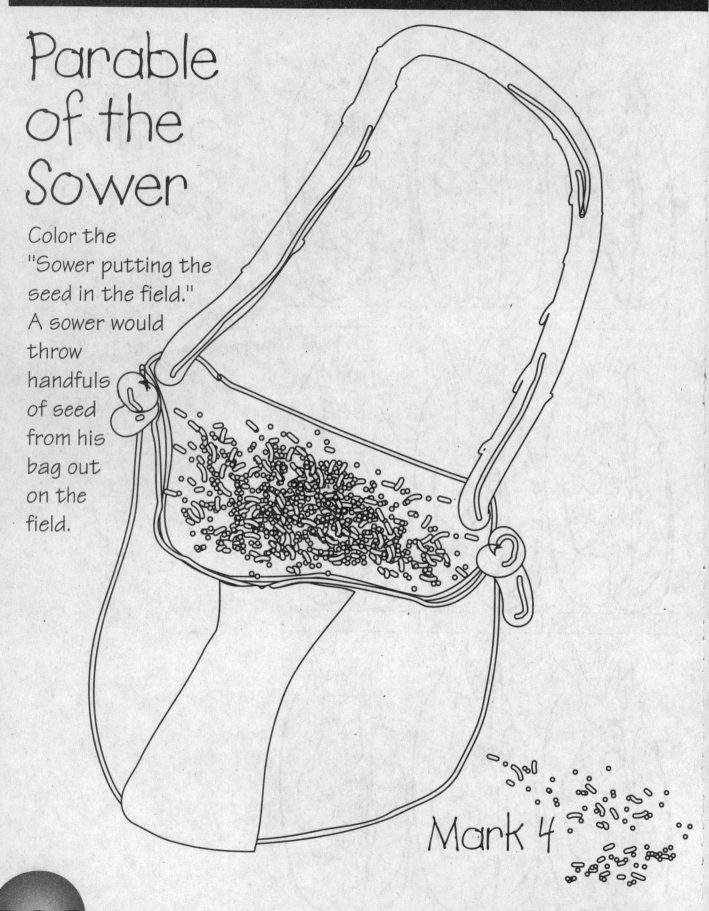

Mark 4

408

Mark 4•1-20

Help this seed get to the fertile soil. Be careful: don't let it get stuck on the rocks or in the thorns.

Start

End

Parable of the Sower

ANSWERS IN BACK

"What's in a seed?"

C	Z	D	L	O	G	I	R	A	M
U	G	A	U	Q	S	C	C	P	O
C	A	R	Z	T	A	R	U	A	P
U	O	Z	A	R	H	E	Z	U	Z
M	T	T	R	S	N	P	M	Z	E
B	Z	O	A	R	S	P	A	L	Z
E	T	U	O	M	K	E	P	W	K
R	Q	C	B	I	O	P	E	A	R
S	T	A	N	R	A	T	S	G	L
W	A	T	E	R	M	E	L	O	N

All these plants have something in common: they come from a seed. Find and circle them in the puzzle above.

Watermelon   Pear
Pumpkin   Marigold
Grass   Carrot
Tomato   Pepper
Corn   Cucumber
Apple   Squash

Parable of the Sower

410

ANSWERS IN BACK

"Harvest"

Cool·Things to Know

Did you know that in ancient times when the seed was sown and the crops had grown, grains such as wheat and barley were cut down with a "Sickle." A sickle is like a round knife. Then the stalks were tied into sheaves. They were then beaten to loosen the grain. Another way to loosen the grain was to toss the stalks in the air with a large fork, called a "winnowing fork."

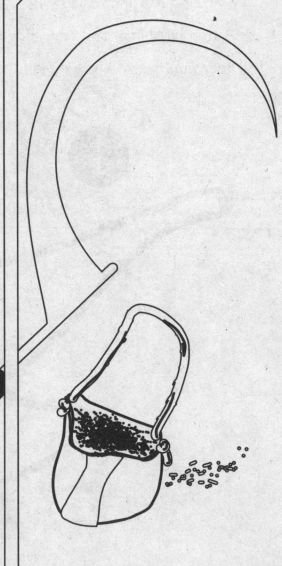

4·11

BibleTells

Jesus asked ...

...the question, "When you light a lamp, do you hide it under a basket or under a bed? Isn't it meant to be set on a lampstand and so it's light can shine?" Jesus is referring to things that are hidden which will be brought into the light and revealed.

Parable of the Lamp

STORY PAGE 1

Mark 4•21-25

412

ANSWERS IN BACK

Parable of the Lamp

Mark 4•21-25

413

"Hidden Picture"

The lamp on the nightstand is bright enough to help reveal the hidden objects.

Mark 4•21-25

Can you find: a spoon • fish • fork • worm • dollar bill • marshmallow
toilet paper • sponge • ball bat • screwdriver • snake • log • flag
saw • paint brush • ice cream cone • pencil • nail • football • candy cane

ANSWERS IN BACK

"Spot the Light"

Wherever you are right now, look around and
see how many sources of light you can find.

Mark 4•21-25

Draw them here. You may try to draw each item you see using one
continuous line. Try not to look at your hand while you draw.

"Mix & Match"

Match the source of light where you most commonly find it.

ANSWERS IN BACK

"Golden Rule"

Jesus spoke about the rules of the kingdom: to love our enemies, to pray for those who persecute us. The most well known rule is the Golden Rule, which tells us to treat others the way we would like for them to treat us.

Can you think of ways to be kind to a person and do things for them that you would want them to do for you? Write them down and look at them again every now and then to remind yourself to be kind.

Luke 6•31

"Do unto others as you would have them do unto you."

The Golden "Ruler"

Finish drawing the ruler. Then complete the Bible verse.

If you can't remember the words, look at the "Golden Rule" page.

"Golden Rule"

"Do unto others as

1 2 3 4

BibleTells

The Bible has ...

...two stories about Jesus feeding the masses of people who came to hear him and to see his miracles of healing. In one of the stories 5,000 people had gathered to hear Jesus and there was very little to eat. Jesus had compassion on all the people because He knew they were hungry and had not eaten for a while. Some of them would not even make it home because they would be so weak from not eating. Jesus asked the disciples how much food they had. The disciples said, "We have seven loaves and a few small fish." Jesus told them to begin to divide the loaves and fishes and amazingly the food multiplied and fed the whole crowd with twelve baskets of food left over.

Loaves and Fishes

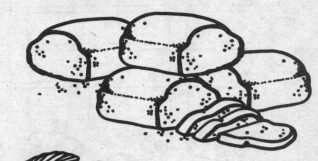

STORY PAGE
1

Mark 6•30-44

Loaves and Fishes

Count the number of loaves and fish in each row. Now color that many squares in the row.

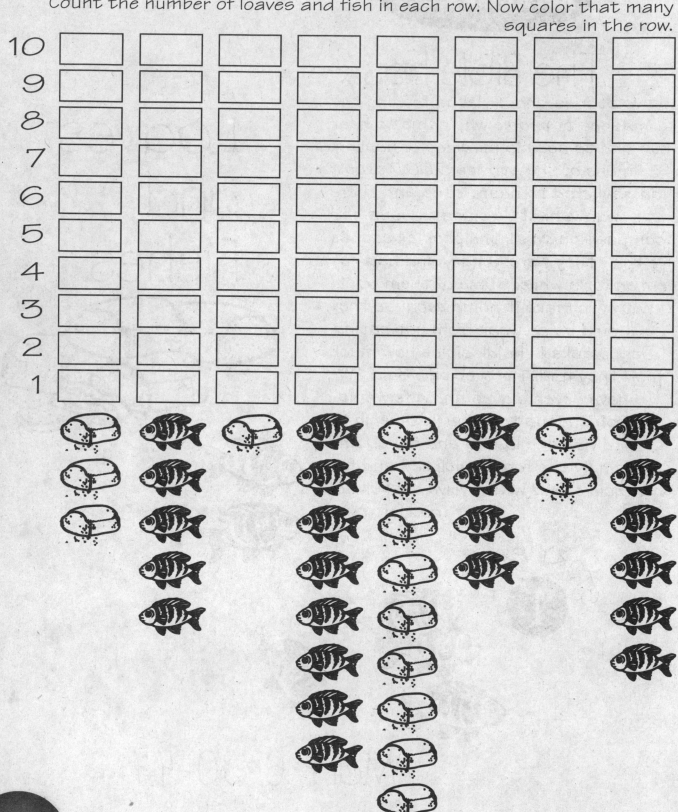

420

ANSWERS IN BACK

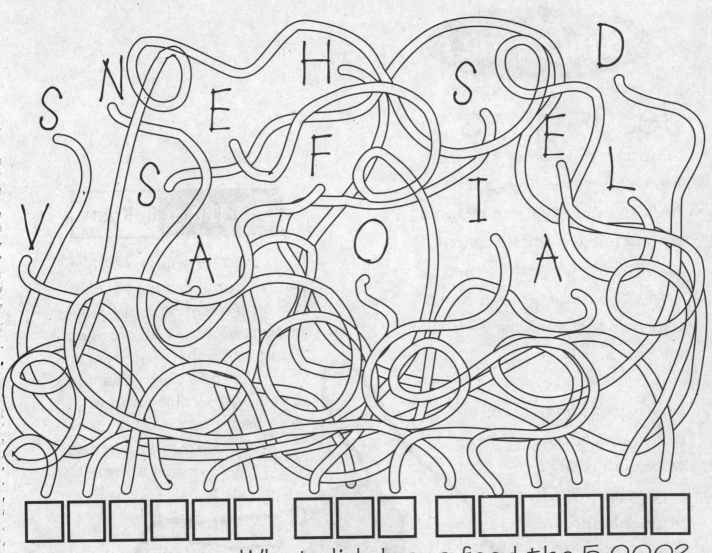

What did Jesus feed the 5,000?

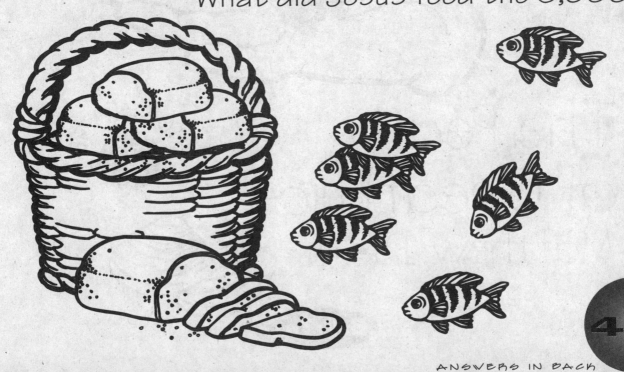

421

BIBLE TELLS

Jesus gives ...

...us the parable of the pearl. He tells of the kingdom of heaven being like a merchant who is looking for a beautiful, very expensive pearl. When he finds the most precious and valued pearl, he sells everything he has and buys it.

Jesus is telling us that once you discover God, there is no need for any other worldly possessions. He takes care of our every need.

Cool•Things to Know

Did you know that pearls come from oysters? When a grain of sand gets in the oyster's shell, it creates an irritation. The oyster eases the irritation by coating the sand with a substance that forms a smooth round ball that we call a "pearl."

The Pearl of Great Price
Matthew 13•45

STORY PAGE 1

422

BIBLE TELLS

The Pearl of Great Price

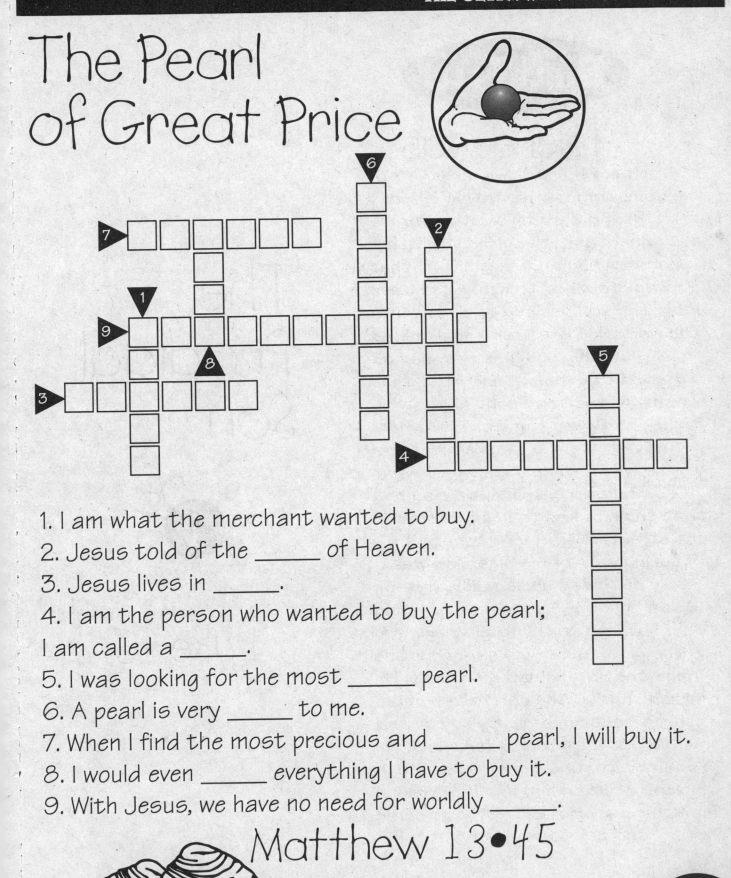

1. I am what the merchant wanted to buy.
2. Jesus told of the _____ of Heaven.
3. Jesus lives in _____.
4. I am the person who wanted to buy the pearl; I am called a _____.
5. I was looking for the most _____ pearl.
6. A pearl is very _____ to me.
7. When I find the most precious and _____ pearl, I will buy it.
8. I would even _____ everything I have to buy it.
9. With Jesus, we have no need for worldly _____.

Matthew 13•45

BibleTells

There was ...

...a man who had two sons. One of the sons came to his father one day and asked his father for his inheritance early. So the father honored him and gave him all that was promised to him. A few days later the son decided to go out into the world. He left his home and lived very lavishly on the money he had received from his father. After time went by, the son spent all that his father had given him. The land where he lived was in a famine and there was no way for him to get back what he had spent. Things were so bad that the son had to beg for bread in the streets. A farmer gave him a job taking care of his pigs. This was a very dirty and unclean job. The son was hungry — so hungry he would even have eaten the food being given to the pigs. As he was caring for the pigs one day, he had a thought. He realized that all the caretakers of his father's house had plenty to eat and did not have to beg for bread. He realized at that moment how much his father loved him and how special his home was. He decided to go home and ask to be a servant in his father's house.

The Prodigal Son

STORY PAGE 1

Luke 15

The
Prodigal
Son

Start

"I will go
back to my
father's
house."

End

425

As he ...

...approached his home, his father saw him from a distance. His father became overjoyed and ran to meet him and hugged him and told his son how happy he was he had come home. The son asked his father for forgiveness and told him he was sorry for sinning against him. The father told his son to relax and he called for the finest things to be put on him: a special robe, a ring for his hand, and a new pair of shoes for his feet. Then the father said to the housekeepers to kill the fattest calf they had because he wanted to have a feast to celebrate the "homecoming" of his son.

In the meantime, the other son had come in from the fields to see what all the excitement was about. When he saw that his brother had returned home and that he was receiving royal treatment from his father, the other son grew angry and jealous. He reminded his father that he had not gone astray and had been good and respectable. Yet his father had never done anything like this for him. The father said, "Son, everything I have is yours and you are precious to me. But your brother was lost and now he is found; he was dead but now he is alive!"

The Prodigal Son

STORY PAGE 2

Luke 15

This phrase should read "The prodigal son has come home," but I've got one too many letters. Can you tell me which is the extra letter?

The Prodigal Son

ANSWERS IN BACK

Draw a circle around all the things the father gave the prodigal son when he returned home.

The Prodigal Son

ANSWERS IN BACK

BibleTells

Once again ...

...Jesus was in a multitude of people. The people began bringing up their little children for Jesus to bless, but the disciples asked the people to stop doing this. This made Jesus a little upset because he loved the little children so much. Jesus told the disciples "Let the little children come to me and do not keep them from doing so, for such is the kingdom of God." He also pointed out to the disciples that child-like faith is the key to entering the kingdom of God. Jesus then gathered the little children and hugged them and blessed them.

Jesus blesses the Little Children Luke 18•15-18

STORY PAGE 1

The children knew that Jesus loved them. What are some things that your family does to tell you how much they love you?

ANSWERS IN BACK

"Love is Spelled"

1	1	1	1	1	1	1	1	1	1	1	1
1	2	1	1	2	1	1	1	1	1	2	1
1	2	1	1	1	2	1	1	1	2	1	1
1	2	1	3	3	3	2	1	2	1	1	1
1	2	1	3	1	3	1	2	3	3	3	1
1	2	1	3	1	3	1	1	3	1	1	1
1	2	1	3	1	3	1	1	3	3	1	1
1	2	1	3	3	3	1	1	3	1	1	1
1	2	1	1	1	1	1	1	3	3	3	1
1	2	1	1	1	1	1	1	1	1	1	1
1	2	2	2	2	2	2	2	2	2	1	1
1	1	1	1	1	1	1	1	1	1	1	1

Color the squares below and see the hidden word when you're finished.

1 = Yellow
2 = Red
3 = Blue

424

"Love is the Star"

I LOVE

Jesus loves the little children, all the children of the world
Red, Yellow, Black, and White...

"Telephone"

When the shepherds saw Jesus, they spread the word concerning what had been said by the angels about this child.

The shepherds were so excited about baby Jesus that they told everyone. Do you think everyone heard correctly?
Play this fun game with friends and create lots of giggles.
Sit in a circle. One person whisper in another person's ear, "Glory to God in the Highest, Peace on earth, goodwill towards men!" Each person should only whisper this once.

When it reaches the end of the circle, have the last person say the sentence out loud and see how it comes out. You can do this with any saying or sentence.

Luke 2•17

Jesus ...

Zacchaeus Luke 19

...traveled to many cities to tell people about the kingdom of God. He was in Jericho and again people were everywhere. There was a man in the city who was a tax collector. His name was Zacchaeus. Zacchaeus was very rich because he cheated the people out of more taxes than they were supposed to pay, and kept the rest for himself. He was a man of short stature, which means he wasn't very tall. When Jesus was in Jericho, Zacchaeus was curious and wanted to see Him. He had to push his way through the crowd because everyone knew who he was and didn't want to let him by. Zacchaeus saw a big sycamore tree and climbed up in the tree so he could see and hear Jesus. Much to his surprise, when Jesus passed by him he called to Zacchaeus, "Zacchaeus come down from that tree, and hurry; I want to stay at your house."

STORY PAGE 1

Zacchaeus ...

...was so excited he couldn't get out of the tree fast enough. So Jesus went home with Zacchaeus and all the people began to talk and complain that Jesus had gone to a sinner's house. Zacchaeus repented to Jesus and said he would give half of everything he had to the poor and if he had cheated anyone he would repay them four times what he had taken. Jesus was pleased with Zacchaeus and said "Salvation has come to your house today." Jesus blessed Zacchaeus' household and went on His way.

Zacchaeus
Luke 19

STORY PAGE
2

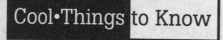

Cool•Things to Know

Did you Know?
A tax is a sum of money the government requires you to pay to help run the government. The amount of tax is determined by the amount of income or possessions you have.

"Zacchaeus in a Tree"

Draw what you think Zacchaeus saw from the tree.

Jesus came ...

...to earth for a reason. He was sent by God as a way for people to come closer to God. This is how much God loved us: He sent his only Son to come to earth and to tell us about His Father in heaven. In John 3:16, the scripture tells us, "God so loved the world that he gave His only begotten son, that whoever believes in Him should not perish but have everlasting life." This is why Jesus talked in parables and healed the sick and taught us how we should live according to God's word. But Jesus had not completed his mission just by talking to the people. He had come to be the sacrificial lamb for us to God. If you remember, in the Old Testament people would give offerings to God to have God forgive their sins. Sins are when you do things that are not pleasing to God and not according to the way of living that He has set for us. So when we sin, it separates us from God. Jesus is often called the Lamb of God because He was offered to God for our sins. Jesus had to die on the cross and be buried, but after three days He rose from the grave and went to live with His Father in heaven. His precious blood was shed for us to cover our sins once and for all. Hallelujah!!

Lamb of God

BibleTells

Matthew 26-28
Mark 11

STORY PAGE

1

"Donkey & Colt"
Matthew 21•2

Jesus told the disciples to look for a donkey with its colt tied to a doorway and bring it back to him.

Help the disciples find the donkey and colt.
(Going under bridges one street width is allowed)

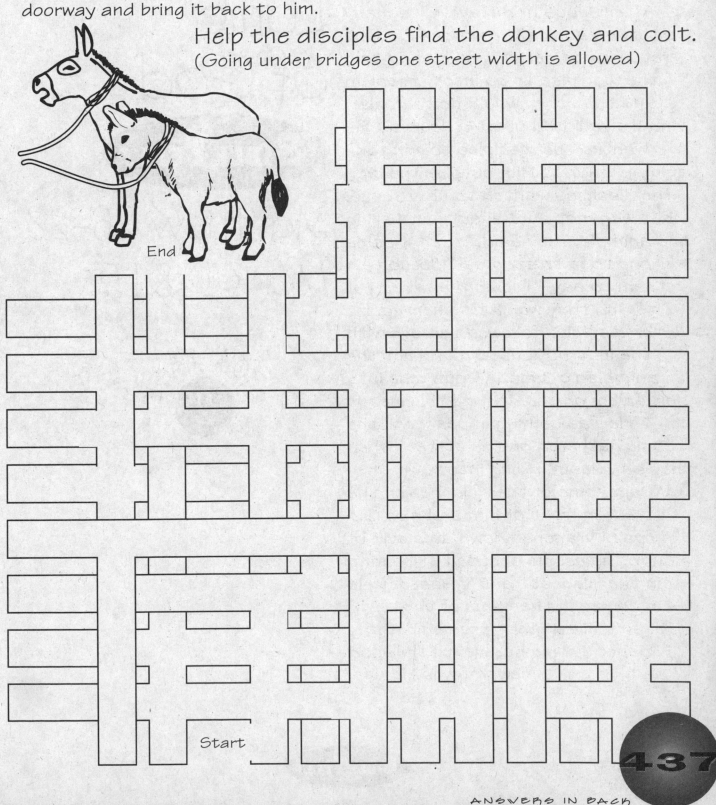

End

Start

437

It was a ...

...difficult thing for Jesus to do because he knew that dying would not be easy. But He also knew that the reward after would be great. After Jesus had traveled to many cities preaching the word of God, he returned to Jerusalem. He had told the disciples to go into Jerusalem and that they would find a donkey and its colt tied up at a doorway. He wanted the disciples to bring the animals back to Him outside the city. The disciples wanted to obey Jesus, but were not sure about just taking the animals. They said, "What if some one tries to stop us?" Jesus told them to say, "The Lord has need of it," and they would let them go. So the disciples followed through with the instructions and brought the animals to Jesus. Jesus rode into Jerusalem on the donkey: this meant He was coming in peace. All the people gathered on the streets when they saw Jesus riding into town. They laid some of their clothes on the street in front of him and also laid palm branches down as a sign of honor. The people shouted, "Hosanna in the Highest," and "Blessed is He who comes in the name of the Lord!" Jesus received great praise that day because people had heard the good news of who He was.

Lamb of God

BibleTells

Matthew 26-28
Mark 11&15

STORY PAGE
2

BibleTells

"Jerusalem"
Matthew 21•10-11

Jesus entered Jerusalem and the whole city was stirred. They asked, "Who is this?" Some in the crowd answered, "He is Jesus, the prophet from Nazareth in Galilee."

Help Jesus and the donkey get through the street of Jerusalem.

ANSWERS IN BACK

Some of the ...

...people had not heard, and asked "Who is this? Why is he receiving such praise and honor?" The people replied, "It is Jesus, the Prophet from Nazareth in Galilee." Jesus loved the praise of the people, but knew what was about to take place and that these very people that were praising Him now would later call for his death.

After spending time in Jerusalem, Jesus went to Bethany, a city outside of Jerusalem, to visit his friends Martha, Mary, and their brother Lazarus. (You can read about Jesus raising Lazarus from the dead in John 11.) Jesus' friends were very happy to see him. Mary brought out a very precious and expensive jar of oil, broke the jar, and began to rub it on Jesus' feet. Judas Iscariot, one of the disciples, was very upset because he thought Mary was being very wasteful. He told her she could have sold that oil and given the money to the poor. Jesus told him to leave her alone because what she was doing was a kind act. It also symbolized the fact that Jesus was about to die because this kind of oil was often used to prepare people's bodies for burial.

Lamb of God

Matthew 26-28
Mark 11&15

STORY PAGE
3

"Precious Oil"

Mary came to him with an alabaster jar of very expensive perfume, which she poured on his head and feet.

Matthew 26•7

The precious oil Mary used to anoint Jesus feet with was called Spikenard. It is found in India and is very expensive and not so easy to get.

Cool•Things to Know

The jar that held the perfume was called an "Alabastron." Its name came from the alabaster stone from which it was made.

Cut on gray lines to make a puzzle.

In the ...

...meantime, the officials in Jerusalem were plotting against Jesus and trying to figure out how to arrest him. They didn't like the fact that he had such great influence on the people. Judas had made a deal with these officials that he would turn Jesus over to them for thirty pieces of silver. When the hour came, Judas kissed Jesus to show the officials which one He was. Jesus knew that he was being betrayed and asked Judas, "Do you betray the Son of Man with a kiss?" When the officials tried to arrest Jesus, Peter d.. his sword and cut off one of the men's ears. Jesus rebuked, Peter and healed the mans ear.

The time was drawing near for Jesus to die on the cross. He was also betrayed by another disciple, Peter, who eventually said he didn't even know Jesus. Jesus had a last meal with the disciples known as the Last Supper. He spoke with them about the things to come and reminded them how much He loved them. The next day Jesus went to the cross and was hung there to die for our sins. He was buried in a tomb, which was like a big rock cave. All of Jesus' friends were very sad He had to die. They loved him very much.

Lamb of God

BibleTells

Matthew 26-28
Mark 11&15

STORY PAGE

4

"Victory"

"For anyone that is born of God has victory in life through the Son of God, Jesus."

1 John 4•4

Connect the dots to see something that in ancient times represented victory.

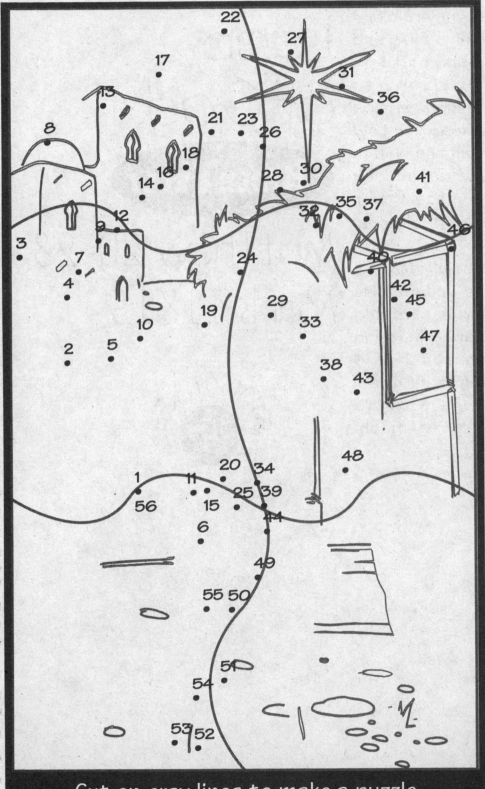

437

ANSWERS IN BACK

But after He ...

...was laid in the tomb, the big rock that covered it was opened after three days and when they looked in Jesus was gone. They rejoiced because this meant He was alive and not dead, just like Jesus had said would happen. Jesus reappeared to the disciples to confirm He was alive and had risen from the dead. He told them to go and tell of all the things He had taught them, and reminded them they were witnesses to all that He had done.

We in modern times celebrate the resurrection of Jesus because He rose from the dead and is alive and sits at the right hand of God in heaven, just like He promised. This is a symbol of our life with Christ. Rejoice in the fact that Jesus is alive and loves us very much!

Lamb of God

BibleTells

Matthew 26-28
Mark 11&15

STORY PAGE
5

"God Loves Me"

God wants me to be kind to others.
Find the words in this puzzle that describe how I should act toward others and toward Him.

```
C Q S H J V B L P N B K L C P N S
V R I G H T E O U S L M E E C L T
U N D E R S Q L H T Y W V E O S L
T E R N B P N T V S R T I N M E K
U G N I D N A T S R E D N U P R N
M R C F I F U L V N O R H J A I S
E V E O L R I G H J T E O U S S E
M E R C I F U L M P L A S I S O N
F A L I R E D N E T H H T E I O S
P R O U E E K N R I G U P O U R R
T U V R S H T E F A J T L S N O Z
V W E N T D G J I V H K S B D C P
N Z S V W N M E R C I F L U Y U T
R D N E T I V E O E L D I K R N S
T O E N J K H C D M S A S E I T N O
G E N L T H T I A F V E O L G D O
```

trust   understanding   love   pure
kind   compassion   merciful   tender
gentle   faith   meek   righteous

445

"God Made this"

Ann went to the park and saw all of the wonderful things God had made. Help her find them all.

Can you find: a bird • squirrel • ant • basket worm • caterpillar • fish • and butterfly?

ANSWERS IN BACK

"God Made Me"

God created me special and unique.

1. help bend my legs

2. this is in my mouth

3. help bend my arms

4. ten per foot

5. where my lips are

6. I do this when I'm sleepy

7. this pumps my blood

8. I hug with these

9. they help me breathe

10. I smell with this

11. I cannot see without these

12. where my food goes

13. I feel with these

14. I run with these

"God Made Me"

447

"Someone Special"

God made us in His image, so that makes us extra special!

Fill in the fun facts about yourself
and see how unique you are.

Name
Age
Hair Color
Eye Color
Height
Favorite Color
Favorite Food
Characteristic I like most about myself

Things that make me smile and feel happy

Something nice I have done for someone today

Something nice I plan to do soon

"Bible Bingo"
Play Bingo with Bible Character's

Rules to play the game by:

1. Gather old loose buttons or pennies as your Bingo Tokens.

2. Cut out all the "Bible Character Names", put in a plastic bowl or basket.

3. Get several friends to play this with you, pick one person to be the "Caller".

4. The caller will draw one character name at a.time, then call it out.

5. The "Players" then look at their bingo card to see if they have that name on it.

6. If the do they put a button or a penny over that square.

7. Who ever get's 4 straight button or pennies in a row has a "Bingo" and wins,

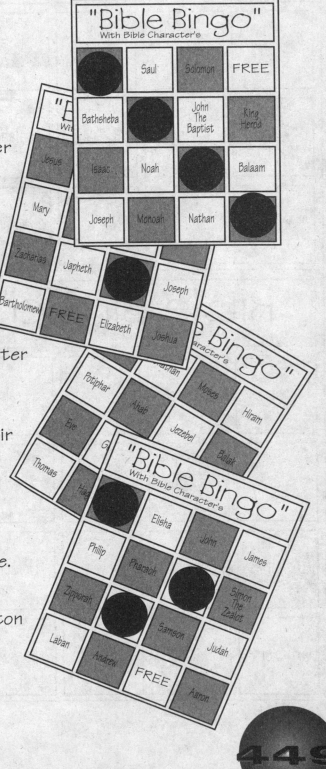

449

"Bible Bingo"
With Bible Character's

God	Saul	Solomon	FREE
Bathsheba	Adam	John The Baptist	King Herod
Isaac	Noah	Delilah	Balaam
Joseph	Monoah	Nathan	Sarah

"Bible Bingo"
With Bible Character's

Shem	Jonathan	Moses	Hiram
Potiphar	Ahab	Jezebel	Balak
Eve	Goliath	Elijah	Zorah
Thomas	Hagar	Jacob	FREE

"Bible Bingo"
With Bible Character's

Jesus	Ishmael	Ham	Leah
Mary	Esau	Simon Peter	Abner
Zacharias	Japheth	Gabriel	Joseph
Bartholomew	FREE	Elizabeth	Joshua

"Bible Bingo"
With Bible Character's

Rebekah	Elisha	John	James
Philip	Pharaoh	Rachel	Simon The Zealot
Zipporah	Abraham	Samson	Judah
Laban	Andrew	FREE	Aaron

450

ANSWERS IN BACK

"Bible Bingo"

With Bible Character's

"Bible Bingo"

With Bible Character's

"Bible Bingo"

With Bible Character's

"Bible Bingo"

With Bible Character's

ANSWERS IN BACK

"Bible Bingo"
With Bible Character's

Abraham	Saul	Hiram	Gabriel
Bathsheba	Ham	Simon The Zealot	King Herod
Isaac	Thaddeus	FREE	Mary
Ahab	Monoah	Nathan	Sarah

"Bible Bingo"
With Bible Character's

Shem	Jonathan	Moses	Elizabeth
FREE	Ahab	Isaac	Balak
Noah	Judas	Matthew	Zorah
Martha	Zipporah	Jacob	Mary

"Bible Bingo"
With Bible Character's

Jesus	Zacchaeus	Isaac	God
Eve	FREE	King Herod	Abner
Zacharias	Japheth	Benjamin	Peter
David	Andrew	Elizabeth	Joshua

"Bible Bingo"
With Bible Character's

Elijah	FREE	Jacob	James
Philip	Lazarus	Rachel	King Herod
Esau	Abraham	Solomon	Judah
Jezebel	Andrew	Judas	Aaron

452

"Bible Bingo"

With Bible Character's

"Bible Bingo"

With Bible Character's

"Bible Bingo"

With Bible Character's

"Bible Bingo"

With Bible Character's

ANSWERS IN BACK

"Bible Bingo"
With Bible Character's

Abraham	Bathsheba	Hiram	Gabriel
FREE	Ham	John The Baptist	Simon Peter
Rebekah	Thaddeus	FREE	Mary
Ahab	Eve	Noah	Jesus

"Bible Bingo"
With Bible Character's

Bartholomew	FREE	Andrew	Elizabeth
Simon The Zealot	Jesus	Isaac	Shem
Noah	Judas	Matthew	James
Martha	Zipporah	Potiphar	Mary

"Bible Bingo"
With Bible Character's

Abraham	Zacchaeus	Isaac	God
Eve	Joseph	Simon Peter	FREE
Jesus	Ishmael	Benjamin	Elisha
David	Andrew	Pharaoh	Esau

"Bible Bingo"
With Bible Character's

Elijah	Gabriel	Jacob	Aaron
James	Lazarus	God	Simon Peter
Esau	FREE	Solomon	Judah
Jesus	Zacharias	Judas	Philip

ANSWERS IN BACK

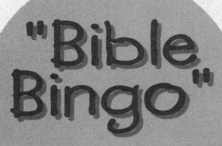

"Bible Bingo"

With Bible Character's

"Bible Bingo"

With Bible Character's

"Bible Bingo"

With Bible Character's

"Bible Bingo"

With Bible Character's

ANSWERS IN BACK

"Bible Bingo"
With Bible Character's

Leah	Bathsheba	FREE	Sarah
Jonathan	Jacob	John The Baptist	King Herod
Esau	Eve	Saul	Rachel
Laban	God	Noah	Jesus

"Bible Bingo"
With Bible Character's

Rebekah	Abner	God	Abraham
Simon The Zealot	Jesus	Balaam	Shem
Joshua	FREE	Samson	James
Goliath	Isaac	Potiphar	Delilah

"Bible Bingo"
With Bible Character's

Abraham	Shem	Ishmael	Potiphar
Judah	Joseph	King Herod	Jonathan
Jesus	God	FREE	Ham
Benjamin	Noah	Pharaoh	Esau

"Bible Bingo"
With Bible Character's

Joseph	FREE	Pharaoh	Balak
James	Hagar	Adam	Simon Peter
Moses	God	Zipporah	Japheth
Jesus	Zacharias	Aaron	Philip

456

"Bible Bingo"

With Bible Character's

"Bible Bingo"

With Bible Character's

"Bible Bingo"

With Bible Character's

"Bible Bingo"

With Bible Character's

457

Cut out all the "Bible Names" and put in a plastic bowl or basket.

God	Ishmael	Judah	Zorah	Hiram	Elizabeth	Mary
Adam	Isaac	Potiphar	Samson	Ahab	Andrew	Martha
Eve	Rebekah	Pharaoh	Delilah	Elijah	James	Lazarus
Noah	Rachel	Moses	Goliath	Elisha	John	Zacchaeus
Shem	Jacob	Zipporah	Saul	Jezebel	Philip	Peter
Ham	Esau	Aaron	Jonathan	Jesus	Bartholomew	David
Japheth	Laban	Balak	Abner	Mary.	Thomas	King Herod
Abraham	Leah	Balaam	Bathsheba	Joseph	Matthew	John The Baptist
Sarah	Joseph	Joshua	Nathan	Gabriel	Thaddeus	Simon The Zealot
Hagar	Benjamin	Monoah	Solomon	Zacharias	Judas	Simon Peter

ANSWERS IN BACK

Genesis 1•1

What did God create?

In the beginning
God created the _h_ _e_ _a_ _v_ _e_ _n_ _s_
and the _e_ _a_ _r_ _t_ _h_.

Can you get through the Heavenly Maze & the Earthly Maze?

START

END

God created?

Down
1 In the beginning, God _____
2 We live on a planet called _____
3 It's always up.
4 Usually more than two legs
5 When it's not day
6 Grown-up Girl

Across
7 What are the four _____ ?
   (Spring, Summer, Fall, Winter)
8 Twinkle, twinkle little _____
9 What has seven days in it?
10 When it's not night
11 Grown-up Boy
12 Earth is one of the _____
   of the solar system.
13 Twelve _____ in one year

All the words below
have to do with creation.
Can you find and circle them?

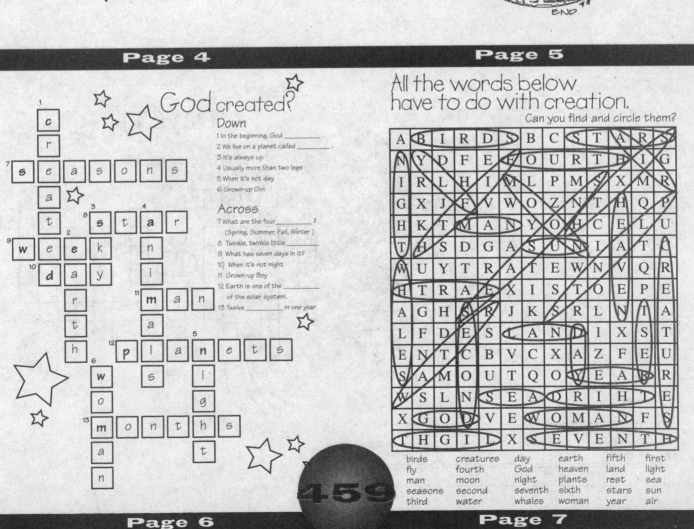

birds	creatures	day	earth	fifth	first
fly	fourth	God	heaven	land	light
man	moon	night	plants	rest	sea
seasons	second	seventh	sixth	stars	sun
third	water	whales	woman	year	air

459

Genesis 1•3
Day ①

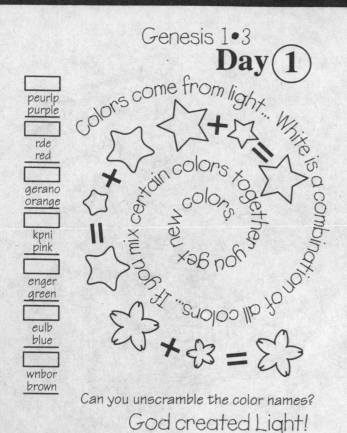

Colors come from light... White is a combination of all colors... If you mix certain colors together you get new colors.

peurlp
purple

rde
red

gerano
orange

kpni
pink

enger
green

eulb
blue

wnbor
brown

Can you unscramble the color names?

God created Light!

Genesis 1•8
Day ②

God called the sky heaven...

odlscu	clouds
idnw	wind
dbisr	birds
nsu	sun
omon	moon
astrs	stars
oerwrksfi	fireworks
nlpea	plane
olnalob	balloon
itgnhilgne	lightening
biwanor	rainbow
wosn	snow
veaenh	heaven

You can find many of these things in the sky!
Can you unscramble these words?

Sometimes clouds can look like funny things!

What do you think these clouds look like?

Next time you're outside,
look at the clouds and see if you can see some funny things!

ice cream cone	teddy bear
dog	face
fish	whale

Genesis 1•9-13
Day ③

God created the seas, land, and vegetation...

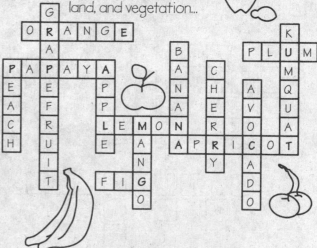

At this time God created fruit trees.
Can you put the fruit in its proper place?

apple • lemon • plum • papaya • cherry
avocado • fig • kumquat • peach • banana
orange • mango • apricot • grapefruit

460

Genesis 1•11-13

God said they would grow after their kind because of the seed he put in the fruit...

Each tree was created to grow one kind of fruit. In this orchard some of the trees are growing the wrong kind of fruit. Can you find and circle them?

God made sure that an apple tree would only grow apples and a plum tree would only grow plums.

Genesis 1•14

"Let there be stars in heaven to separate day from night, and to make known the seasons, days and years."

START

In 1 year we have 4 seasons: Winter, Spring, Summer, and Fall.

Skate into Winter, Jump into Spring, Swim into Summer, and blow into Fall where you will be the winner of all!

YOU WIN

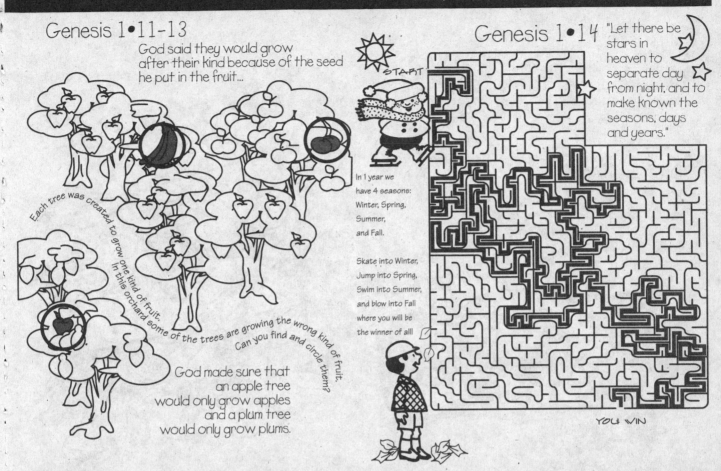

Page 13

Page 14

The earth is where we live. Can you build off the word blocks starting here?

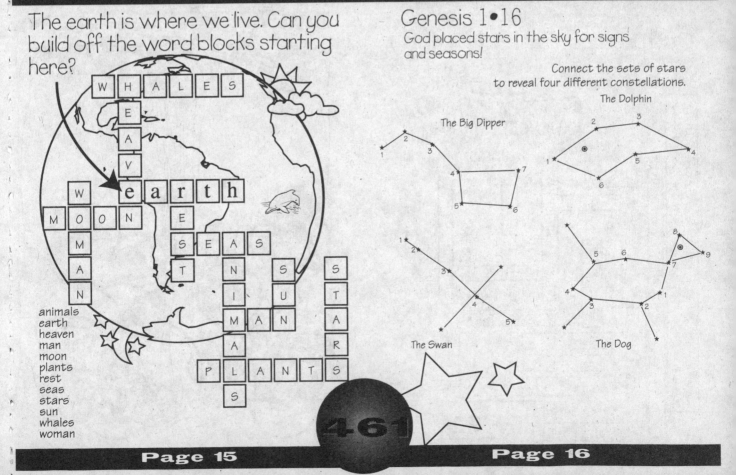

animals
earth
heaven
man
moon
plants
rest
seas
stars
sun
whales
woman

Genesis 1•16

God placed stars in the sky for signs and seasons!

Connect the sets of stars to reveal four different constellations.

The Big Dipper

The Dolphin

The Swan

The Dog

461

Page 15

Page 16

Genesis 1•20
Day (5)

God said, "Let there be living creatures in the water and in the sky..."

What's wrong with this picture?
Find and circle all the funny things!

There are many kinds of creatures in the ocean...

...can you match these creatures with their name!

Whale
Sea Horse
Starfish
Dolphin
Shark
Sea Turtle
Octopus
Sea Snail
Clam
Swordfish
Sea Lion
Sea Otter
Eel
Crab
Squid
Jellyfish
Lobster
Seal

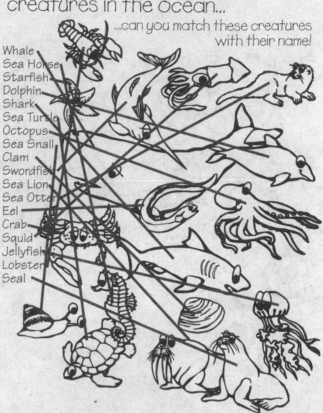

Genesis 1•24
Day (6)

God created cattle and living creatures to fill the earth.

Can you circle the creatures after decoding the symbols

Ant
Beetle
Bull
Cat
Cow
Deer
Dog
Elk
Goat
Horse
Lamb
Lizard
Mouse
Pig
Sheep
Snake
Spider
Toad
Turtle
Worm

God gave man dominion...

... over all the animals.
Help the man by finding as many animals and creatures as you can!

462

God created Eve as a friend and helper for Adam...

... Can you tell Adam which path he should take to find Eve?

This creature moves very slowly. Can you help him reach the pond in the Garden?

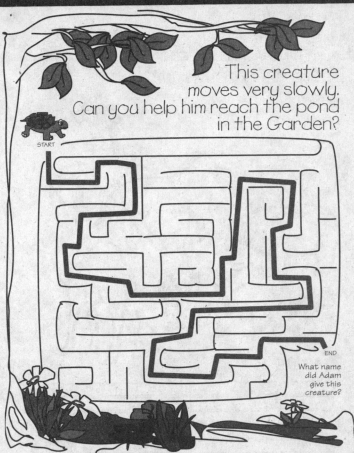

START

END

What name did Adam give this creature?

God made the Garden of Eden for man to live in...

Adam
animals
birds
Eden
Eve ✔
figs
fruit
garden
God
knowledge
leaves
life
plants
rivers
Satan
serpent
tree
water

K	N	O	W	L	W	D	G	E	F
G	L	E	A	V	E	S	T	D	I
O	S	A	T	A	N	N	D	E	G
L	D	T	E	O	E	S	V	N	S
E	R	S	R	P	R	E	F	I	L
T	I	Y	R	E	O	U	S	O	A
I	B	E	V	E	E	D	M	V	M
U	S	I	E	R	O	Y	A	M	I
R	R	U	C	G	A	R	D	E	N
F	P	L	A	N	T	S	A	H	A

...Find all the words about the Garden of Eden in this puzzle. Then fill in the secret phrase below with the uncircled letters!

GOD • LOVES • YOU • SO • VERY • MUCH !

Adam lived to be a very old age!

Do the math and get the answer!

Add 657 and 242 then subtract 503

$$657 + 242 = 899$$
$$899 - 503 = 396$$

Take that number and divide it by 3

$$3\overline{)396} = 132$$

Take your number and add 846

$$132 + 846 = 978$$

Now subtract 132

$$978 - 132 = 846$$

Take this number and divide it by 2

$$2\overline{)846} = 423$$

Take your number and add 452

$$423 + 452 = 875$$

Now subtract 410 and add 465

$$875 - 410 = 465$$
$$465 + 465 = 930$$

How old was Adam?

Can you guess Adam's age?

Genesis 2•8

God planted the garden of "Eden" and put Adam there.

One of the first things God asked Adam to do was to name all the animals!

Can you help give names to these animals?

L A M B	L I O N
S H E E P	C A M E L
D O G	H O R S E
H I P P O	D E E R
C O W	F R O G

GENESIS 2•8

On the following pages...

...you will be asked to guess what type of animals you see.

A	B	C	D	E	F	G	H	I	J	K	L	M	N	O	P	Q	R	S	T	U	V	W	X	Y	Z

If you don't know...

...just use 1 of the 3 codes on this page.

try out this phrase for practice

P R A C T I C E

M A K E S

P E R F E C T

Genesis 2•8

God created the animals!

God brought the animals to the man one by one and asked what he would name them.

Do you know what name Adam gave to this animal? Use the code!

T A P I R

Genesis 1•21

God brought forth...

...every winged fowl after its kind.
Unscramble the names of these winged fowl.

ARPORT
PARROT

LEJY BUA
BLUE JAY

LCRIAADN
CARDINAL

ODEKRWOPCE
WOODPECKER

ODUNRRARNE
ROADRUNNER

How are bird babies born?

OINBR
ROBIN

464

Genesis 2•19
God created the animals...
...and brought them to Adam
to see what he would name them.

HUMMING BIRD

Looking at the picture above,
can you draw this bird?

Cool•Things to Know

Did you know that this
is the only bird that
can fly backward!?

God created the animals!

What is this
animal called?
What type of sound
does it make?

ELEPHANT

End
Genesis 2•19

What would Adam...
...call this little creature when God
brought it to him?

SQUIRRELS

Can you help point the way
to the acorn?
Start

Genesis 2•19
Adam called these?

FROGS

Cool•Things to Know

Did you know that this
animal is in a group called "amphibians?"
This means they live
both in water
and on
land.

What sound do they make?

465

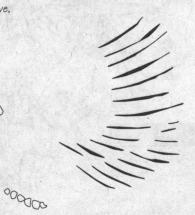

God created the animals!

God brought the animals to the man one by one and asked what he would name them.

PANDA BEAR

Genesis 2•19

How many Horses do you see on this page?

19

Cool•Things to Know

Did you know that except for the ostrich, the horse has the largest eyes of any other land animal? These eyes can move separately from each other so a horse can look forward and backward at the same time.

God is so creative!

God created the creeping things that crawl on the earth.

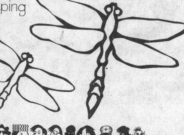

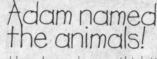
DRAGONFLY

BEES

He created the tiniest insect...

SPIDER

Adam named the animals!

How long do you think it took for Adam to name all the living creatures?

HIPPOPOTAMUS

...to the largest animals.

466

God created unique and individual animals!

Some animals seem fun and friendly.

Just connect the dots to see what comes from down under.

Cool·Things to Know

Did you know that a nickname given to the kangaroo is "Joey?"

Cool·Things to Know

Did you know that this animal is mentioned in the bible 9 times?

UNICORN

God created the animals!

Help the little camel catch up to mom.

Finish

Start

God gives us joy...

Help this creature hop up this maze to get to the carrot. He may not stand on any step that has a star on it or climb up or down a wall with a star on it.

...as we watch his creation.

End

Start

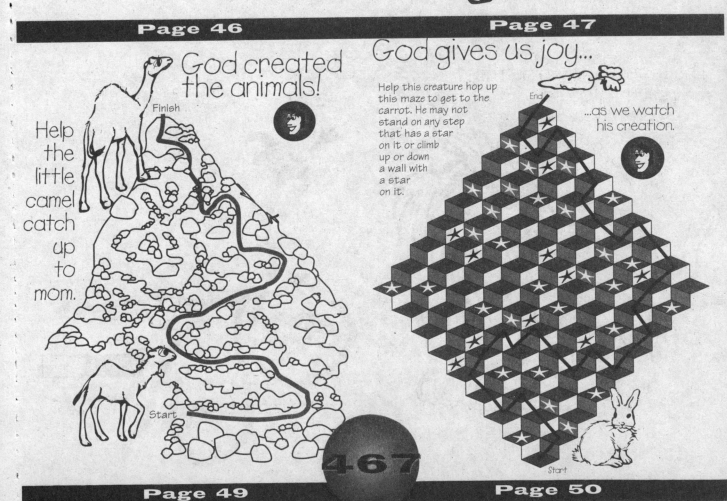

467

Adam took care...
...of the garden for God, and you can take care of the garden here.

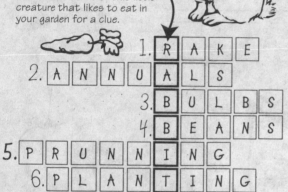

RABBIT

Decode the name of this little creature that likes to eat in your garden for a clue.

1. R A K E
2. A N N U A L S
3. B U L B S
4. B E A N S
5. P R U N N I N G
6. P L A N T I N G

1. When the leaves fall you use this to put the leaves in a pile.
2. These grow from seed, flower and die in one year.
3. Within each one is a flower and all its leaves just waiting for spring.
4. This vegetable sometimes has the word "string" in front of it.
5. This is another word for "trimming the trees."
6. This is what you're doing when you put a seed or plant in the ground.

"Word Games"
Combine these pictures to find the animal name! You may want to draw and color it in.

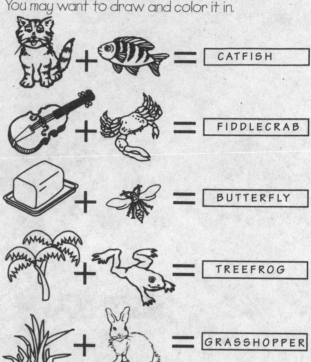

+ = CATFISH

+ = FIDDLECRAB

+ = BUTTERFLY

+ = TREEFROG

+ = GRASSHOPPER

The Lion is known as the King of the Jungle.

Connect the dots and color him COOL!

Start

End

What sounds do Lions make?

Genesis 2•10-14

• A river ran through Eden to water the garden and then split off into four separate rivers.

Garden of Eden

• The first was Pison, which means to surround the land of Havilah. This land was rich in gold.

• The second river was called Gihon and it surrounded Ethiopia.

• The third river was called Hiddekel as it went towards the east of Assyria.

• And the fourth river was called Euphrates.

NSPOI
PISON

Havilah

UHRESTRPE
EUPHRATES

IDKLEEDH
HIDDEKEL

Cool•Things to Know
Did you know that the Euphrates river can still be found on a map of the middle east?

INGHO
GIHON

Ethiopia

468

Genesis 2•17

God's one rule was that Adam and Eve could not eat of the tree of the knowledge of good and evil

God said "For on that day you shall surely <u>die</u>!"

God kept them from eating from the tree of <u>life</u>.

Page 56

Genesis 3•23
Because Adam & Eve disobeyed...
...they were forced out of the garden.

Help Adam & Eve out of the garden.

Start   End

At The Entrance To The Garden Is A Flaming Sword To Keep All Out!

Page 59

Genesis 4•3-5

God was very pleased with Abel's offering and accepted it. But Cain's offering did not please God because it was not his best.

How can we always give God our best?

MATCH THE WORD WITH THE PHRASE OR FILL IN THE BLANKS!

LIE • I will always try to put others _ _ _ _ _.

LOVE • I will not be _ _ _ _ _ _ _.

COMPASSION • I will _ _ _ _ my Mom and Dad.

SELFISH • I will have _ _ _ _ _ _ _ _ _ _ towards others.

TRUTH • I will _ _ _ _ to God.

FAITH • I will _ _ _ _ God.

PRAY • I will have _ _ _ _ _ in God.

OBEY • I will not _ _ _.

FIRST • I will always tell the _ _ _ _ _.

Page 61

"Cain & Able," being brothers,...
...had a rivalry and would compete with each other. Have fun competing with a friend. See who can get through the maze first.

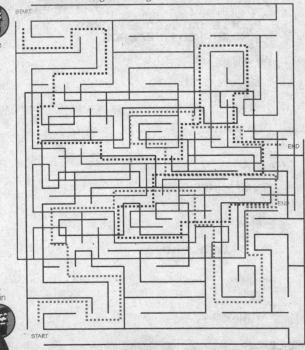

Able

START   END   END

Cain

START

469

One of you take the gray trails, the other the black. If you're gray you can cross black lines, if you're black you can cross gray lines!

Page 62

Cain & Able Genesis 4

Can you find all of the words listed below in this puzzle?
Color in the letters

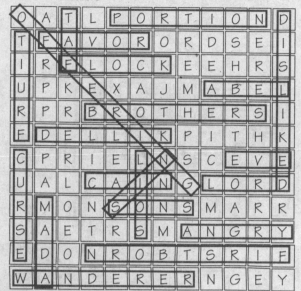

ADAM • EVE • SONS • CAIN • ABEL • FLOCK • SOIL • FRUIT
OFFERING • FAT • FIRSTBORN • PORTION • FAVOR • LORD
DISLIKED • ANGRY • SIN • KILLED • BROTHERS • CURSE
WANDERER

Cain   Able

Genesis 5
The generations of Adam to Noah.

Figure out the centuries,
decades, and years each person lived.

Cool·Things to Know

Did you know that a DECADE = 10 years
and a CENTURY = 100 years?

Description	Centuries	Decades	Years
Adam Lived 930 years	9	3	0
Adam had a son named Seth. He lived 912 years.	9	1	2
Seth had a son named Enosh. He lived 905 years.	9	0	5
Enosh had a son named Kenan. He lived 910 years.	9	1	0
Kenan had a son named Mahalalel. He lived 895 years.	8	9	5
Mahalalel had a son named Jared. He lived 962 years.	9	6	2
Jared had a son named Enoch. He lived 365 years.	3	6	5

Why is Enoch so young compared to the others? Genesis 5:24 says that Enoch walked with God; then he was no more, because God took him away!

Description	Centuries	Decades	Years
Enoch had a son named Methuselah. He lived 969 years.	9	6	9
Methuselah had a son named Lamech. He lived 777 years.	7	7	7

Lamech had a son named Noah…

"Brain Power"
Question & Answers

1. Why did God send the flood?
   PEOPLE HAD BECOME WICKED (AND TURNED FROM GOD)

2. Why did God save Noah?
   NOAH LOVED GOD

3. What did God tell Noah to build to be ready for the flood?
   THE ARK

4. Who helped Noah in his building?
   HIS THREE SONS

5. How many animals did God tell Noah to gather?
   2 OF EACH KIND

6. What sign did God create as a promise between Him and Noah that He would not flood the whole earth again?
   RAINBOW

Noah and the Ark

Noah's son Shem is using the hammer at the far end of the Ark. Can you help Shem get the hammer back to Noah quickly?

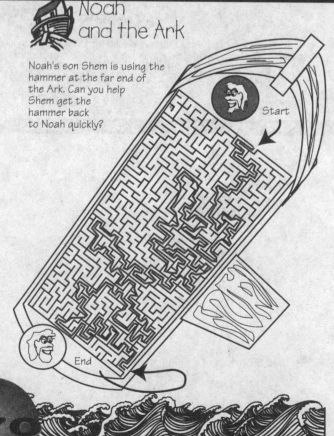

Start

End

470

Noah and the Ark

Noah's 3 sons helped him build the Ark.
Unscramble the letters below and you will know their names.

 SHEM

 HAM

JAPHETH

The Story of Noah and the Ark

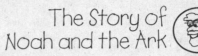

The animals may have gotten a little topsy-turvy after the storm!

Circle the animals that look mixed-up.

Noah and the Ark

GOD   NOAH   ANIMALS   EARTH
EVIL   LOVE   ARK   DOVE
DESTROY   HONEST   RAIN   OLIVE BRANCH
SAVE   FAMILY   FLOOD   RAINBOW

The words above tell the story of Noah and the Ark. Fill in the squares to complete the puzzle!

Noah and the Ark

Have a little animal fun!
Fill in the spaces starting with clue 1.

471

"Two BY 2"

"They went in two by two unto Noah into the ark."
Genesis 7:9

Find the animal names hidden in Noah's Ark!

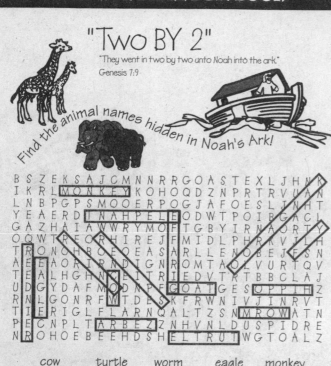

cow turtle worm eagle monkey
zebra elephant fly spider reindeer
giraffe rhino kangaroo hippo goat

"Match Mate"   Noah and the Ark

Help each animal find its mate. Don't get confused and take the wrong path.

Who built the Ark?

___ ___ ___ ___ Look at the puzzle below. How many times can you find his name?

Hint: Look in all directions!

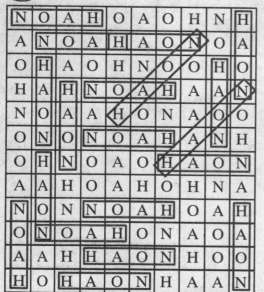

Help Noah navigate...
...these rough ocean waves!

Start

Noah and the Ark

End

472

Search & Read

If you would like to read the story of Noah and the Ark in the Bible, search for the scripture below in the red squares.

N	O	A	H	T	A	O	H	N	H
G	N	O	A	H	H	O	N	O	A
O	E	A	O	H	N	G	O	H	O
H	A	N	N	O	A	H	I	A	N
N	O	A	H	H	O	N	A	E	O
O			GENESIS 3-8						H
O	H	N	O	A	I	G	A	O	N
A	A	H	O	A	U	S	H	N	A
N	O	N	N	O	A	H	S	I	X
O	N	O	R	H	O	N	A	O	A
A	A	H	H	A	O	N	H	O	O
H	T	H	A	O	N	H	A	A	N

Genesis 7•1-3

Noah and the Ark

The Lord told Noah, "Go into the Ark, you and your family. I have found you to be good people in this generation.

Take with you seven of every kind of clean animal, male and female, and two of every kind of unclean animal, male and female. Also take seven of every kind of bird, male and female, to keep them alive throughout the earth.

Clean = God approved for food or sacrifice • Unclean = Not to be eaten or sacrificed

Unscramble the names of these clean and unclean animals

Clean:

UATN	**Tuna**
RUTOT	**Trout**
OUTSCL	**Locust**
ETEBLE	**Beetle**
RSHPERPOSAG	**grasshopper**
XO	**Ox**
HEEPS	**Sheep**
OTGA	**Goat**
ERED	**Deer**
ABLM	**Lamb**
HCENKIC	**Chicken**

Unclean:

AELMC	**Camel**
ABTIBR	**Rabbit**
IGP	**Pig**
OPINHLD	**Dolphin**
OSERTBL	**Lobster**
ALEGE	**Eagle**
UTREULV	**Vulture**
AENVR	**Raven**
WLO	**Owl**
AKWH	**Hawk**
WNAS	**Swan**
EIANCLP	**Pelican**
OSEUM	**Mouse**
OTIESORT	**Tortoise**
IADRZL	**Lizard**

Genesis 7•1-3

From the previous page can you circle which animals and birds were clean? Noah would have seven of these on the Ark.

Noah and the Ark

Help Noah feed the animals!

Draw a line and match the food with the animal.

Cool•Things to Know

One of the largest animals living on land is the elephant. They also have the largest nose (called a "trunk"), the largest ears, and the largest teeth, (called "tusks"). They are very strong and very very smart!

Noah and the Ark

473

"Cow"

Can you find the matching cows that went on Noah's Ark?

Two are the same.

Can you spot them?

Noah
and the Ark

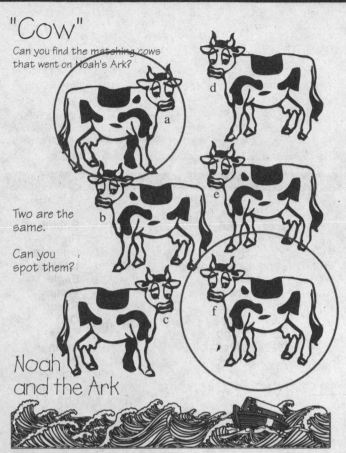

What Kind of animal games might

Draw a line from the letter of the alphabet

A B C D E F G H I J K L M

Noah and his family play on the Ark!

to the animal that begins with that letter!

N O P Q R S T U V W X Y Z

Noah
and the Ark

The Ark was so big that these ants got separated!

Help them find each other.

Start

End

Noah
and the Ark

474

"Bears"

Noah and the Ark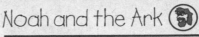

Can you find the matching pair of bears?

Cool·Things to Know

Did you know that Genesis 7:15-16 tells us that pairs of all the creatures came to Noah. When they were all there and in the Ark God shut the door to the Ark!

What are bears known to do in the winter?

Noah and the Ark

"Zebra"

How many Zebras can you find?

Page 106

Page 107

"Animal Guess"

Do you know your animals?

A **SHEEP** is good for wool.

A **CAT** has nine lives.

I never forget: I'm an **ELEPHANT**.

I jump high; I jump low; I'm a **KANGAROO**. I store my baby in a pouch.

The **CAMEL** is known for desert travel.

I swing from tree to tree. You're right— I'm a **MONKEY**.

Is a **ZEBRA** white with black stripes or black with white stripes?

I love to eat hay, and I love to nay. I'm a **HORSE** of course!

Noah and the Ark

Genesis 9•9-11

God's Covenant with Noah

Using the code, read what God's covenant was.

A = ❊
B = ♣
C = 🏛
D = ▲
E = ☆
F = ✿
G = ⊞
H = ⛵
I = ⬠
J = ✟
K = ✠
L = ▢
M = ▟
N = ♣
O = ◗
P = ▽
Q = 🏛
R = ✿
S = ✲
T = ◎
U = ⛺
V = ♣
W = ☙
X = ❖
Y = ♔
Z = ☾

"I NOW ESTABLISH MY COVENANT WITH YOU AND WITH YOUR FAMILIES AFTER YOU AND WITH ALL LIVING CREATURES THAT WERE WITH YOU ON THE ARK: BIRDS, LIVESTOCK, WILD ANIMALS, EVERY LIVING CREATURE ON EARTH. I MAKE MY COVENANT WITH YOU: NEVER AGAIN WILL ALL LIFE BE DESTROYED BY WATERS OF A FLOOD; NEVER AGAIN WILL THERE BE A FLOOD TO DESTROY THE EARTH."

475

Page 108

Page 126

Noah lived to be a very old age!

Do the math and get the answer.

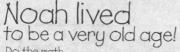

Can you guess Noah's age?

Multiply 400 by 200 then subtract 375

```
  400
   x2
 ─────
  800
 -375
 ─────
```

Take that number and add 95

```
  425
  +95
 ─────
  520
```

Take this number and divide it by 5

```
  104
5/520
```

Take your number and multiply by 10

```
  104
  x10
 ─────
 1040
```

Now subtract 205

```
 1040
 -205
 ─────
  835
```

Take this number and add 175

```
  835
 +175
 ─────
 1010
```

Take this number and divide it by 5

```
  202
5/1010
```

Now multiply your number by 3 then add 344

```
  202
   x3
 ─────
  606
 +344
 ─────
  950
```

How old was Noah?

Genesis 8•11

...and the dove came back to Noah with a newly sprouted _____; Noah knew that the waters had dried from the land.

OLIVE BRANCH

Genesis 11•9
The Lord God confounded all the languages of the earth.

Follow the arrows to reveal why God caused speech to be confused!

End

Start

THE TOWER OF BABEL

Use the code from page 24 to figure out what this says!

476

Cool•Things to Know

There are over 5 million people in the world and they speak over 9,000 languages.

New languages are still being discovered in remote places.

African
Aramaic
British
Celtic
Chinese
Dutch
English
French
German
Greek
Hebrew
Hindi
Irish
Italian
Japanese
Latin
Mandarin
Norwegian
Polish
Portuguese
Russian
Spanish
Swedish

```
A Z W N I R A D N A M E X J
U F R E N C H W E R B E H A
A Z R W A B R I T I S H A P
Y N W I K A C H I N E S E A
N A J E C V A I S Z C H R N
A M E A E A Q N W E A A L E
I R B Z L A N D E A M C A S
G E A C T R A I D A Z A P E
E G J A I W A H I K A A A X
W D U T C H A C S A N H W N
R R U S S I A N H I A W B I
O A K I A Z Q C S A L A P T
N Q L I R I S H A C A G A A
A O B N A I L A T I A V N L
P O R T U G U E S E W Y T E
```

Look at the list of languages and find them in the puzzle - Look backwards and forwards, up then down. Color them in with green or brown!

This **MAN** is lost in the Tower of Babel. He can't find anyone who speaks his language. Can you help him get out?

Start

End

Start with Tower of Babel.
see how many words you can make that have to do with TYPES OF communication. Use the tiles below!

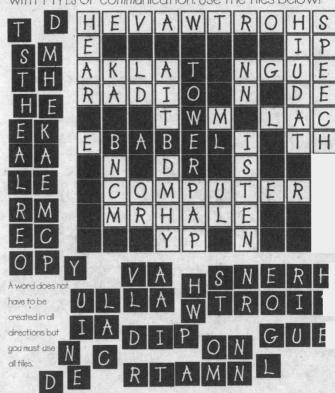

A word does not have to be created in all directions but you must use all tiles.

Genesis 12•1

God tells Abram to move...
...from the land where he and his family lived and to go to a and that God would show him.

Start here

Abram was a very obedient man of God. Can you help him and his family get from Haran to Canaan? Along the way they stopped at Sichem.

Go from Haran to Sichem and then to Canaan.

End here

What's in a name?
Fill in the puzzle below

	A
A B R A M	

A R A H A M

S A R A H

A S A R A I
G A E S
J A C O B S A
R E S A U
B C
K
A

I S H M A E L
O
T

Clues
1. His name before God changed it
2. Her name before God changed it
3. His new name name symbolizing God's promise.
4. Her new name symbolizing Abraham's promise to God.
5. Abram's first born son
6. The son Abraham was told to sacrifice
7. The mother of Ishmael
8. Isaac's wife
9. Isaac's first twin son
10. Isaac's second twin son
11. Abraham's nephew

God changed Abram's name...

...to Abraham. There is a lot to a persons name. Abram means "high" and Abraham means "father of multitudes."

S	P	A	T	R	I	A	R	C	H	S
S	A	B	R	A	H	A	M	O	A	H
I	I	S	A	A	C	E	N	C	S	O
C	S	W	O	R	O	A	R	D	A	B
H	A	R	A	D	N	I	H	W	R	E
E	R	M	R	N	F	S	H	D	O	D
M	A	D	A	I	D	W	O	E	R	I
O	H	C	C	I	S	R	A	E	L	E
E	A	E	O	S	H	A	R	A	N	N
A	B	R	A	M	H	W	H	R	O	T

Look at the list of words. Find and color them in..

Abram	Israel
Obedient	Abraham
Haran	Sacrifice
Canaan	Ram
Sichem	Sarah
Patriarch	Isaac

Camels can carry up to 400 lbs and can travel swiftly through the desert at about 8 to 10 miles an hour.

I love to drink a lot of water- especially when the weather's hotter!

God often used Angels as messengers...

...In fact, angel means 'messenger.'

North
West ✚ East
South

For Sale

478

SHEEP

The Desert night sky is clear and full of stars...

How many triangles can you count in this one?

176

Abraham's servant gave Rebekah beautifully embroidered cloth.

Find your way though the maze.

Start

End

Help the ram get out ot the thicket.

Find your way though the maze.

End

Start

It pleases God when we obey him.

How do we obey God?
Match the picture with the right sentence.

When I help my mom and dad, I am obeying God.

When I pray, I am obeying God.

When I help my friends, I am obeying God.

When I love others and do not fight, I am obeying God.

When I help others who are sick or lonely, I am obeying God.

Can you write some other ways that you obey God?

479

North, south, east, or west: where will Abram stop to rest?

Help Abram get to the land of Canaan.

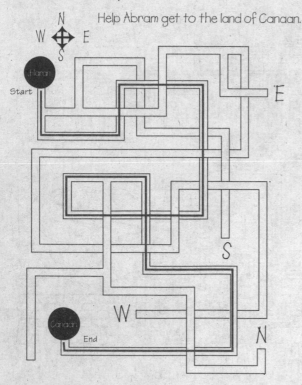

N
W ✦ E
S

Start
Haran

E

S

W

N

End
Canaan

Genesis 12•1-3

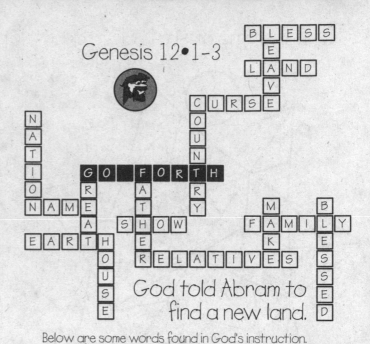

B L E S S
L E A V E
L A N D
C U R S E
C O U N T R Y
N A T I O N
G O   F O R T H
G R E A T
N A M E   F A T H E R
S H O W   M A K E   F A M I L Y   B L E S S E D
E A R T H   H O U S E   R E L A T I V E S

God told Abram to find a new land.

Below are some words found in God's instruction.

Country	Land	Bless	House
Relatives	Show	Name	Nation
Leave	Make	Curse	Blessed
Father	Great	Family	Earth

What did God tell Abram to take with him on his journey?

Unscramble the words below to find out!

1. fWie aSiar   WIFE SARAI
2. pwheeN otL   NEPHEW LOT
3. vsrntSeas   SERVANTS
4. lodG   GOLD
5. lerivS   SILVER
6. nTtse   TENTS
7. hepSe   SHEEP
8. tlaCte   CATTLE
9. nkyoneD   DONKEY

In old times people had to use the sun, moon, and stars to help direct them when they traveled.

If God Told Abram to travel SOUTH, which way would he go?

N
W ✦ E
S

Start

End

480

God told Abram to look to the heavens and count the stars.

This was to show Abram God's promise of multiplying his family, generation to generation.

90

Connect the stars...

...to hear what God would say to you!

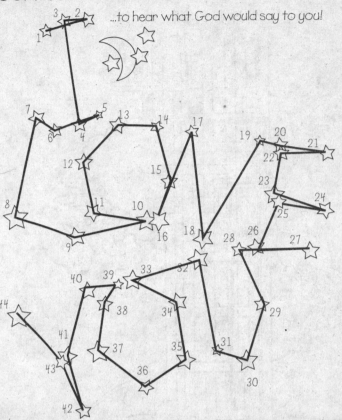

Can you guess what I am?

Clues are in God's promises to Abraham!

What am I?

3. If I were an old man you might think it was my snore: the pounding of waves on the...

SHORE

1. I shine brightly in the sky. When people draw me I have points of 5...

STAR

4. I am what all plants need. Large or small I'm called a...

SEED

2. I touch the ocean, I touch the land, I'm zillions of tiny rocks, called...

SAND

5. Add, subtract, divide: the one word missing is...

MULTIPLY

Isaac and Rebekah had twin boys named Esau & Jacob.

The name Esau means "hairy" and Jacob means "heel-catcher."

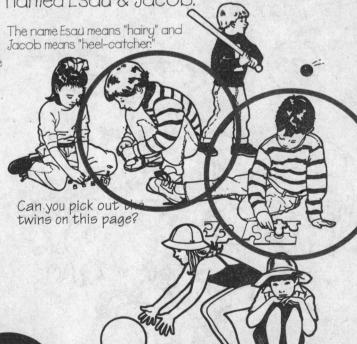

Can you pick out the twins on this page?

481

Genesis 28•10-19
Jacob has a dream of a ladder...

Can you get from the top to the bottom?

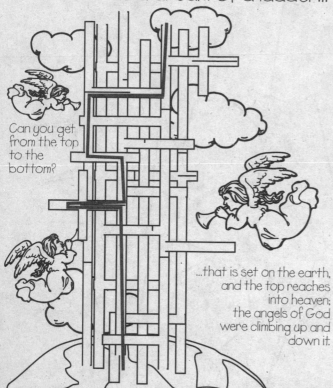

...that is set on the earth, and the top reaches into heaven; the angels of God were climbing up and down it.

Page 171

Genesis 29•1-14
Jacob meets Rachel at the well of Haran...

Rachel is bringing her father's sheep to the well for water. Can you help her get to Jacob?

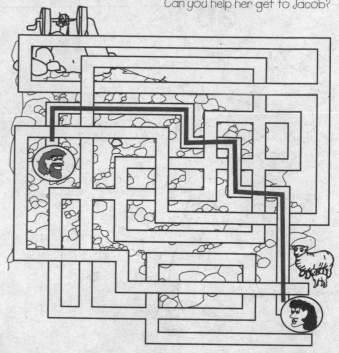

Page 172

Genesis 29•13
Jacob goes with Rachel to meet her dad, Laban.

(23)

To marry Rachel, Jacob must feed and care for Laban's flocks for 7 years.

Jacob has favor with God and God blesses the flock with strength and numbers. How many sheep, lambs and goats do you see?

Page 173

Genesis 31•1-20
After Laban tricked Jacob into marrying Leah...

(14)

...he allowed Jacob to take Rachel as his wife for another 7 years of labor. After that, Jacob contracted to leave with the Speckled and spotted sheep, brown sheep, amd speclked and spotted goats.

Can you help Jacob by coloring the animals so that he can take them?

How many of each should Jacob have?

482

Page 174

Help Jacob, Leah, and Rachel find their way through the desert to Canaan.

End

Start

A ✡
B ✚
C ✣
D ✤
E ◆
F ☆
G ★
H ✩
I ◉
J ✪
K ★
L ★
M ★
N ✰
O ☆
P ✮
Q ✷
R ✳
S ✴
T ✶
U ✵
V ✳
W ✳
X ✳
Y ✳
Z ✳

All of these people are in Jacob's family.

Guess their names using the code!

✡✳✪✳✚ ISAAC is the father of ◉✪✚✣ JACOB.
Jacob has a big brother named ✣✳✪★ ESAU, whom
Jacob and his mother ✣✚✳✚✡✳★ REBEKAH, tricked
into giving Jacob his birthright as the firstborn.
Jacob wants to marry Rachel, but is tricked by ★✪✳✡★
LABAN, Leah's father, into marrying ★✪✪★ LEAH first.
Two weeks after Jacob marries Leah he is then allowed by
Laban to marry ★✪✳★✪✳★ RACHEL.
Jacob and Leah have lots of children. The boys are
✣✪✚✳✪✳★ REUBEN, ★✳✡★★✳★ SIMEON, ✣✣★✩ LEVI,
◉✪✣✪★ JUDAH, ✡★★✪✳✪✣★ ISSACHAR, and
★✪✳★★★✳ ZEBULUN. They also have one daughter.
Her name is ✣✩✪★✪★ DINAH.
Jacob and Rachel do not have as many children. They
have two boys, ◉★★✣✪★ JOSEPH and
✚✣★◉✪★✩★BENJAMIN.

Can you find these colors in the puzzle below?

Cyan
Bone
Ruby
Red
Green
Purple
Blue
Gold
Silver
Orange
Violet
Yellow
Pink
Gray
Taupe
Amber
Teal
Mauve
Olive
Brown
Wine
Plum

B	R	O	W	N	S	C	Y	A	N
O	U	C	K	N	I	P	G	Z	X
N	B	P	Y	E	L	L	O	W	A
E	Y	U	G	T	V	U	L	V	M
D	E	R	B	I	E	M	D	N	B
M	A	I	O	O	R	A	N	G	E
Y	E	L	U	E	A	U	L	S	R
N	E	E	R	G	E	V	I	L	O
T	A	U	P	E	D	E	N	I	W

Know your colors!

Color the objects using the colors listed.
Then draw a line from the color to the matching picture.

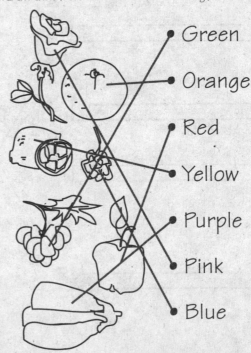

Green

Orange

Red

Yellow

Purple

Pink

Blue

483

The Letter "e" is common in each of the colors from the last page...

...except 1. Which color does not have the letter "e" in it?
Can you fill in the missing letters for all the other colors?

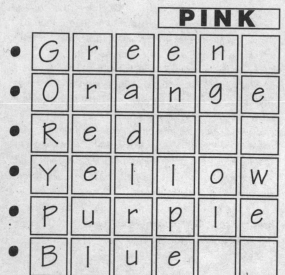

PINK

- G r e e n
- O r a n g e
- R e d
- Y e l l o w
- P u r p l e
- B l u e

Colorful

1. If you go around WEARING ROSE-COLORED GLASSES it means...
   a. you had juice for breakfast.
   b. you think everything in the world is fine.
   c. you are watching a 3-D movie.

2. If your Uncle John has a GREEN THUMB it means...
   a. he is rich.
   b. he is not feeling well.
   c. he can grow plants well.

3. If your sister is GREEN WITH ENVY it means...
   a. she is jealous.
   b. she is lucky.
   c. she is hungry.

4. If your mom is SEEING RED it means...
   a. she is wearing rose-colored glasses.
   b. she is angry.
   c. she is from Russia.

Language

5. If your doctor says you're IN THE PINK it means...
   a. you are cooked medium rare.
   b. you are quite well.
   c. you are out of breath.

6. If your dad says this is a RED-LETTER DAY it means...
   a. you did poorly on your report card.
   b. something important is going to happen
   c. today is your birthday.

A+

7. If a kid on the playground has a YELLOW-STREAK it means...
   a. he is chicken.
   b. his hair is blond.
   c. he has been painting.

8. If your friend is FEELING BLUE it means...
   a. she is sleepy.
   b. she is listening to music.
   c. she is sad.

Genesis 38•26-36

Because Joseph's brothers are so angry and jealous, they decide to sell Joseph into slavery.

God turns this to good and causes Joseph to become a great man in Egypt.

Potiphar, the captain of the royal guards, was Joseph's owner. He gave responsibility for all household matters to Joseph.

God had favor on Joseph and all that he touched prospered.

Joseph has Control of Potiphar's household

Joseph would have been very good with numbers. See if you can figure out these addition blocks.

9	9	3
3	9	9
9	3	9	21

9	9	9	7
9	9	7	9
7	9	9	9
9	7	9	9	34

9	8	9	8
9	9	7	9
8	9	8	9
8	8	9	9	34

484

Joseph lived in Potiphar's house.

What are some of the things he might have seen when he looked out his window?

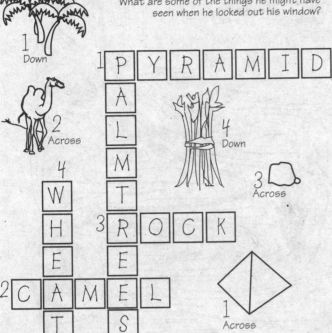

1 Down

2 Across

4 Down

3 Across

4

1 Across

```
1 P Y R A M I D
  A
  L
  M       4
  T       Down
3 R O C K
  E
  E
2 C A M E L
  T
  S
```

Joseph had a very special dinner for his brothers called a feast.

Circle the words in the puzzle below that tell you what you might find at an Egyptian feast!

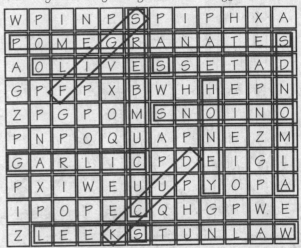

```
W P I N P S P I P H X A
P O M E G R A N A T E S
A O L I V E S S E T A D
G P F P X B W H H E P N
Z P G P O M S N O I N O
P N P O Q U A P N E Z M
G A R L I C P D E I G L
P X I W E U U P Y O P A
I P O P E C Q H G P W E
Z L E E K S T U N L A W
```

cucumbers	garlic	walnuts
duck	olives	dates
leeks	onions	honey
pomegranates	figs	almonds

Joseph hid his cup in his brother's bag of grain.

See if you can find it below

Joseph is no longer a slave in Egypt, but a ruler in the land of the pyramids.

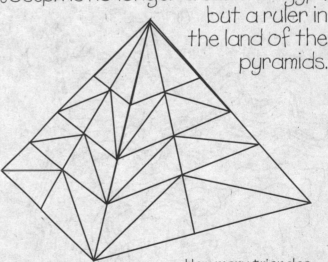

How many triangles can you count?

Cool·Things to Know

The Pyramids in Egypt were built over 4,000 years ago. They served as tombs for the pharaohs.

66

485

Baby Moses...

...was hidden from Pharaoh. Some other things are also hidden! Can you find all 10?

Baby Moses
Pharaoh's Daughter
Mouse
Frog
Crown
Shepherd's staff
Grasshopper
Cup
Bricks
Pyramid

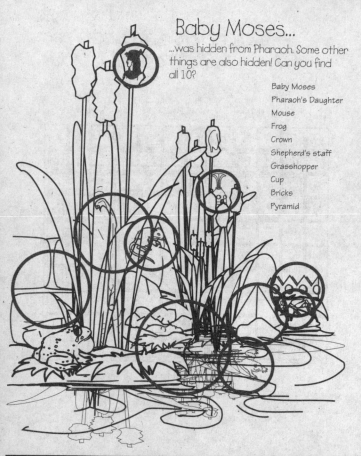

Baby Moses...

Moses' Story

Start

...was too big to hide, so his mom decided to place him in a basket that was made to float in the river.

Can you help baby Moses float down the river?

End

Page 214

Page 215

Help Moses Reach the burning bush!

End

Start

In Exodus 14 God said to Moses

"I AM WHO I AM and WHAT I AM, and I WILL BE WHAT I WILL BE."

We use many names for God. Here are some examples below. Can you unscramble all these names? Do you have a name for God?

God	dolr odg	**LORD GOD**
God Almighty	odg mgythila	**GOD ALMIGHTY**
Living God	l ma	**I AM**
Heavenly Father	dgo fo sohst	**GOD OF HOSTS**
Lord God	vngiil dgo	**LIVING GOD**
I AM	eoahvhj	**JEHOVAH**
Jehovah	dgo fo evaenh	**GOD OF HEAVEN**
King Eternal	aelynveh htfare	**HEAVENLY FATHER**
Most High God	ihytgm odg	**MIGHTY GOD**
God of Hosts	dgo	**GOD**
Father	mgthyila odg	**ALMIGHTY GOD**
Holy One of Israel	leusoja	**JEALOUS**
Mighty God	tralnee odg	**ETERNAL GOD**
Almighty God	lyho eon fo reilsa	**HOLY ONE OF ISRAEL**
Jealous	gikn treanle	**KING ETERNAL**
Father of Light	somt gihh dgo	**MOST HIGH GOD**
Everlasting God	vratngislee dgo	**EVERLASTING GOD**
Eternal God	ehfrat fo ihgtl	**FATHER OF LIGHT**
God of Heaven	cenniat fo asdy	**ANCIENT OF DAYS**
Ancient of Days	tharfh	**FATHER**

486

Page 217

Page 219

In the Book of Exodus God had a message for Pharaoh...
...to be delivered by Moses.

Using the words listed fill in the boxes, one letter in each. When all the letters are in the right place, a message will appear.

Egypt
Israelites
Egyptians
Hardships
Pharaoh
Baby
Boy
Daughter
Plagues
Moses
Death
Freedom
Gave

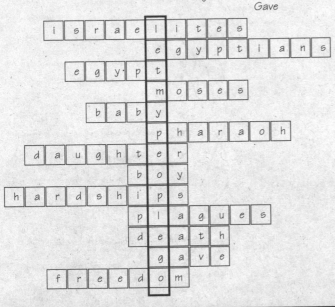

i s r a e l i t e s
e g y p t i a n s
e g y p t
m o s e s
b a b y
p h a r a o h
d a u g h t e r
b o y
h a r d s h i p s
p l a g u e s
d e a t h
g a v e
f r e e d o m

In Exodus when God sent Moses to Pharaoh...
...to ask him to let God's people go, Pharaoh would not let them go.

Because of the hardness of Pharaoh's heart, God sent 10 plagues.

7. h a i l
1. b l o o d
a r k n
8. l i v e s t o c k
5. l o c u s t s
4. f l i e s
10. 2. f r o g s
i n a t s
6. b o i l s

1. Strike the water of the Nile, and it will be changed into ____.

2. Stretch out your hand over streams and ponds and make ____ jump everywhere.

3. Stretch out your staff and strike the dust of the ground and the dust will become ____.

4. God sent swarms of ____ upon all the Egyptians.

5. A terrible plague on your ____ in the fields: cattle, horses, donkeys, and camels.

6. Take handfuls of soot from a furnace and toss it into the air in the presence of Pharaoh. Festering ____ will break out on men and animals of Egypt.

7. Stretch out your hand toward the sky so that ____ will fall over Egypt.

8. Stretch out your hand over Egypt so that ____ will swarm over the land and devour everything growing.

9. Stretch out your hand toward the sky so that ____ will spread over Egypt.

10. At midnight the Lord struck down all the ____ in Egypt.

Exodus 12•1-11

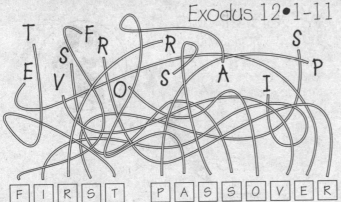

T E S F R O S A S P
S V I

F I R S T   P A S S O V E R

God told the Israelites to have a special meal once a year on the same day. This meal helps them to remember how God saved their ancestors when they were slaves in Egypt.

Follow the paths to find the answer!

Cool·Things to Know

Did you know that God set this celebration to be in the first month of the new year for the Israelites?

487

"Wilderness"
Moses led Israel out of Egypt when Pharaoh finally let them go.

The Israelites wandered through the wilderness for 40 years. Help them to find a message by picking up letters along the way. Only one path has the right letters.

"Red Sea"

By the time Moses got to the Red Sea, Pharaoh realized what he had done and went after them!

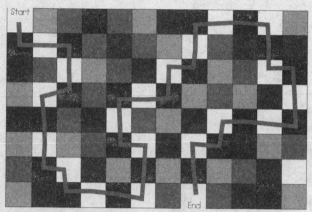

Start

End

The Israelites had to cross the sea to get away from Pharaoh. God instructed Moses to lift his rod and divide the waters of the sea so that the people could walk on dry ground.

Start on the WHITE square and then go to the BLACK square touching it. Then go WHITE, BLACK, WHITE, and so forth. (Do not go corner to corner)

Cool•Things to Know

Did you know that God first knocked off the wheels of the Egyptian's chariots before the Red Sea flowed back together?

"Brain Power"

Question & Answers

Match the right answer with the question...

Pour it upon dry land

Go back to Egypt and set the Israelites free

Sinai

Killed

Fear

To keep him from dying

Freedom from bondage

I am Who I am and What I am and I Will Be What I Will Be

Turned into Blood

Moses' Sister

The Flocks

Snake

Aaron

Pharaoh's daughter

Burning Bush

Leprosy

...by drawing a line between the dots!

Ten

Passover

1. What caused the Pharaoh to be so hard on the Israelites?
2. Why did Moses' mother put him in a basket to float down the river?
3. Who did Moses' mother send to follow the basket down the river?
4. Who found the basket and kept the baby Moses?
5. What did Moses do that was wrong and resulted in his running away from Egypt?
6. After Moses left Egypt, the Israelites kept crying out to God for what?
7. When Moses fled to Midian and married Zipporah he took care of what?
8. What did Moses see on the mountain of God?
9. What is this mountain called?
10. When Moses spoke to God, who did God say He was?
11. What did God ask Moses to do?
12. God caused Moses' Shepherd stick to turn into something. What was it?
13. God also caused Moses' hand to get a disease called _____.
14. What did God tell Moses to do with the water from the Nile River?
15. What happened to the water when Moses obeyed God?
16. What was Moses' brother's name?
17. How many plagues did God send upon Egypt before Pharaoh let God's people go?
18. At the last plague God, provided a way to protect the firstborn of those who loved God. What was this called?

"The Tabernacle"

A place to worship God in the desert.

Exodus 25

The Lord asked Moses to build a tabernacle. He tells Moses to take an offering from all the Israelites and ask them to give of their gold, silver, bronze; blue, purple and scarlet yarn and fine linen; goat hair; ram skins dyed red; acacia wood; olive oil and spices; and onyx stones and other gems.

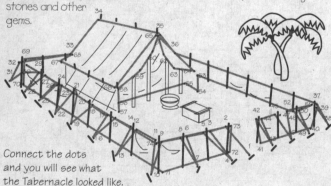

Connect the dots and you will see what the Tabernacle looked like.

Cool•Things to Know

Did you know that all the precious items used to build the tabernacle were given to the Hebrews by the Egyptians? You can read about this in Exodus 12•35-36.

Moses lived to be very old!

Moses lived long, but not as long as his ancestors. Why do you think that is?

Do the math and find out how old Moses lived to be.

Add 50 and 49 together

$$\begin{array}{r} 50 \\ +49 \\ \hline 99 \end{array}$$

Take that number and add 139

$$\begin{array}{r} +139 \\ \hline 238 \end{array}$$

Take this number and subtract 50

$$\begin{array}{r} 238 \\ -50 \\ \hline 188 \end{array}$$

Take your number and add 20

$$\begin{array}{r} 188 \\ +20 \\ \hline 208 \end{array}$$

Can you guess Moses' age?

Take this number and subtract 100

$$\begin{array}{r} 208 \\ -100 \\ \hline 108 \end{array}$$

Now add 12

$$\begin{array}{r} 108 \\ +12 \\ \hline 120 \end{array}$$

How old was Moses?

Cool•Things to Know

There have been many great prophets since Moses, but Moses was the last prophet to have a very special face to face relationship with God. God gave Moses many special miraculous signs and wonders to do while he was in Egypt. All of these helped in getting Pharaoh to let God's people go. If you want to read about this, read Deuteronomy 34.

488

"Deuteronomy 33"
Before Moses died he blessed the tribes of Israel.

Below are listed the names of the twelve tribes.

Can you find all the names in the boxes below?
Circle them or color them in.

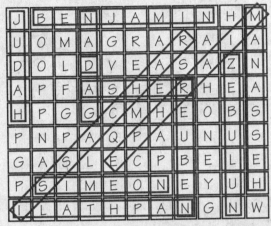

| Asher | Benjamin | Dan | Ephraim | Gad | Issachar |
| Judah | Manasseh | Naphtali | Reuben | Simeon | Zebulun |

"Basketful of Blessings"
In the basket, unscramble the words to discover a multitude of blessings Moses enjoyed through his life!

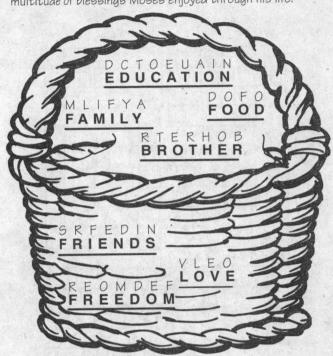

DCTOEUAIN
EDUCATION

MLIFYA
FAMILY

DOFO
FOOD

RTERHOB
BROTHER

SRFEDIN
FRIENDS

VLEO
LOVE

REOMDEF
FREEDOM

"Pillar of Smoke"
By day the Lord went before the children of Israel in a pillar of cloud.

Start

End

Cool·Things to Know   Exodus 13•21 also says that God watch over them by night from a pillar of fire.

"Scramble"
The scrambled message below reads God said, "Let my people go.."

There is one letter missing.
Can you find which one?

GOD SAID, "LET MY PEOPLE GO."

O

489

"God is Everywhere"

By day the Lord was there in a pillar of cloud. By night the Lord was there in a pillar of fire. When they where hungry, God brought manna from heaven.

How many times can you find God hidden in the puzzle? Look every direction you can.

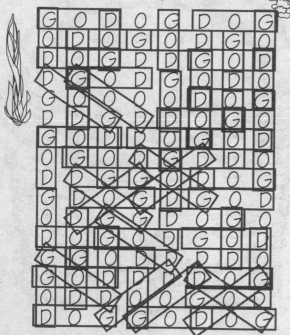

"Manna from Heaven"

Every day God's people would go out and gather Manna in the morning. In the evening the Lord brought Quail.

Exodus 16•2-13

"Donkey Maze"

Numbers 22:23 The donkey sees the angel of the Lord standing in the road.

Balaam's donkey takes the wrong path to get away from the angel of the Lord. Help her to find a path where Balaam can see the Angel.

Balaam and the Donkey

"Speaking Blessing"

Numbers 23•11 Balak wanted Balaam to curse the Israelites, but instead Balaam blessed them. What did God say to Balaam to keep him from speaking curses?

Balaam and the Donkey

By using multiplication you can figure out the code and solve the answer below.

$4 \times 4 =$ **16** (T) $6 \times 9 =$ **54** (C) $4 \times 6 =$ **24** (Y)
$6 \times 8 =$ **48** (A) $7 \times 8 =$ **56** (P) $12 \times 3 =$ **36** (M)
$8 \times 4 =$ **32** (B) $3 \times 6 =$ **18** (R) $5 \times 3 =$ **15** (U)
$3 \times 7 =$ **21** (G) $3 \times 3 =$ **9** (O) $4 \times 15 =$ **60** (D)
$9 \times 9 =$ **81** (H) $7 \times 4 =$ **28** (N) $8 \times 9 =$ **72** (S)
$6 \times 7 =$ **42** (E) $4 \times 3 =$ **12** (I) $8 \times 12 =$ **96** (L)

"   24 9 15   36 15 72 16   28 9 16   56 15 16
Y O U   M U S T   N O T   P U T

48   54 15 18 72 42   9 28   16 81 9 72 42
A   C U R S E   O N   T H O S E

56 42 9 56 96 42   32 42 54 48 15 72 42
P E O P L E ,   B E C A U S E

16 81 42 24   48 18 42   32 96 42 72 72 42 60
T H E Y   A R E   B L E S S E D   "

490

"Jericho"

Walls of Jericho

The Walls of Jericho came falling down!

The City of Jericho sat on top of a hill. The walls of the city were so big that many of the people who lived in Jericho built their homes in the wall.

Connect the dots to see what the city might look like!

"Joshua 5&6"

Walls of Jericho

The Walls of Jericho came falling down!

God told Joshua to march around the city walls with his army one time a day for six days. While they marched, seven priests carried horns in front of the ark of the covenant. On the seventh day they marched around the city walls seven times and the priests blew on the trumpets. When the people heard the loud blast of the horns they shouted very loudly. Then the walls of Jericho came falling down!

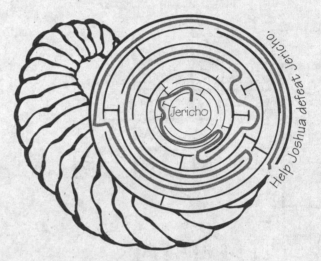

Help Joshua defeat Jericho.

"Joshua obeyed..."

Walls of Jericho

...the instructions God gave him, and the walls of Jericho came falling down.

Fall
Jericho
Sword
Army
Lord
Wall
City
Delivered
King
March
Trumpets
Ram's Horn
Seven
Shout
Ark
Priests

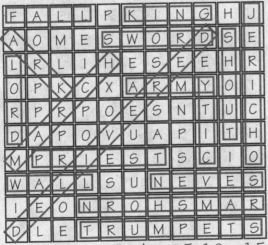

Joshua 5: 13 - 15
and 6:1 - 5

"Jericho"

Walls of Jericho

Find these hidden items in the walls of Jericho...

Sword
Angel
Sandals
King's crown
Ram's Horn
Silver coin
Gold Cup

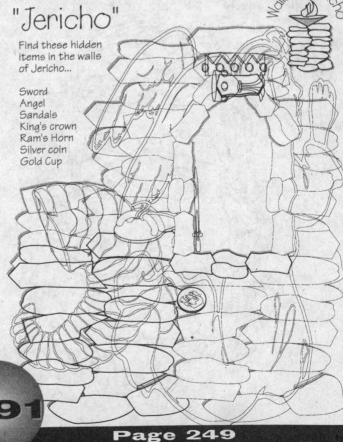

491

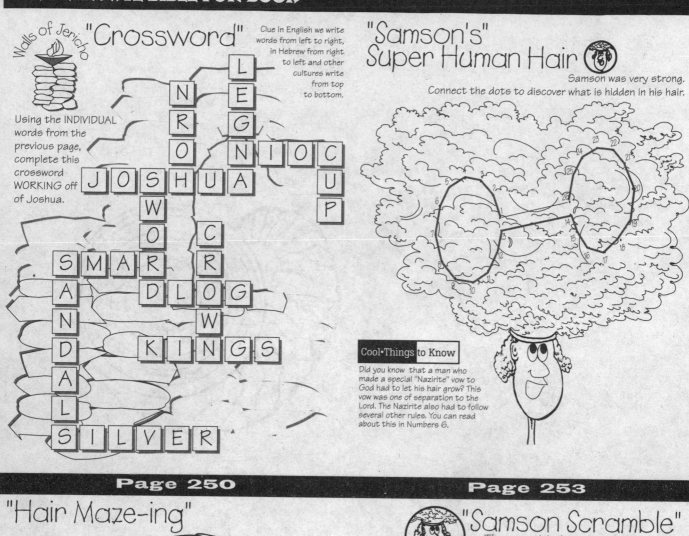

"Crossword"

Walls of Jericho

Clue In English we write words from left to right, in Hebrew from right to left and other cultures write from top to bottom.

Using the INDIVIDUAL words from the previous page, complete this crossword WORKING off of Joshua.

"Samson's" Super Human Hair

Samson was very strong.
Connect the dots to discover what is hidden in his hair.

Cool•Things to Know

Did you know that a man who made a special "Nazirite" vow to God had to let his hair grow? This vow was one of separation to the Lord. The Nazirite also had to follow several other rules. You can read about this in Numbers 6.

"Hair Maze-ing"

Samson's hair was very, very long.

How long will it take you to get through this hairy maze?

Start

End

"Samson Scramble"

The scrambled message below reads "Samson's hair makes him very strong."

Oops! There's one letter missing. Can you find which one?

492

m

What do you remember?

Using the Samson story, fill in the blanks to these sentences.

1. An A N G E L of the Lord appeared to Samson's mother and father, telling them they were going to have a S O N.

2. Samson's mother, Z O R A H, could not drink wine or eat any unclean thing while she was pregnant.

3. They were also told never to C U T Samson's H A I R.

4. Samson would one day begin the D E L I V E R A N C E of Israel from the P H I L I S T I A N E S, their enemies.

5. Samson was very S T R O N G because his hair had never been cut.

6. Samson fell in love with D E L I L A H, a Philistine.

7. Samson said if his head was S H A V E D his strength would L E A V E him and he would become as W E A K as any man.

8. Delilah told the Philistine rulers and they shaved Samson's hair while he was A S L E E P.

9. Samson was put in P R I S O N by the Philistine.

10. One day the Philistines were having a big C E L E B R A T I O N, and brought Samson to it.

11. Samson asked G O D to give him S P E C I A L strength just one more time so he could D E F E A T his enemies.

12. Samson put his arms out toward the two main P I L L A R S on which the Philistine T E M P L E stood.

13. Samson pushed the pillars over with all his M I G H T and the temple came D O W N.

Samson

David and Goliath

Follow each step to see David's answer!

David went into battle against Goliath, a	**PHILISTINE**
The "P" needs to leave, make it an "S."	**SHILISTINE**
We have too many "I's;" remove the first and the last.	**SHLISTNE**
Now the "H" is all wrong; move it between "S" and "T."	**SLISHTNE**
The "N" needs help getting between "I" and "S."	**SLINSHTE**
The "E" needs to change to the letter after "F" in the alphabet.	**SLINSHTG**
Oh my! We forgot the "O" between "H" and "T."	**SLINSHOTG**
You are almost there, but the "G" needs to move between "N" and "S."	**SLINGSHOT**
Now we are sure you can see where a space needs to be.	**SLING SHOT**

But David said to King Saul, "This Philistine is defying the army of the living God. Do not be afraid, I will go and fight him."

David...

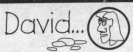

1. Do you know what Goliath wore into battle?

2. Do you know what King Saul wanted David to wear in his fight with Goliath?

3. Why was David so sure of himself?

4. David believed the battled belonged to who?

Unscramble the words for your answers. Then circle as many question numbers you think apply.

	Scrambled	Answer
1 • 2 • 3 • 4	EORBZN EMHLTE	**BRONZE HELMET**
1 • 2 • 3 • 4	ZOBENR ORRMA	**BRONZE ARMOR**
1 • 2 • 3 • 4	OZBERN DEHLIS	**BRONZE SHIELD**
1 • 2 • 3 • 4	APRES	**SPEAR**
1 • 2 • 3 • 4	RWDOS	**SWORD**
1 • 2 • 3 • 4	RHDSDPEH FTFAS	**SHEPHERD STAFF**
1 • 2 • 3 • 4	TOSHOM EOSSNT	**SMOOTH STONES**
1 • 2 • 3 • 4	NLGIS OSTH	**SLING SHOT**
1 • 2 • 3 • 4	DGO	**GODS**

If you need help you can look in your Bible at 1 Samuel 17•5-7, 38-40, 47

...and Goliath

David and Goliath

"David has faith in God"

is what this message is supposed to read. But one of those Philistines ran off with one of my letters. I don't know which one it was. Can you help me find it?

1 Samuel 17•45-47

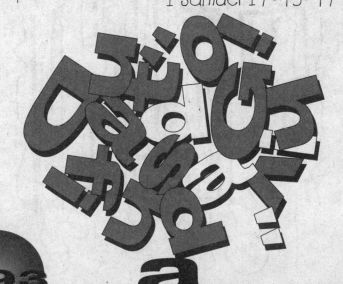

493

"Hide & Find"

In this drawing of shapes (6 items) are hidden

sword

shield

shepherd staff

spear

five smooth stones

sling shot

Can you find them?

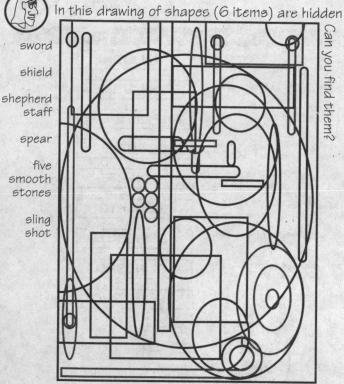

David and King Saul

Using the David & King Saul story, solve the crossword puzzle.

1. What did Saul keep when David killed Goliath?

2. What was the first item Jonathan gave David?

3. Saul sent David on many tasks and each time David was very _____.

4. Who came out to meet King Saul and David after the battle?

5. The women sang a song that made Saul very mad and _____.

6. Who was with David that caused him to be so successful?

7. Who was the king's daughter that married David?

8. Jonathan and David were good _____.

9. David's wife did something to help David escape during the night. What was it?

10. David had opportunities to kill King Saul but would not do it. He did cut something off of Saul's robe. What was it?

11. David would not kill King Saul because he was God's _____

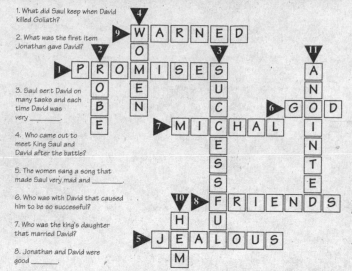

1 Samuel 18

David and King Saul

Help David get away from King Saul!

Start

End

David and King Saul

What did the women sing that made King Saul so jealous of David?

Using the information on the opposite page, find each letter by moving in the given direction, always beginning at the ✸ symbol.
The first one is done for you.

1 Samuel 18•7

				S	A	U	L
H	A	S		S	L	A	I	N		H	I	S

| T | H | O | U | S | A | N | D | S |

| | | | | A | N | D |

| | | | D | A | V | I | D |

| H | I | S | | T | E | N | S | | O | F |

| T | H | O | U | S | A | N | D | S |

494

David becomes King over Judah & Israel

2 Samuel 5

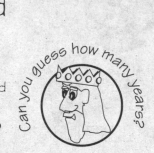

Start

End

Use the Maze to help David lead all the people to Hebron.

"Unscramble"
David becomes King over Judah

2 Samuel 2

Can you unscramble the names of these people that Ish-Bosheth was made king over? If you need help you can find the answers in the story you just read.

Scrambled	Answer
ALGDEI	**Gilead**
RHAIUS	**Ashuri**
ERELEZJ	**Jezreel**
IRPMAHE	**Ephraim**
IANBNMJE	**Benjamin**
ERILAS	**Israel**
IADVD ASW NKGI	**David was king**
EVRO AUHDJ	**over Judah**

David reigned for many years as king!

David was king in Hebron and in Jerusalem.

Do the math to get the answer.

Can you guess how many years?

Add 190 and 220 together

$$190 + 220 = 400$$

Take this number and divide it by 2

$$2\overline{)400} = 200$$

Take this number and subtract 80

$$200 - 80 = 120$$

Take your number and multiply by 3

$$188 \times 3 = 360$$

Take this number and divide it by 3

$$3\overline{)360} = 120$$

Take this number and subtract 85

$$120 - 85 = 40$$

How long did King David reign?

"What's Wrong"
2 Samuel 6:5

While the ark was being moved, David and the tribes of Israel were celebrating with all their might before the Lord with songs, lyres, harps, tambourines, castanets, and cymbals.

...ple are playing instruments, but what's wrong here? C.. you find .t least 10 ...at are wrong in this group of musicians? (wrong colors a.. .ot an answer)

495

"What's Wrong"
2 Samuel 6

vid brought the ark to the City of David in hopes that it would prosper the kingdom of Israel.
e picture below shows a very prosperous city today.

David brings
the Ark to Jerusalem

CAN YOU FIND: a backward hat • triangle • musical note • coat hanger •
funny face • mailbox • open book • screwdriver • butterfly

• marshmallow • donut • slipper • baseball • saw • log
• yo-yo • flower • rabbit • pencil • comb • and a fish.

Page 286

King David brings the Ark of the
Covenant to Jerusalem

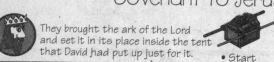

They brought the ark of the Lord
and set it in its place inside the tent
that David had put up just for it.

• Start

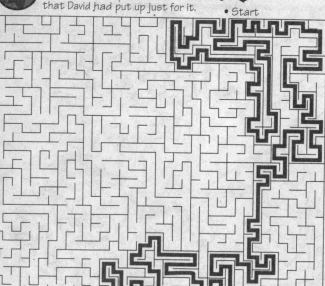

End •

2 Samuel 6:1

Page 287

David
Makes Solomon
King

See if you can solve this crossword puzzle by
using the "David makes Solomon King" story.

1 Kings 1•30

5 T R U M P E T

2 S O L O M O N

T H R O N E

3c B E N A I A H

8 E S T A B L I S H E D

1. Who was David's wife that
came and made a request?

2. David made this son the
one to follow in his footsteps
as king.

3. David called these 3 people
to him so they could go and
anoint Solomon King.
Who were they?
3a = Priest
3b = Prophet
3c = Son of Jehoiada

4. What did David have
Solomon ride on?

5. What instrument were
they to blow?

6. What did the new king
sit on?

7. David instructed Solomon
to walk in the ways of God. If
Solomon would do this then
God would keep his _____ to
David.

8. When David died, Solomon's
rule was firmly _____.

496

David Makes Solomon King

Connect the dots and you will see what Solomon sat on. Then color it with beautiful, royal colors.

Purple is a color used to show royalty.

1 Kings 1•30

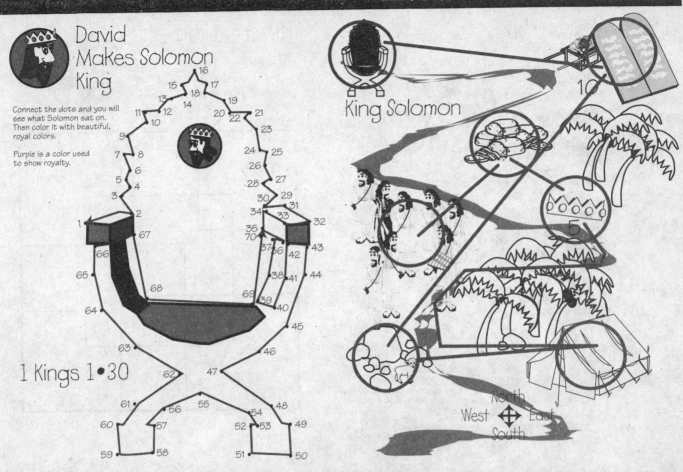

King Solomon

North
West ✛ East
South

Page 294

Page 297

Solomon Asks God for Wisdom
1 Kings 3•6-11

See if you can find and circle all of them!

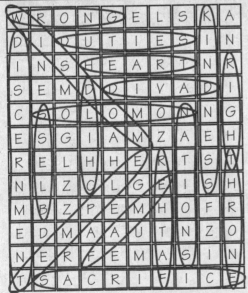

Solomon
Wisdom
David
Father
Throne
Child
Duties
Right
Wrong
Discernment
Bless
Kindness
Fame
Nations
Heart
Sacrifice
Temple

All of the words listed come from the story "Solomon asks God for wisdom."

King Solomon

Solomon asked God for wisdom and was well-known for being a fair king thoughout the land.

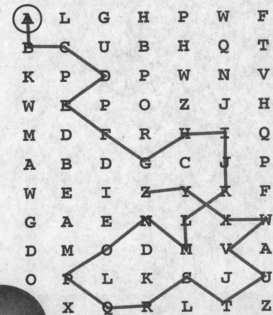

How wise are you? Put on your thinking cap for this one.

Start at the top with 'A.' Move up, down, right, left, or diagonally to the nearest 'B.' Continue with 'C' and so forth until you have found the entire alphabet.

497

King Solomon

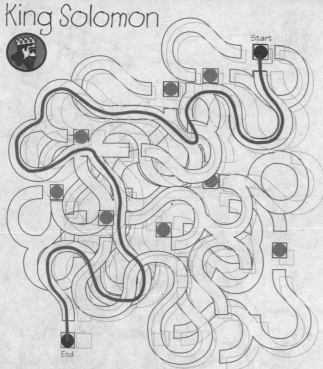

This maze looks hard, but if you think ahead
you'll whip right through it.

Start at the black circle at the top and jump onto the maze.
You may make 1 more jump to and from a grey circle intersection.
You may go under a road that looks like it follows through.
You may crossover grey lines.

"King Solomon's wisdom"

Solomon was always solving problems for all kinds of people. Can you solve how many boxes are in the one big box?

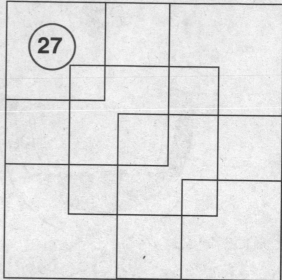

27

Solomon needs...

...some of these from this forest to build the temple. But before he can cut them down they have to be cleared of all the objects that don't belong!

CAN YOU FIND: a piece of pizza • fish • nail • rocket • saw
pair of scissors • 2 arrow heads • pencil • ice cream cone • log

"It Adds Up"
Solomon Builds the Lord's Temple

All these numbers are written with words in the story,"Solomon Builds the Lords Temple." Can you write them using numbers? When you're done add them up to see one really big number!

Four hundred and eighty years	480
Fourth year	40
Ninety feet long	90
Thirty feet wide	30
Fortyfive feet high	45
One hundred twentyfive thousand bushels of wheat	125,000
One hundred fifteen thousand gallons of pressed olive oil	115,000
Thirty thousand men	30,000
Ten thousand	10,000
Seventy thousand carriers	70,000
Eighty thousand stone cutters	80,000
Thirtythree hundred foremen	3,300
	433,985

498

King Solomon builds the Temple

1 Kings 7•48-50

Solomon also made all the furnishings that were in the Lord's temple: golden altar, golden table for the showbread, the ten lampstands of pure gold, the gold floral work and lamps and tongs, the pure gold basins, wick trimmers, sprinkling bowls, dishes and censers, and the gold sockets for the doors of the innermost room, the Most Holy Place and also the doors of the main hall of the temple.

What am I? Match the items with the correct description:

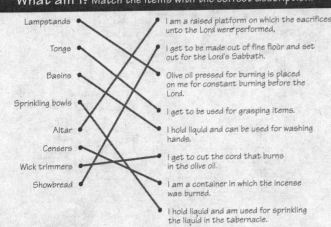

Lampstands

Tongs

Basins

Sprinkling bowls

Altar

Censers

Wick trimmers

Showbread

I am a raised platform on which the sacrifices unto the Lord were performed.

I get to be made out of fine flour and set out for the Lord's Sabbath.

Olive oil pressed for burning is placed on me for constant burning before the Lord.

I get to be used for grasping items.

I hold liquid and can be used for washing hands.

I get to cut the cord that burns in the olive oil.

I am a container in which the incense was burned.

I hold liquid and am used for sprinkling the liquid in the tabernacle.

Solomon Builds the Lord's Temple

1 Kings 6:11 - 13

When all was done on the temple, God spoke to Solomon saying, "As for this temple you are building, if you do all I have commanded, follow my decrees, obey and keep my commands, I will fulfill through you the promise I gave to David your father..."

To find what the promise is, solve this puzzle. The secret decoder is "F" means go forward, "B" go backward. Start with "I."

A B C D E F G H (I) J K L M N O P Q R S T U V W X Y Z

I WILL LIVE AMONG
THE ISRAELITES AND
WILL NOT ABANDON
MY PEOPLE ISRAEL

"A-Mazing"

1 Kings 8•10-13

When the priests put the ark in the Most Holy Place and withdrew from there, the cloud filled the temple of the Lord. The priests could not perform their service because of the cloud, for the glory of the Lord filled his temple. Then Solomon said, "The Lord has said that he would dwell in a dark cloud; I have indeed built a magnificent temple for the Lord, a place He will dwell forever."

Start

End

Can you find your way through this a-mazing glory cloud of God?

 Elijah & Elisha

All of these words have to do with the miracles Elijah performed. Can you find them in the puzzle?

C	R	I	E	D	O	U	T	T
Z	A	P	G	W	A	T	E	R
X	T	N	I	A	T	P	A	C
U	L	Z	Z	N	P	O	W	H
S	A	C	R	I	F	I	C	E
O	R	S	Z	Q	L	L	Z	A
N	A	W	I	D	O	W	T	L
V	I	U	Z	Q	U	J	Z	E
K	N	Z	F	I	R	E	Q	D

Rain
Widow
Son
Healed
Oil
Flour
Altar
Sacrifice
Fire
Water
Cried Out
Captain

1 Kings 17-19
& 2 Kings 1 & 2

499

"Word Sramble"

Elijah & Elisha

Ravens	AIEHJL
Ahab	IRNA
False-gods	EAHDLE
Provoke	ILO
Elijah	EAHNVE
Rain	HOPTEPR
Morning	EJEELBZ
Bread	ENAGL
Double	ASLHIE
Evening	ROFUL
Meat	DORL
Feed	DGO
Brook	TOUDIC-ER
Whirlwind	TUNCLSO
Widow	ALRTA
Son	AMTE
Healed	EFDE
Oil	ORKOB
Heaven	NWRHDILIW
Flour	OIWWD
Lord	CFRAEIICS
God	RFEI
Cried-Out	RTEWA
Consult	SEANVR
Altar	BHAA
Sacrifice	DGSOELF-SA
Fire	GIRMNNO
Water	DEBAR
Captain	EBOLUD
Cloak	GIEENNV
Prophet	NSO
Jezebel	EOOPKVR
Angel	NAPCITA
Elisha	KOCAL

All of these words are in the Elijah and Elisha story.

Can you match the unscrambled word with the scrambled word?

Elijah & Elisha

Can you help the raven get through the maze to feed Elijah?

START
END

1 Kings 17:6

The ravens brought food to Elijah: bread in the morning and meat in the evening.

Elijah & Elisha

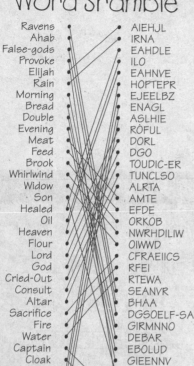

WHIRLWIND
MOUNT CARMEL
CHARIOT
DOUBLE
RAIN
THREE
TWELVE
GOD
FIRE
CLOAK
AHAB
WATER
RAVEN
TRIBES

MEN OF GOD

Using the letters in grey outlined boxes, match the correct word number to the correct box number, find out what Elijah and Elisha were called.

1 Kings 17-19 & 2 Kings 1 & 2

Shadrach, Meshach, & Abednego

King Nebuchadnezzaar said, "Look! I see four men walking around in the fire, unbound and unharmed, and the fourth looks like a son of the gods."

"Daniel 3•25"

Can you find the 4 men in the furnace and a man that looks like a son of the gods?

300 "to the fiery furnace"

"Into the Furnace"
Daniel 3

N	E	B	U	C	H	A	D	N	E	Z	Z	A	R
S	O	A	M	A	Z	E	M	E	N	T	D	S	E
H	R	L	E	H	E	W	O	R	S	H	I	P	S
A	P	K	S	X	G	L	Y	Y	O	I	N	A	C
D	I	R	H	O	G	O	D	T	U	C	T	U	U
R	D	P	A	V	U	A	P	I	T	H	R	E	E
A	O	R	C	E	M	U	S	I	C	O	C	I	D
C	L	L	H	S	F	A	I	T	H	F	U	L	S
H	E	F	O	U	R	H	S	Z	X	V	R	G	R
A	B	E	D	N	E	G	O	X	A	N	G	E	L

Nebuchadnezzar   Amazement
Idol   Three
Music   Four
Worship   Angel
Shadrach   Rescued
Meshach   Faithful
Abednego   God

Shadrach, Meshach, & Abednego

Can you find all these words in the squares above and circle them?

"A-Mazeing Alphabet"

Work the maze, picking up letters along the way. What did it spell?

Start

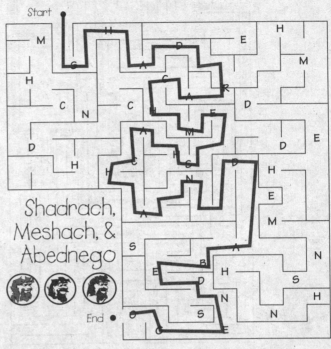

Shadrach, Meshach, & Abednego

End

SHADRACH, MESHACH, & ABEDNEGO

"The writing on the wall."

All of the these words are from the "writing on the Wall" story. Can you find them and CIRCLE THEM?

K	I	N	G	B	E	L	S	H	A	Z	Z	A	R
S	T	E	L	B	O	G	M	N	N	T	D	A	E
H	N	L	E	H	D	W	D	R	S	H	Z	P	S
C	E	M	P	L	E	D	R	A	W	Z	R	A	W
N	E	B	O	S	D	R	A	W	E	R	Z	M	R
S	U	G	M	A	Z	Z	M	N	N	R	A	R	E
H	Q	L	E	H	E	W	D	R	I	L	I	S
A	P	Z	S	X	G	A	V	Y	L	E	N	T	S
S	I	Z	R	E	H	T	A	P	U	C	L	I	R
E	D	P	A	C	U	A	P	Z	T	R	N	E
L	O	R	U	E	M	U	Z	I	C	T	C	G	G
B	L	B	A	N	Q	U	E	T	H	F	U	L	N
O	E	F	S	I	L	V	E	R	X	I	R	G	I
N	B	G	D	E	N	E	T	H	G	I	R	F

Daniel 5

Belshazzar   Silver   Wall   King   Gifts
Banquet   Goblets   Writing   Father   Reward
Nebuchadnezzar   Queen   Nobles   Temple   Read
Frightened   Fingers   Daniel   Gold

The writing on the wall said:
"Mene, Mene, Tekel, Uparsin"

This writing is believed to have been Aramaic. The meanings to these words would have been:
• Mene - 'numbered or unit of money' • Tekel - 'weighed' • Uparsin - 'divided or half a shekel.'

You have been given by the king:
• 3 Talents
• 240 Minas
• 160 Shekels

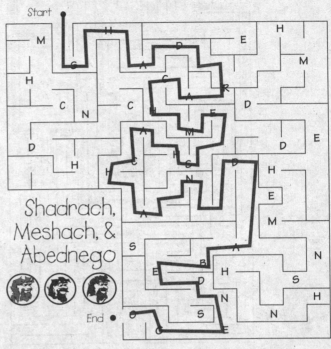

Cinnamon Sticks = 1 Talent

Bag of Grain = 1 Mina

Olive Oil = 5 Shekels

Perfume = 2 Talents

Do you have enough money to buy the following items on your list?

Shopping list:
1. 3 Bags of grain
2. 2 Bottles of Olive Oil
3. 5 Cinnamon Sticks
4. 1 Bottle of Perfume

Answers: Daniel 5:25

Yes
150 Shekels,
10 Shekles
1 Talent and 240 Minas
2 Talents

You can solve the problem using these biblical units.
lent = 60 Minas • Mina = 50 Shekels • Shekel = 2 Bekas • Beka = 10 Gerahs

Royal Grocery Store

Daniel & the Lion's Den

Because Daniel loved God, he was thrown into the lions' den. Help him walk out.

Start

End

Daniel 6•23

Jonah & the Big Fish!

Connect the dots to discover what swallowed Jonah when he jumped from the ship into the turbulent waters.

Jonah 1•15

Jonah & the Big Fish!

God provided a great fish to swallow Jonah. He stayed in the belly of the fish three days and three nights

Jonah 1•17

Jonah & the Big Fish!

By providing Jonah with the plant to shade his head and then having the worm come and eat the plant, God was teaching Jonah how to have mercy on the people of Nineveh.

ROW:	COLOR IN SQUARES WITH:		
1	numbers greater than 10	11	even numbers
2	odd numbers	12	numbers greater than 10
3	even numbers	13	numbers less than 10
4	numbers greater than 8	14	numbers with 2
5	numbers less than 5	15	numbers with 3
6	numbers greater than 20	16	odd numbers
7	odd numbers	17	numbers with 5
8	numbers with 8	18	numbers with 8
9	numbers with 6	19	numbers with 4
10	numbers with 1	20	even numbers

Follow the directions to discover what animal taught Jonah a great lesson.

In this picture can you find ten ways that people are helping others?

502

Jonah 3

Jonah & the Big Fish!

Follow each step to see Jonah's answer!

When Jonah did not obey God, God was	**DISPLEASED**
Move the "ED" at the end to the front.	**EDDISPLEAS**
Now you can remove one "D."	**EDISPLEAS**
Change the "AS" to an "OB."	**EDISPLEOB**
S & E need to swap places. Make sure to use the second "E!"	**EDIEPLSOB**
That "P" is no help; it needs to leave	**EDIELSOB**
Say the alphabet and when you get to "M" write the next letter in place of the "L."	**EDIENSOB**
You have come very far and it's not too hard. Change the "S" to the next letter in the alphabet	**EDIENTOB**
Move the "OB" to the front of the line and you will find how Jonah changed his mind.	**OBEDIENT**

"Unscramble"
Luke 1•63
Unscramble the words that Zachariah wrote on his tablet.

ISH
MNEA
SI
HJNO

HIS
NAME
IS
JOHN

Cool•Things to Know

More than likely, Zachariah wrote John's name on Papyrus. This is a material which is made from the aquatic papyrus plant found in the Nile valley in Egypt. The "paper" is made from the pith of this plant by taking strips of the pith, laying them together, soaking them, then pressing the material and drying it. This was commonly used by ancient Egyptians, Greeks, and Romans. Now you understand where our word for "paper" comes from.

"Off to Elizabeth's"

Help Mary get to her cousin Elizabeth's in Judea!
Remember - she is so excited about her good news she wants to get there quickly.

Start

Luke 1•39

"Good News"

Complete the dot to dot and you will see where Mary and Elizabeth shared their good news with each other.

Cool•Things to Know

In Judea and other parts of that area the houses were built from bricks made with mud or big rough stones. The houses were built with flat roofs because the people could dry things there in the sun, like fruits and vegetables and even their clothes. Sometimes if it was really hot, they would sleep on the roof.

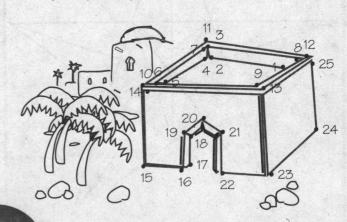

503

"The Census"

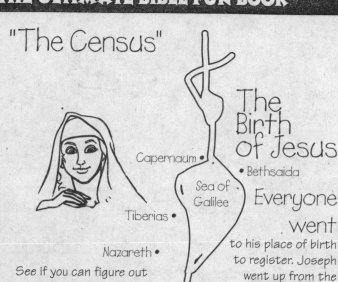

The Birth of Jesus

Everyone went to his place of birth to register. Joseph went up from the town of Nazareth to Judea, then to Bethlehem, the town of David, because he belonged to the house and line of David.

Luke 2•3-4

See if you can figure out these word problems.

It is 80 miles from Galilee to Bethlehem. Mary and Joseph probably walked the distance. If the trip took them 5 days, how many miles a day did they travel?

Answer 16

If you took an 80 mile trip today by car, and the speed limit is 65 miles per hour, how long would it take you?

Answer 1 hour 15 min

The Birth of Jesus

The scrambled message below "Glory to God in the highest," is what the angels sang when Jesus was born. There is one letter missing. Can you find which one?

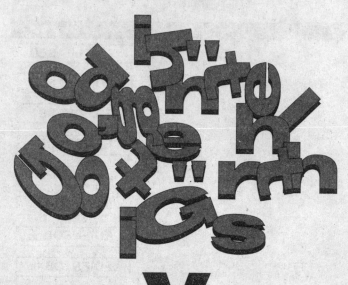

Page 361   **Page 365**

"Signs in the Heavens"

How many triangles can you count in this star?

(120)

A bright star shone in the heavens as a sign that the child of promise was born.

"Meanwhile,"
back at the manger

Luke 2•16

Name the animals that were at the manger with Mary & Joseph!

And they came with haste and found Mary and Joseph, and the babe lying in a manger.

504

Page 368   **Page 369**

"Animals in Stable"

You normally would find all kinds of animals at the stables. Our Stable is full, boarding animals for all of the people in town, and it's feeding time!

Can you count the right number of animals we have to feed?

22

"His Name is Called"

Jesus was also called "Emmanuel," which means "God with us."

Matthew 1•23

Unscramble the names to find out their meanings.

Scramble	Name	Meaning
AAMD	ADAM	= Red Earth
IANBNMJE	BENJAMIN	= Son of my right hand
ENDLIA	DANIEL	= God is my judge
IADDV	DAVID	= Loved by God
ERALIBG	GABRIEL	= God's Hero
HJNO	JOHN	= God's Mercy
EHILACM	MICHAEL	= Who can be like God?
TBHE	BETH	= Breath of life
VEE	EVE	= Life-Giving
NNHHAA	HANNAH	= God's Favor
AAHRS	SARAH	= Princess
ETERHS	ESTER	= Star

"Help the Wise Men"

After leaving King Herod, the 3 Wise men need to find their way to Mary and Joseph's home.

Start

End

The Wise Men Came Bearing Gifts

Gold, Frankincense, and Myrrh

Which 2 of these items match the picture on the left?

505

"Baby Gifts"
Matthew 2•11
Jesus received very unusual baby gifts: Gold, Frankincense, and Myrrh.

Fill in the puzzle below to find baby gifts for today.

A	1
B	2
C	3
D	4
E	5
F	6
G	7
H	8
I	9
J	10
K	11
L	12
M	13
N	14
O	15
P	16
Q	17
R	18
S	19
T	20
U	21
V	22
W	23
X	24
Y	25
Z	26

DIAPERS
4 9 16 5 18 19

RATTLE
18 1 20 20 12 5

TOYS
20 15 25 19

PACIFIER
16 1 3 9 6 9 5 18

BOOTIES
2 15 15 20 9 5 19

BLANKET
2 12 1 14 11 5 20

GOWNS
7 15 23 14 19

CLOTHES
3 12 15 20 8 5 19

WASHCLOTHS
23 1 19 8 3 12 15 20 8 19

BOTTLES
2 15 20 20 12 5 19

"Luggage"
When Mary and Joseph traveled to Bethlehem from Galilee and the wise men traveled from Jerusalem to Bethlehem, did they have a suitcase for their trip?

Luke 2•4

Can you find: a fish • worm • slice of pizza • baseball banana• flower • hamburger • seashell • hammer • and an ice cream cone

"Who Am I"
Read the clues carefully, write the name in the space provided.

1. I appeared to Zachariah and to Mary to tell them of their children to come.   **Gabriel**

2. I was unable to speak until my son was born.   **Zacharias**

3. I'm very old; but God blessed me and my husband Zachariah with a son.   **Elizabeth**

4. I was born to tell people about the Savior. My name is_____?   **John**

5. I was not married, but the Holy Spirit blessed me with the Son of God.   **Mary**

6. I love Mary very much and want her to be my wife.   **Joseph**

7. We were afraid of the bright light in the sky, but were comforted by the news from the angels.   **Shepherds**

8. We followed the star in the east to find baby Jesus to worship him.   **Wise men**

"Test Your Counting Skills"
How many of each item or thing do you see?

Can you solve this crossword puzzle?

Answer all the questions regarding Jesus Birth for the answers to the puzzle...

1. What do you give someone when it's their Birthday?

2. Silver & ____

3. Gift to baby Jesus that burns and smells good.

4. A stable is for?

5. Jesus was called ____ of the Jews.

6. The wise men followed a ____ in the east.

7. A ____ was Jesus' crib.

8. A gift to baby Jesus that is a sweet smelling oil.

9. Jesus' earthly father.

10. The son of God.

11. Town where Jesus was born

12. Watching their flocks at night

13. Jesus' mother

Crossword grid:
```
G I F T
O   R
L   A N I M A L S       M
D   N         T         Y
    K     M A N G E R   R
  K I N G     R         R
    N       J E S U S   H
    C       H
J O S E P H E
    N       P
  B E T H L E H E M
            E     A
            R     R
            D     Y
            S
```

"What Am I?" Read the clues carefully and write the name in the space provided.

1. Zachariah was burning me in the temple when and angel appeared to him. **Incense**

2. My name is Gabriel. I am an ____ of the Lord. **Angel**

3. I am the town where Mary and Joseph lived. **Nazareth**

4. Zacharias wrote his son's name on me. **Tablet**

5. Mary and Joseph went to this town to be counted. **Bethlehem**

6. I carried Mary on the journey. **Donkey**

7. I house the animals and also provided a place for Jesus' birth. **Stable**

8. Mary used strips of me to wrap baby Jesus in. **Linen**

9. I'm used for feeding animals, but I was the crib for Baby Jesus. **Manger**

10. I shone brightly in the sky over baby Jesus. **Star**

"Jesus' Natural Family"

Can you find all of the names of Jesus' family members?

```
E L I Z A B E T H B
M M A J E J A M E H
A A O R T O D X S A U
R R B Y S K J R I W O
Y Y I E L W K R A I S
X P M N I A B V L E
H E I O H J U D A S
P L S C N B Z E T H
E I A F G N O M I S
A Z A B E S E M A J
```

Mary — James
Joseph — Joses
Elizabeth — Simon
Zachariah — Judas

Matthew 13•55

"J" is for Jesus

Can you circle all the things below that start with the Letter "J"?

Jumprope

Jelly Beans

Jacks

507

"Rules for Living"

Jesus had so many people around him that wanted to hear him speak, that he had to walke up a mountainside so he could be seen and heard.

To finish each sentence you will need to unscramble the letters on the next page. Here is a hint: use the matching letter style and you will find the answers.

1. Blessed are the poor in **SPIRIT**, for theirs is the kingdom of **HEAVEN**.

2. Blessed are those who **MOURN** for they shall be **COMFORTED**.

3. Blessed are the **MEEK**, for they shall inherit the **EARTH**.

4. Blessed are those who **HUNGER** and **THIRST** for righteousness.

5. Blessed are the **MERCIFUL**, I F U L, for they shall obtain **MERCY**.

6. Blessed are the pure in **HEART** for they shall see **GOD**.

7. Blessed are the **PEACE MAKERS**, for they shall be called **SONS** of God.

8. Blessed are those who are **PERSECUTED** for righteousness' sake, for theirs is the **KINGDOM** of heaven.

Matthew 5

Parable of the Sower

In the "ears" of corn, UNSCRAMBLE the letters you find in the kernels to find a MESSAGE!

HE | WHO | HAS

EARS | TO | HEAR

LET | HIM | HEAR

Mark 4•1-20

Help this seed get to the fertile soil. Be careful: don't let it get stuck on the rocks or in the thorns.

Start

End

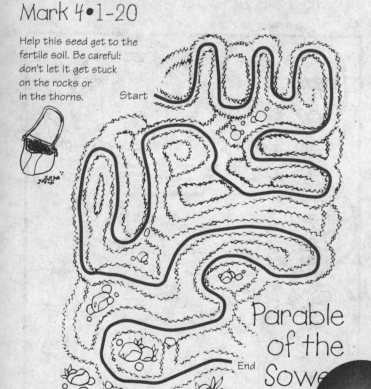

Parable of the Sower

"What's in a seed?"

All these plants have something in common, they come from a seed. Find and circle them in the puzzle above.

Watermelon
Pumpkin
Grass
Tomato
Corn

Pear
Marigold
Carrot
Pepper
Cucumber

Parable of the Sower

508

"Hidden Picture"

The lamp on the nightstand is bright enough to help reveal the hidden objects.

Mark 4•21-25

Can you find: a spoon • fish • fork • worm • dollar bill • marshmallow
toilet paper • sponge • ball bat • screwdriver • snake • log • flag
saw • paint brush • ice cream cone • pencil • nail • football • candy cane

"Mix & Match"

Match the source of light where you most commonly find it.

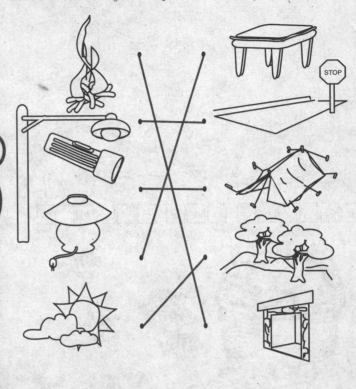

STOP

The Golden "Ruler"

Finish drawing the ruler. Then complete the Bible verse.

"**Golden Rule**"

"Do unto others as you would have them do unto you."

If you can't remember the words, look at the "Golden Rule" page.

Loaves and Fishes

Count the number of loaves and fish in each row. Now color that many squares in the row.

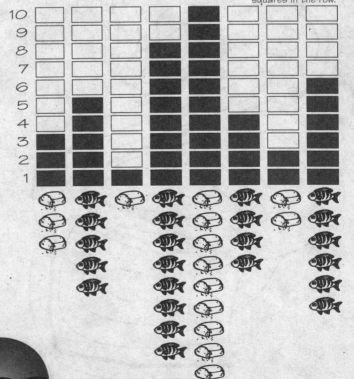

509

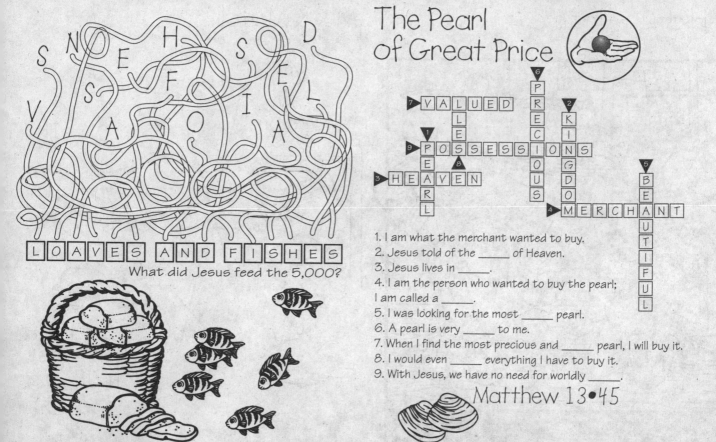

LOAVES AND FISHES

What did Jesus feed the 5,000?

The Pearl of Great Price

1. I am what the merchant wanted to buy.
2. Jesus told of the _____ of Heaven.
3. Jesus lives in _____.
4. I am the person who wanted to buy the pearl; I am called a _____.
5. I was looking for the most _____ pearl.
6. A pearl is very _____ to me.
7. When I find the most precious and _____ pearl, I will buy it.
8. I would even _____ everything I have to buy it.
9. With Jesus, we have no need for worldly _____.

Matthew 13•45

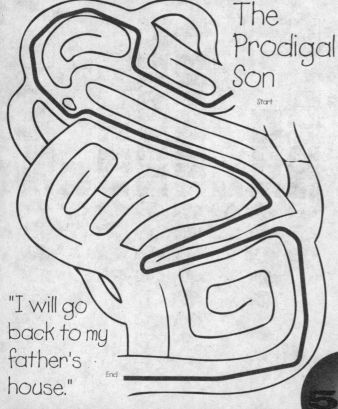

The Prodigal Son

Start

"I will go back to my father's house."

End

This phrase should read "The prodigal son has come home," but Iv'e got one too many letters. Can you tell me which is the extra letter?

The Prodigal Son

510

m

Draw a circle around all the things the father gave the prodigal son when he returned home.

The Prodigal Son

"Love is Spelled"

Color the squares below and see the hidden word when you're finished.

1 = Yellow
2 = Red
3 = Blue

Page 428

Page 430

"Donkey & Colt"
Matthew 21•2

Jesus told the disciples to look for a donkey with its colt tied to a doorway and bring it back to him.

Help the disciples find the donkey and colt.
(Going under bridges one street width is allowed)

End

Start

"Jerusalem"
Matthew 21•10-11

Jesus entered Jerusalem and the whole city was stirred. They asked, "Who is this?" Some in the crowd answered, "He is Jesus, the prophet from Nazareth in Galilee."

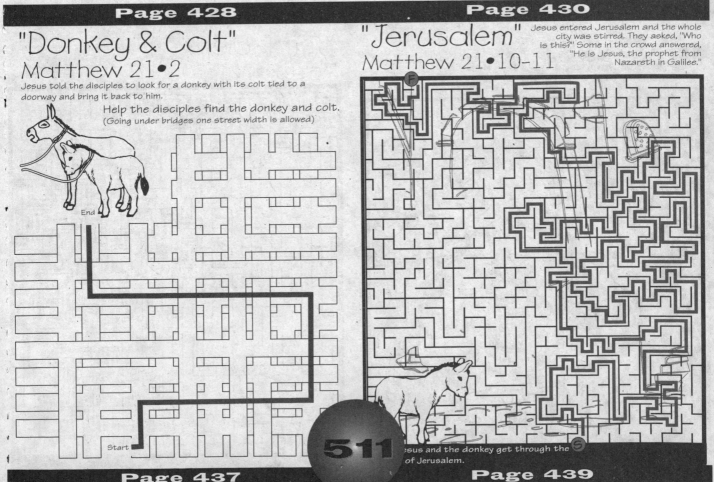

511

esus and the donkey get through the of Jerusalem.

Page 437

Page 439

"Victory"

"For anyone that is born of God has victory in life through the Son of God, Jesus."

1 John 4•4

Connect the dots to see something that in ancient times represent victory.

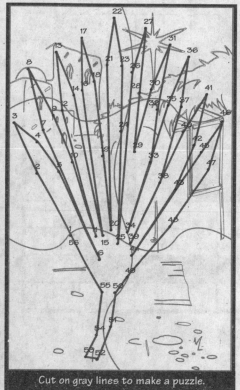

Cut on gray lines to make a puzzle.

Page 443

"God Loves Me"

God wants me to be kind to others.
Find the words in this puzzle that describe how I should act toward others and toward Him.

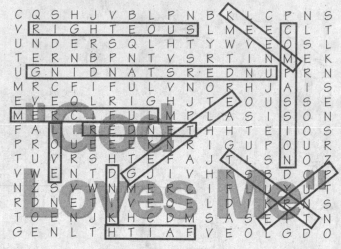

```
C Q S H J V B L P N B K L C P N S
V R I G H T E O U S L M E E C L T
U N D E R S Q L H T Y W V E O S E
T E R N B P N T V S R T I N M R L
U G N I D N A T S R E D N U P R K
M R C F I F U L V N O R H J A I N
E V E O L R I G H J T E O U S I S
M E R C I F U L M P L A S I O N E
F A L I R E D N E T H H T E I O N
P R O U E E K N R I G U P U O U R
T U V R S H T E F A J T L S O Z Z
V W E N T D G J I V H K S B D C P
R N Z S W N M E R C I F L U Y U T
R D N E I V E O E D K R N A I S N
T O E N J K H C D M S A S E T T N
G E N L T H T I A F V E O L G D O
```

trust   understanding   love   pure
kind   compassion   merciful   tender
gentle   faith   meek   righteous

Page 445

"God Made this"

Ann went to the park and saw all of the wonderful things God had made. Help her find them all.

Can you find: a bird • squirrel • ant • b...

Page 446

"Jerusalem"
Matthew 21•10-11

Jesus entered Jerusalem and the whole city was stirred. They asked, "Who is this?" Some in the crowd answered, "He is Jesus, the prophet from Nazareth in Galilee."

...esus and the donkey get through the...

Page 447